# Beyond the Welfare State?

For my parents, John and Margaret

# Beyond the Welfare State?

## The New Political Economy of Welfare

**Christopher Pierson**

The Pennsylvania State University Press
University Park, Pennsylvania

Originating publisher, Polity Press, Cambridge, England

First published in the United States of America by The Pennsylvania
State University Press, Suite C, 820 North University Drive, University
Park, PA 16802

ISBN 0–271–00820–2 (cloth)
ISBN 0–271–00821–0 (paper)

*Library of Congress Cataloging in Publication Data*
A CIP catalogue record for this book is available from the Library of
Congress.

Typeset in 10 on 12 pt Palatino
by Graphicraft Typesetters Ltd, Hong Kong
Printed in Great Britain by TJ Press, Padstow, Cornwall

It is the policy of The Pennsylvania State University Press to use acid-free
paper for the first printing of all clothbound books. Publications on
uncoated stock satisfy minimum requirements of American National
Standard for Information Sciences—Permanence of Paper for Printed
Library Materials, ANSI 239.48–1984.

# Contents

# Acknowledgements

I have incurred many debts in writing this book. While I have benefited from the research of many earlier students of welfare state development, I want to acknowledge the especial value of the work of Peter Flora and his collaborators. Their heroic efforts to collect and collate details of the comparative historical development of the welfare state have proven an invaluable service to every student of welfare state development. A number of people have been kind enough to read and comment upon a part or the whole of the manuscript. These were: Virginia Bovell, Anthony Giddens, David Held, John Keane, Desmond King, Meridee Pierson; and participants at the British Sociological Association Annual Conference, at the American Sociological Association Annual Conference, and at seminars in the Departments of Politics and Sociology at the Universities of Edinburgh and Stirling. I have benefited from discussion with several cohorts of students on my course in the Politics of the Welfare State at the University of Stirling. I am grateful to the Carnegie Trust for the Universities of Scotland and the University of Stirling, whose support enabled me to undertake a period of research in the United States.

I am grateful to all the extraordinarily efficient staff at Polity Press, and especially to David Held and Anthony Giddens. Above all, I am grateful to Meridee and Ailsa May for their constant support and forbearance.

I dedicate the book to my parents, John and Margaret, with whom I have been in amicable political disagreement for half a lifetime. I hope that they will find something here with which they can agree.

Christopher Pierson
Glasgow, 1991

The author and publisher would also like to thank the following for permission to reproduce material in the book:

*The Political Quarterly* for Table 5.2, from P. Pulzer, 'The Paralysis of the Centre-Left: A Comparative Perspective', *The Political Quarterly*, 58/3, 1987, p. 387; Oxford University Press for Table 5.3, from J. Alber, 'Is there a Crisis of the Welfare State? Cross-national Evidence from Europe, North America and Japan', *European Sociological Review*, 4/3, 1988, p. 194; Basil Blackwell and Harvard University Press for Table 5.1, from M. Bruno and J. D. Sachs, *Economics of Worldwide Stagflation*, 1985, p. 2; HarperCollins Publishers for Figure 2.1 from C. Offe, *Contractions of the Welfare State* (Chatto and Windus, 1984), p. 52, and for Table 4.8 from R. E. Goodin and J. Le Grand, *Not Only the Poor: The Middle Classes and the Welfare State* (Unwin Hyman, 1987), p. 92; Transaction for Figure 4.1 from A. Flora and A. J. Heidenheimer, *The Development of Welfare States in Europe and America*, 1981, p. 85; OECD, Paris for Figure 4.3 from *Social Expenditure 1960–1990: Problems of Growth and Control* (1985), p. 19, and for Table 4.5 and Figure 4.2 from *The Future of Social Protection* (1988), pp. 10 and 13; Harvester-Wheatsheaf for Table 4.7 from M. Godfrey, *The Economic Approach to Social Policy*. First edition, London: Harvester-Wheatsheaf, 1986, p. 2. Reprinted by permission of the publisher. *Evening Standard* for D. Low, 1950 cartoon, 'This is the Road', on p. viii.

Every effort has been made to trace all copyright holders, but if any has been inadvertently overlooked the publishers will be pleased to make the necessary arrangement at the first opportunity.

# Introduction

Recent years have seen the welfare state, once a seemingly immovable fixture in the liberal democratic order, drawn increasingly towards the centre of an ever more contentious political debate. For a long time, the dominant academic view was that the emergence of the welfare state was to be seen either as the completion of the centuries-long movement towards full and equal citizenship or else as the price exacted by the organized labour movement for a cessation of open hostilities with the powers of capital. For some, the institutionalization of the welfare state represented a decisive victory of the political forces of the labour movement, a vindication of the 'positive-sum' reformism of social democracy. For others, it was the technologically rather than politically determined concomitant of industrial and economic progress, the final act in the process of 'civilizing' the brute forces of industrialization. Again, while for some it consummated the transformation of capitalism into a distinctively new form of social and political organization (which might or might not be called socialism), for others it represented the further and benevolent development of capitalism. For the latter, the welfare state constituted a form in which the excesses of nineteenth-century *laissez-faire* capitalism had been curbed and a more rational, equitable, sociable (and thus secure) basis for the private ownership of the economy put in its place. As we shall see, such views were never universally shared, still less unequivocally welcomed. Some on the left insisted that the rise of the welfare state sapped the transformative energies of the working class while subsidizing the reproduction costs of capital. At the same time, critics to the right maintained that the welfare state undermined the fundamental premises of the liberal society that had been created by the great revolutionary movements of the seventeenth and eighteenth centuries. But despite these dissenting opinions, enough of a common view prevailed in the post-war years of Western economic growth and welfare state expansion for us to speak of a widespread (though often unarticulated) professional consensus upon the broad lines of welfare state development.

Just as certainly, we may speak of the last twenty years having seen an extremely widespread challenge to this orthodoxy. This dissent has been heard from most points of the political compass. In the heyday of 'post-war consensus', outright hostility to the welfare state settlement was widely characterized as a maverick disposition of the political extremes of both left and right. But this was to alter under the pressure of the economic reverses and social upheavals of the late 1960s and early 1970s, and the political changes these brought in their wake. In this period, the belief that the welfare state was 'in crisis', indeed, that many of the social, economic and political ills of the modern era were directly attributable to the continuing growth of the welfare state, established itself, with astonishing rapidity, as something like a new orthodoxy. Elements of both the New Left and the New Right found common ground in identifying the incompatibility of a working market economy with the state provision of welfare. At the same time, criticism of the particular consequences of the welfare state for women and for ethnic minorities, long a suppressed undercurrent in social policy, gained a new prominence with the general resurgence in feminist and anti-racist writing and thinking from the early 1970s onwards. Still more recently, the impact of the green movement, with its characteristic concern for the harmful consequences of unsustainable economic growth and bureaucratized public services, has represented a further challenge to the benign assumptions of the defenders of the social democratic welfare state.

Paralleling this increased political interest and controversy has been a change in the academic study of the welfare state. However wrongly, the welfare state was for long seen as the worthy, if rather dull, province of a group of concerned specialists, mostly in the fields of social policy and social administration, working on a particular and practical agenda of (diminishing) poverty and (expanding) welfare provision. By contrast, in recent years, the welfare state has increasingly been colonized by students of political theory and the 'new political economy' who have drastically broadened the domain of welfare state studies, seeking, under this rubric, to construct broad explanations of the general nature of the social, economic and political arrangements of advanced capitalism.

From both these political and academic sources has come, in

recent years, increasing support for the claim that the advanced capitalist societies are undergoing a process of transformation which is carrying them towards social and political arrangements which are, in some sense, *beyond the welfare state*. Most prominent among these claims are the following:

---

## Proposition 1

In the long term, the welfare state is incompatible with a healthy market-based economy. Only the exceptionally favourable circumstances for economic growth of the post-war period allowed simultaneously for an expansion of the economy *and* the welfare state. Under changed international economic conditions this means, for the political right, that economic growth can only be restored by severely lessening the drain of the welfare state upon the productive economy. For the left, it implies that the welfare aspirations embodied in the idea of a welfare state can only be met by the transformation of society towards socialism.

---

## Proposition 2

The development of the welfare state was an integral part of the evolution of modern capitalist societies. However, the period of its remarkable growth was also historically unique. The welfare state has now 'grown to its limits'. Wholesale dismantling is neither necessary nor likely, but any further (costly) growth will begin to undermine the basis of its popular support.

---

## Proposition 3

Changes in the international political economy have increasingly undermined the circumstances for the promotion of national welfare states. The powers of national governments, national labour movements and nationally based capital – between whom agreements about national welfare states were typically constructed – have been undermined by the greater internationalization and deregulation of the modern world economy. The Keynesian Welfare State is incompatible with this new international political economy.

---

## Proposition 4

The post-war welfare state represented an 'historic compromise' between the powers/interests of capital and organized labour. While at one time welfare state policies served both their interests, it is now becoming increasingly unattractive to both and will be able to mobilize decreasing support within both camps. Under these circumstances, the only appropriate strategy for contemporary social democratic movements is to reactivate their traditional commitment to socialization of the capital investment function, 'bracketed out' in the (temporary) compromise of the Keynesian Welfare State.

## Proposition 5

The development of welfare state provision (especially in public health and public education) has itself generated social changes which undermine the continuing necessity for state welfare provision and itself attenuates the basis of continuing support for public provision. In particular, the development of the welfare state has transformed the *class* structure of advanced capitalism in such a way as to undermine the *class* basis for its own continuation. Most significantly, these changes undermine that alliance between middle and working classes upon which the welfare state was built, and furnish for an ever growing section of the population an incentive to *defect* from (the support of) public welfare provision.

## Proposition 6

The welfare state represented an appropriate institutional means for delivering certain welfare services at a given level of social and economic development. Continued economic growth has rendered these forms of welfare provision increasingly inappropriate. Most notably, the expansion of consumer choice/affluence within Western industrialized economies engenders increasing dissatisfaction with state-administered welfare and a greater defection of consumers to market-provided welfare services.

## Proposition 7

While the welfare state political project should be understood as historically progressive, further progress cannot be effected through the continued promotion of conventional welfare state policies. This is because the welfare state is tied to a productivist/economic growth strategy which is not (any longer) consonant with the meeting of real human needs and the securing of genuine social welfare.

It is with these claims about development 'beyond the welfare state' that this book is principally concerned. It is not however a study in futurology. Future 'tendencies' in the welfare states must depend upon their historical evolution and those powers and structures that they currently embody. This is reflected in the structure of the book. The first three chapters deal with the major theoretical approaches to the welfare state out of which prognoses for its future development arise. More specifically, they are concerned with the relationship between the welfare state, social democracy and the structure of advanced capitalism. To assist the reader through this minefield of competing explanations, I include at the end of each section a brief thesis summarizing the main claims that have been outlined. Chapter 4 reviews major trends in the international development of welfare states down to the early 1970s.

For most commentators, the conditions for moving 'beyond the welfare state' have only ripened or become manifest over the last fifteen to twenty years. This is the period that has been dominated by the spectre of a 'crisis in the welfare state'. Correspondingly, the fifth chapter gives detailed consideration to varying explanations of this crisis and measures these against the actual experience of developed welfare states since the early 1970s. The final chapter returns explicitly to our propositions about developments 'beyond the welfare state' and makes an assessment of these in the light of the evidence considered in the rest of the study. While we shall see that the casual elision of social democracy and the welfare state is historically and theoretically misplaced, especial attention is directed throughout the book to the changing relationship between the welfare state and social democracy.

# 1
# Capitalism, Social Democracy and the Welfare State I: Industrialism, Modernization and Social Democracy

The purpose of these first three chapters is to establish how the (contested and changing) relationship between capitalism, social democracy and the welfare state has been understood. It would perhaps be as well to begin by clarifying how these terms will be employed within this study. *Capitalism* refers to an economic (and social) system based upon the production and exchange of privately owned commodities. *Advanced capitalism* refers to this economic (and social) system as it has evolved within the most developed societies of North America, Western Europe, Japan and Australasia. Both systems are seen to be more or less dependent upon markets, but neither is premised upon pure 'free' markets in either labour and/or commodities. *Social democracy* refers to those political movements, ideologies and practices which are founded upon the reformist promotion of the interests of organized labour within a developed capitalist economy. It tends to afford definitive status to the development of representative democratic institutions within capitalist societies as the means of gradually reforming these societies in the direction of greater fairness and equality, largely through the promotion of welfare state strategies.

Use of the expression *welfare* has always been inexact. At its simplest, *welfare* may describe 'well-being' or 'the material and social preconditions for well-being' (*Shorter Oxford English Dictionary*; Weale, 1983, p. 23). As such, it may be distinguished from three common subclassifications: (1) *social welfare*, which broadly refers to the collective (and sometimes sociable) provision or receipt of welfare, (2) *economic welfare*, which usually describes those forms of welfare secured through the market or the formal economy and (3) *state welfare*, which refers to social welfare provision through the agency of the state. A good deal of confusion has arisen from the tendency of commentators to argue as if one of these subclassifications was exhaustive of *all* forms of welfare or as if they were interchangeable (as, for example, in the supposition that state welfare is the same as social welfare). These definitional issues have been extensively discussed elsewhere (see Titmuss, 1963; Madison, 1980, pp. 46–68; Weale, 1983, pp. 1–21; Jones, 1985, pp. 13–14; Rose, 1981; on classical definitions of economic welfare, see Pigou, 1912, 1929). Here, comment can be confined to two points. First, in this study the primary focus of attention is upon *state*-provided forms of welfare and their interconnection with the structure of the formal economy. Secondly, and given this emphasis, it should be stressed that the ways in which welfare is delivered *outside* of the state or the formal economy, through the church, through voluntary organizations and, above all, through the family, is just as important.

In a narrow sense, the *welfare state* may refer to state measures for the provision of key welfare services (often confined to health, education, housing, income maintenance and personal social services). Increasingly broadly, the welfare state is also taken to define (1) a particular form of state, (2) a distinctive form of polity or (3) a specific type of society. In this study, the *welfare state under capitalism* is generally understood in this third sense as defining a society in which the state intervenes within the processes of economic reproduction and distribution to reallocate life chances between individuals and/or classes.

## Capitalism Against the Welfare State: Classical Political Economy

In this book, attention is focused upon the nature of the relationship between capitalism, the welfare state and social democracy. In considering the competing ways in which this relationship has been understood, perhaps the most primitive line of division is between those who perceive the welfare state to be *incompatible* with the principles and practices of (any form of) capitalism and those who understand the welfare state as a possible or even as a *necessary* component of any developed capitalist economy. Both forms of explanation can be seen to focus upon (differing) aspects of capitalism as a market-based form of economic organization. For both, social democracy may be either an indispensable third term or else largely irrelevant.

The conviction that state responsibility for social welfare is incompatible with the efficient working of a capitalist economy can be persuasively retraced to capitalism's greatest advocate – Adam Smith. In common with many later commentators, Smith understood welfare, or the means to welfare, rather narrowly, as being secured primarily through the production and exchange of goods and services within the formal economy. Since, he argued, the general welfare of society is but the sum of the welfare of the individuals within it, social welfare would be best secured by maximizing the sum of individual welfares. Such maximization could best be achieved by allowing individuals, within an overall legal framework of tort and contract, to pursue their own economic interests without external restraint. The form for such economic maximization was a freely competitive market economy in which production was directed solely by the laws of supply and demand and in which each sought to maximize his/her welfare within the marketplace by selling dear and buying cheap such marketable resources or 'commodities' (including labour) as lay within his/her command. The great beauty of the market economy – its 'cunning of reason' – was that though every man entered into market transactions solely to serve his own selfish (and generally short-term) ends, in so doing he was 'led by an invisible hand to promote an end which was not part of his intention', that is the maximization of general social welfare or the common good (Smith, 1976a). If not quite the product of either God or Nature, markets nonetheless maximized the liberty of the individual and effectively directed man's (natural) self-interest and greed towards the optimization of general social welfare.

Smith, like the more thoughtful of his latter-day followers, was not an uncritical admirer of the market. He noted, for example, the pernicious effect that the minute division of labour might have upon the labouring poor. Nor did he discount the importance of a state exercising centralized political authority. However, the proper exercise of such state power was limited to: (1) the defence of the realm against external assault, (2) the guarantee of the rule of law and (3) the maintenance of 'certain public works and certain public institutions' which the market could not competently provide. Even were the latter to include some sort of state responsibility for the relief of destitution, it is clear that the state could not have a *duty* to provide (nor its citizens a corresponding *right* to claim) generalized social welfare.

Just why such a welfare-securing state was incompatible with a capitalist market economy is made clear in the work of other classical political economists – notably by Nassau Senior and Thomas Malthus (Senior, 1865; Malthus, 1890; see also Bowley, 1967, pp. 282–334; Rimlinger, 1974, pp. 38–47). Within a capitalist economy, the 'free' owners of labour power – as Marx ironically noted, 'free' in the twin sense of being legally at liberty to sell their labour power to an employer and being 'free' of any other means of supporting themselves – must be obliged to sell this labour power *at the prevailing market price* in order to support themselves and their families (Marx, 1973a, pp. 270–1). Without this compulsion to work – the requirement to undergo the disutility of labour in order to enjoy the utility of welfare – an efficient (and welfare-maximizing) market economy could no longer function. If welfare were to be granted, still more were it to be guaranteed, independent of the willingness (and/or capacity) to work, there would remain no incentive for the worker to sell his or her labour power. Workers could then dissipate themselves (as Malthus feared) in idle living (and breeding) at the expense of the productive members of society and the economy would in turn be undermined to the eventual ruination of the whole society. Thus, it was the very uncertainty of the wage-earner's continued welfare that was the mainspring of capitalist economic growth.

## Capitalism Against the Welfare State: Marx

Marx was perhaps the most sophisticated (and admiring) critic of this classical political economy. In turning to his account of the relationship between capitalism and welfare, we find broad agreement about the structure and dynamics of the capitalist economy and about its incompatibility with state-secured welfare. As the status of his definitive study of *Capital* as 'a critique of political economy' suggests, Marx's intention was to take the work of the classical political economists and to press what he saw as their authentic premises to radically new conclusions (Marx, 1973a). The radical divergence between Marx and classical political economy lies not in his view of the relationship between capitalism and the welfare-securing state, but in his account of the (ever more acute) inability of capitalist economic organization to secure 'genuine' individual and social welfare.

At the heart of Marx's critique of capitalism were three basic claims drawn from classical political economy: first, that capitalism is an economic system based upon the production and exchange of privately owned commodities within an unconstrained market; secondly, that the value of any commodity is an expression of the amount of human labour power expended upon its production. Upon these premises, Marx develops an account of capitalism as a necessarily exploitative and class-based system, one in which unpaid labour is extracted from the sellers of labour power by the owners of capital under the form of a 'free and equal exchange' in the marketplace. Such market exchanges do not however optimize individual (and thus social) welfare. Rather, the radically unequal exchange (the extraction of surplus value) that is masked by a formally 'free and equal' market in commodities means that capitalist economic organization only secures the welfare of the capitalists (as individuals and as a numerically declining class) while prescribing *dis*welfare for the great majority of the exploited working class.

The third element that Marx derives from classical political economy is the claim that capitalism is a dynamic system in which the competitive search for profit and responses to the long-term tendency for the rate of profit to fall lead to the intensification of exploitation and the heightening of class conflict. It is also a system chronically prone to periodic crises (of overproduction). While such crises do not straightforwardly occasion the economic collapse of capitalism, they do determine a cyclical intensification of the contradictions that are to lead to its eventual demise. As a part of this process, capitalism in its historically 'declining' phase comes to be ever less efficient and less equitable in delivering individual and collective social welfare.

This radical inequality of welfare outcomes is endemic to capitalism and, for Marx, not open to remedy or amelioration by an interventionist state. As we shall see later, views on the welfare state in twentieth-century Marxism are complex and sometimes contradictory. However, the most essential points of Marx's own understanding of the state, and of its capacity to secure general social welfare, may be summarized as follows:

1   While some insist that Marx's central works of political economy constitute not an economic but a *materialist* critique of capitalism, the core of Marx's historical materialism depicts the political in general, and the state in particular, as derived from essentially economic relationships.
2   That economic relationship which the state and politics expresses is one of systematic class-based exploitation. In every age, the state mobilizes *exclusively* the interests of the ruling class. This is true of the capitalist state, as it will be of the proletarian state

under a transitional socialist order. Only under communism, with the final elimination of class oppression, will the state 'wither away'.

3 The state cannot serve two masters (or classes) nor can the transformation from one type of state to another be peaceful and/or gradual (other than under very exceptional circumstances). The bitter historical experience of the workers' movement has been that the existing state has to be 'smashed' and replaced with new and distinctively proletarian state institutions. (Marx, 1973b, pp. 125, 71; Pierson, 1986, pp. 7–30)

4 This relationship is not changed by the winning of popular parliamentary democracy. Certainly, Marx held democracy to be a progressive principle but he rejected the claim that the winning of parliamentary democracy so transformed the existing order that it became possible to effect transition through the institutions of the existing state. (Marx, 1973b, pp. 238, 190)

In summary, the state under capitalism might intervene in the reproduction of social relations; however it could not (1) intervene in such a way as to undermine the logic of the capitalist market economy or (2) act against the long-term interests of the capitalist class. Whatever institutional form the state under capitalism might take (and even under the governance of social democratic forces) it remained in essence a *capitalist* state. For Marx, securing the *real* welfare of the broad working population and articulating their *real* needs were simply incompatible with the structure of a capitalist economy.

It is possible then to find in the work of classical political economy and its fiercest opponent a broadly shared view of the incompatibility between capitalist economic organization and the state provision of welfare. The distribution of utilities under capitalism is taken to reflect not 'needs', however these are understood, but market capacity. It was not so much this analysis of the nature of the capitalist economy that divided socialists from capitalism's defenders. Rather it was the socialists' argument that responsiveness to markets rather than 'needs' made capitalism unacceptable and required that it be replaced by a form of social organization of production (whether communal, co-operative or state-directed) in which the distribution of welfare reflected 'real need' rather than 'market capacity'. Down to the early twentieth century and the prospect of the welfare state as an alternative socialist strategy, this was a view embraced not just by revolutionary Marxists but also by most other (and more circumspect) species of socialism. The defenders of liberal capitalism responded to this criticism by insisting that, while not perfect, markets were the most effective way of promoting general and improving levels of welfare. If the anonymous and impersonal 'coercion' of the market were to be removed and society's material needs still to be met, this would require *more* oppressive and directive forms of coercion by the state (Kristol, 1978).

## Capitalism and the Welfare State: Symbiosis and Support

There were those writing in the eighteenth and nineteenth centuries who believed that capitalist economic organization was compatible with securing collective provision for the welfare of the working class (Owen, 1927; Paine, 1958, pp. 246ff.). However, down to the last third of the nineteenth century there was widespread agreement among both the defenders and the detractors of capitalism that state welfare was incompatible with the dynamics of a capitalist economy. The twentieth century has seen opinion much more evenly divided. Indeed, in certain phases, there has been a broadly based consensus, again shared on both left and right, that the state provision of welfare is fully compatible with, or even indispensable to, a developed capitalist economy. This mutual compatibility of capitalism and state welfare is not always welcomed and some see the welfare state as a way of reinforcing the inequitable welfare outcomes dictated by the market economy. But, whether for good or ill, in the period after the Second World War, the logic of *symbiosis* between the welfare state and capitalism came to define the prevailing orthodoxy.

The context for this changed approach to the relationship between capitalism and the welfare state was the emergence or maturing of a series of deep-seated economic, social and political changes in the structure of the developing capitalist societies towards the end of the nineteenth century. For those who perceive a symbiotic relationship between capitalism and public welfare, the emergence of the welfare state can be understood in terms of those societal changes which arose out of the great historical transformation from essentially agrarian, localized and traditional to definitively industrialized, (inter)-national and modern societies that occurred between the eighteenth and twentieth centuries. More specifically, these transformations could be traced to the interaction between industrial revolution (expanding from its origins in eighteenth century Britain) and political revolution (most spectacular in America and France in the eighteenth century, but just as important in the widespread extension of democracy in the late nineteenth and early twentieth centuries).

To summarize, the most important of these societal developments were:

1  **The impact of industrialization.** The coming of large-scale industrial production led to:
   (a)  a long-term decline in agricultural employment and the rural population
   (b)  extensive urbanization; the growth of large cities and of typically urban 'ways of life'
   (c)  the creation of a landless (manual) urban working class, concentrated in particular economic sectors and based in distinctive urban neighbourhoods
   Its *further* development led to:
   (d)  the requirement for a (partially) skilled, literate and reliable work-force
   (e)  the recognition of 'unemployment' as a condition in which workers were *involuntarily* unable to find paid work
   (f)  the growth of white-collar employment and the middle classes
   (g)  the creation of societies of historically unprecedented wealth (however inequitably this wealth might be distributed) and of sustained and long-term economic growth

2  **Population growth and the changing social composition of the population.** Everywhere industrialization was accompanied by a rapid growth of population. It was also associated with other demographic changes:
   (a)  changing patterns of family and community life
   (b)  a growing division between working and non-working populations and between 'home' and 'work'
   (c)  decreasing infant mortality and increased life expectancy, (at least in the long run)
   (d)  the emergence of publicly sanctioned non-participation in the labour force (through retirement in old age, sickness, disability, child-rearing, involvement in full-time education)

3  **The growth of nation states.** The locus of industrialization consisted increasingly of nations and states. In some cases, state formation and nation-building were directly associated with the management and co-ordination of industrial development (as, for example, in Germany and Italy). The growth of industrialized nation states was itself widely associated with:
   (a)  internal pacification
   (b)  the centralization of governmental powers
   (c)  the development of a 'professional' civil service

(d)   growing state competence through new techniques of surveillance and advanced communications

For most (though certainly not for all) significant commentators, one
further element should be added to these basic characteristics of
industrialization:

4 **The growth of political democracy/the rise of political
citizenship:**
(a)   the expansion of legal citizenship
(b)   the extension of the franchise
(c)   the development of social democratic parties
(d)   the increased salience of 'the social question' or the political
'problem' of the working class

For the great majority of more recent commentators, these constitute
the necessary, but not sufficient, bases for an explanation of the
development of the welfare state. There is some disagreement about
which of these constitute the more important causes. For example,
some commentators dismiss the independent impact of *political*
forces in shaping the welfare state, while others regard political
mobilization as indispensable. There is also violent disagreement
about those other variables whose interaction with industrial development can persuasively account for the emergence of the welfare state. But it is widely maintained that without these basic
processes of industrialization (the growth of industrial production,
economic growth, urbanization, demographic change, state development) it would be impossible to imagine the modern welfare state.

## Industrialism and the Welfare State

For some, the principal mobilizing force behind the growth of the
welfare state was a *moral* one, based upon public or elite reactions
against the excessive hardships inflicted by early industrialization.
In such accounts, particular stress is laid upon the growth of huma-
nitarian and charitable sentiment among the governing and middle
classes, the growth of knowledge of social and medical conditions
affecting the industrial population and a growing awareness of the
nature and importance of public health provision. Thus Penelope
Hall, in a standard British text of the 1950s (and beyond), insists that
the basis of the welfare state rests in 'the obligation a person feels to
help another in distress, which derives from the recognition that
they are in some sense members one of another' (Hall, 1952, p. 4).
In a more historical mode, Derek Fraser writes of 'the public conscience ... shocked into action' and Malcolm Bruce of the welfare state

as 'the result of a fit of conscience' (Fraser, 1973, p. 23; Bruce, 1968, p. 294).

However much this 'moral' approach may continue to reflect popular justifications of the welfare state, its intellectual authority has been rapidly eroded over the past twenty years. Perhaps more lastingly influential have been those who depict the coming of the welfare state as a product of *'the logic of industrialism'*. From the perspective of (Anglo-Saxon) functionalist sociology in the post-war period, the rise of the interventionist state and the curtailment of the 'excesses' of liberal capitalism could be seen as a response to the new 'needs' generated by the development of industrial societies. Upon such an explanation, the origins of the welfare state were seen to lie in secular changes associated with the broad processes of industrialization and, particularly, the breakdown of traditional forms of social provision and family life. These changes included economic growth and the associated growth in population (especially of an aged population), the developed division of labour, the creation of a landless working class, the rise of cyclical unemployment, changing patterns of family and community life and industry's increasing need of a reliable, healthy and literate workforce.

The most authoritative advocate of this industrialism thesis has been Harold Wilensky, whose early work concluded that 'over the long pull, economic level is the root cause of welfare-state development'. Its effects are expressed 'chiefly through demographic changes ... and the momentum of the programs themselves once established'. The effects of 'political elite perceptions, mass pressures, and welfare bureaucracies' may hasten its coming, but the welfare state is essentially a product of the 'needs' of an industrialized society. While Wilensky allows some weight at the margins to the influence of 'democratic corporatism', in essence, political ideology and political systems are largely irrelevant in explaining a technologically determined development which occurs more or less independently of the will of either political elites or mass publics (Wilensky, 1975, p. 47; Wilensky, 1976, pp. 21–3).

This thesis on the welfare state, which achieved its greatest prominence in the 1950s and 1960s, belonged within a much broader explanation of the evolution of industrial societies. This broader account enjoined that conventional political divisions between capitalist and socialist (or communist) societies were increasingly irrelevant. What characterized societies in the developed world (capitalist or communist) was that they were *industrial* societies, the nature of whose social and economic arrangements were given by the technological logic of industrial production and economic growth. Thus, Wilensky argued economic growth and its demographic and bureaucratic outcomes are the root cause of the general emergence of the welfare state ... such heavy brittle categories as 'socialist' versus 'capitalist' economies, 'collectivistic' versus 'individualistic' ideologies, or even 'democratic' versus 'totalitarian' political systems ... are almost useless in explaining the origins and general development of the welfare state. (Wilensky, 1975, p. xiii)

Accordingly, such theorists maintained both that the welfare state was an indispensable part of this structure of the industrial societies and that 'the primacy of economic level and its demographic and bureaucratic correlates is support for a convergence thesis: economic growth makes countries with contrasting cultural and political traditions more alike in their [welfare state] strategy' (Wilensky, 1975, p. 27).

---

**Thesis 1**

The welfare state is a product of the *needs* generated by the development of industrial societies.

---

## Commentary: The Industrialism Thesis

As the orthodoxy of the 1950s and 1960s, the industrialism thesis – with its central claim that the welfare state was a product of both the new *needs* and the new *resources* generated by the process of industrialization – has received considerable attention. A series of empirical surveys (most influentially those of Cutright and Wilensky) suggested 'the primacy of economic level and its demographic and bureaucratic correlates' in determining welfare state development. In a survey of seventy-six nation states outside Africa, Cutright found that 'the degree of social security coverage is most powerfully correlated with its level of economic development' (Cutright, 1965, p. 537). Wilensky's later survey among a range of twenty-two developed and underdeveloped nation states maintained that economic level, when combined with the dependent effects of the proportion of aged in the population and the age of the social security system, explained in excess of 85 per cent of the international variance in social security effort. Accordingly, 'there is not much variance left to explain' by other causes (Wilensky, 1975, pp. 22–5, 48–9).

However, this view has been frequently challenged. In a survey of seventeen developed Western capitalist democracies, Stephens argues that Wilensky's 'finding that public spending is heavily influenced by the demographic and bureaucratic outcomes of economic growth does not hold' (Stephens, 1979, p. 101). Similarly, O'Connor finds very limited evidence of convergence in the OECD countries, and then only upon a very particular definition of 'welfare effort' and for a very limited period (O'Connor, 1988). In a survey of the long-term experience of four Western European states, Hage, Hanneman and Gargan find that 'previous research has overestimated the importance of GNP in welfare state development'. While 'social need is an important determinant of the growth in welfare expenditures ... the availability of resources has no relationship to the growth in welfare expenditures' (Hage, Hanneman and Gargan, 1989, pp. 104–8). Indeed, in certain contexts, Hage, Hanneman and Gargan and David Cameron find that the growth of welfare expenditure is in fact *counter*-cyclical, that is it is negatively related to economic growth. (For France and the UK, respectively, see Hage, Hanneman and Gargan, 1989, p. 107; Cameron, 1978, p. 1245).

Most recently, Manfred Schmidt has adapted the 'industrialist' thesis developed by Dethev Zollner to assess social policy development in a range of thirty-nine 'rich and poor countries'. Zollner's original thesis was that the share of social spending as a percentage of GDP (as a surrogate of welfare state development) could be correlated with 'the non-agricultural dependent labour force–population ratio' (as an index of industrialization). Amending the thesis so as also to include previous levels of affluence and of social expenditure, Schmidt finds that, in its amended form, Zollner's industrialism thesis will explain about 75 per cent of total variation in social spending effort among his thirty-nine nation sample. The fit between the amended Zollner thesis and the empirical data is thus 'remarkably good'. However, for a small subsample of nine nations (both 'underspenders' and 'overspenders'), the fit was 'remarkably bad'. In the case of these 'social policy-surplus' and 'deficit' nations, Schmidt insists that an explicitly political explanation is required (Schmidt, 1989).

Schmidt's assessment may in fact direct us towards a more general conclusion about the utility of the industrialism thesis. Undoubtedly, the experience of industrialization and economic growth has had a profound impact upon the development of welfare states. Even among those who challenge the relationship of economic development to welfare state growth, there is widespread recognition of changing social need as a spur to social policy innovation. However, following Uusitalo, it is clear that the significance of economic development in explaining *variation* in social policy between nations depends very substantially upon the size and diversity of the sample under review. It may also depend upon the precise ways in which crucial variables, such as 'welfare effort', are specified (O'Connor and Brym, 1988). In samples which draw upon a wide range of very differently developed nations (as when, for example, contrasting the first and third worlds), economic development emerges as a very powerful indicator of welfare state growth. However, among similarly developed nations (for example, in studies confined to OECD countries), much less can be explained by variation in level of economic development (Uusitalo, 1984). Correspondingly, we can argue that the industrialism thesis (stripped of its teleological functionalist element) demonstrates that economic and industrial development has been a necessary background condition for the development of welfare states. However, given this premise, especially within the developed capitalist states, the *particular form* that the welfare state takes may be crucial, and it is here that the space remains for other forms of explanation.

This is an insight which has been developed with particular effect in the recent work of Goran Therborn. Concentrating upon the logic of market economies rather than the logic of industrialism, Therborn insists that the dominance of capitalist markets, far from eliminating the necessity for state institutions, generates new and pressing demands for (welfare) state intervention. He draws attention to what he calls 'the modern *universality* of welfare states', as the form which all developed and industrial societies (and not only capitalist ones) must necessarily take. For Therborn, such universality necessarily arises from a uniform feature of all such societies, namely *'the failure of markets in securing human reproduction'*. Echoing the classical analysis of Karl Polanyi on the coming of a market society, he insists that 'markets require states'. He identifies a 'double historical process, in which the modern welfare state emerged, a process of market expansion and a countermovement of protection against the market' (Therborn, 1987, p. 240). As feminist writers have done most to establish, the market has never provided competently for the reproduction of human labour power. For this it has always had to rely upon either private provision (through the family) or public provision (through the state's education and health services). Welfare states then are the necessary corollary of the rise of the market economy.

This account of the welfare state as provider of those conditions of human reproduction not secured by the market is developed through a further distinction between *public* goods and *private* goods.[1] Therborn argues that state provision for simple human re-production and some provision for expanded reproduction consti-tutes a public good in virtually all developed countries. Some other public goods – beyond the simple reproduction of the species – are widely acknowledged (for example, in the area of natalist or health policies). Others have become more or less deeply institutionalized as 'national norms' or 'social citizenship rights'. However, the state provision of private (rivally consumed) goods is seen to constitute a much more fiercely contested area of welfare state policy. The provision of private goods, whether progressive or regressive, is, by definition, redistributive. It is here, over the redistribution of re-sources through taxation, pensions, social security transfers and so on, that the fiercest disputes occur.

In essence, Therborn's view is that a minimum of state provision of welfare (broadly, that which can be understood as constituting public goods) is a necessity dictated by the structure of societies dependent on markets and is not vulnerable to political retrench-ment. Only the form and extent of the welfare state, rather than its very existence, is a political issue in market-dependent societies, and this form will be largely determined by the balance of social forces in conflict. This may be illustrated through Therborn's own 'ideal types' of the welfare state as these might reflect the conflicting interests of owners and workers (see table 1.1).

A strong, interventionist welfare state is seen to be closer to the working-class model and better able to resist pressure for retrench-ment. By contrast, a market-oriented, weak welfare state is closer to the bourgeois model. However, the conflict engaged in is over the *form* or *extent* of the welfare state, not over the welfare state set against some other state form.

In this way, Therborn characterizes the welfare state as 'irreversi-ble' or as a 'functional necessity'. It is an indispensable means of overcoming the limitations of market provision under *any* social formation. However, its actual form may represent the interests of either capital or organized labour. The balance of interests repre-sented will be determined by the effective strengths of these (and other) opposing political forces. Therborn's account thus shares with the original industrialism thesis the claim that the welfare state is a product of the needs generated by the development of market-based

---

1  *Public goods* are 'non-rivally consumed' goods or goods the exclusion from which by non-paying consumers is impractical. *Private goods* are those which, even if provided by the state, are rivally consumed.

**Table 1.1**   Two types of Welfare State

| 'Proletarian' welfare state | 'Bourgeois' welfare state |
|---|---|
| (1) Welfare state arrangements to assert workers' right to a livelihood | Welfare state arrangements adjusted to needs of capital accumulation, incentives to work, and so on |
| (2) Right to work, right to safety at work, leisure, and so on | Primarily geared to provision of skilled, able, loyal and fit work-force |
| (3) Statutory public social insurance, public income maintenance, worker-controlled; (state-controlled a second-best option) | Limited (discretionary) system, administered by employers; (state-controlled a second-best option) |
| (4) A wide coverage and uniform/universal provision on a class (rather than 'social citizenship') basis | No uniform/universal provision; provision on a 'needs' basis |
| (5) Redistributive financing | Financed on (actuarially sound) insurance principles |

*Source*:   Therborn (1986) pp. 155–6

societies. But he also maintains that the actual level of welfare state provision will be an expression of the strength of social democratic forces.

The industrialism thesis, in either its original or this amended form, remains of considerable importance. It is clear that massive changes in the social and industrial character of capitalist societies in the nineteenth century did transform the context for state action, and the view that the dominance of capitalist markets, far from eliminating the necessity of state intervention, generates new and pressing demands for state involvement carries considerable conviction. Nonetheless, such accounts are very significantly weakened by the misplaced assumption that the identification of changing 'needs' in itself explains the development of new institutions to meet such needs. In the case of Therborn's work, it is not clear that the identification of potential public goods makes their (indefinitely continued) provision unproblematic. Public choice theory makes it clear that there is no guarantee that a public good will be produced even if it is in the interests of every member of society to have such a good provided (Offe, 1987, p. 516; Olson, 1965). Furthermore, many of Therborn's proposed public goods, resting on 'national norms' or 'social citizenship rights' look extremely vulnerable to political retrenchment or 'redefinition'. Too often, the 'logic of industrialism' has been seen as a sufficient explanation of the rise of welfare state institutions, without identifying the political and historical actors and forces which were to make such changes happen.

## Modernization and the Welfare State

The modernization approach may be represented, simply if rather approximately, as a politicized version of the industrialism thesis. It too is concerned with what distinguishes modern from traditional societies and sees the welfare state as a part of that complex which defines modern society. It too is shaped by a progressive–evolutionary logic, an historical transition towards more complex and developed societies which is seen to be carrying all traditional societies towards some variant of the modern form. But it can be distinguished from the industrialism thesis by the (differing) ways in which it complements the logic of industrialism with the dynamics of democratization. Thus modern societies are to be defined as much by the processes of institutional change that they have undergone under the rubric of political democratization as by the technological changes that have followed upon industrialization.

The modern world (including the welfare state) is seen to be the product of two revolutionary changes – not just the 'industrial revolution' but also the political revolution that transformed national publics from subjects to citizens. The latter process – most explicit in the revolutionary experience of France and the US – saw its more prosaic but equally important fulfilment in the widespread universalization of the franchise around the turn of the twentieth century. In the words of Flora and Heidenheimer, the welfare state is 'a general phenomenon of modernization ... a product of the increasing differentiation and the growing size of societies on the one hand and of processes of social and political mobilization on the other'. Thus, 'the historical constellation in which the European welfare state emerged' was one of 'growing mass democracies and expanding capitalist economies within a system of sovereign nation states' (Flora and Heidenheimer, 1981a, pp. 8, 23, 22).

Theorists of modernization have not fought shy of identifying capitalism (as opposed to industrialism) as an important and independent component in the shaping of (at least western) modern societies. They also confer considerable importance upon political mobilization and especially the mobilization of the emergent working class as an important component in the rise of the welfare state, particularly in the period before 1945.[2] However, at least in the modernization writing of the 1950s and 1960s, such political mobilization was depicted less as the implementation of the class aspirations of the organized working class than as the natural correlate of full citizenship (Lipset, 1969; Flora and Heidenheimer, 1981a). Certainly, the expansion of the franchise around the turn of the twentieth century did bring the working class more fully into political life. But perhaps more importantly for the modernization theorists, it tended in the longer term to de-emphasize class politics through (1) the social concessions made to the working-class public (partly through social welfare) and (2) the shared status which everyone then enjoyed as full citizens of the nation state. Thus, the securing of the early welfare state was seen both to constitute a success for working-class politics but also to lessen the requirement for further class-based political action. Indeed, it was suggested that in a reformed polity, the equality of political citizenship might predominate over the economic inequalities that arose within the capitalist marketplace. Thus Reinhard Bendix wrote 'it may appear ... that the growth of citizenship and the nation-state is a more significant dimension of modernization than the distributive inequalities underlying the formation of social classes', while 'the growth of the welfare state ... provides a pattern of accommodation between competing social groups' (Bendix, 1970, p. 313).

Upon this account, the coming of the welfare state is one aspect of a more widespread process of modernization. It is associated historically with the extension of political citizenship and especially the rapid expansion of suffrage (and the consequent development of mass political parties) of the turn of the twentieth century. It is seen as a response to working-class political pressure (or, at least, the anticipation of such pressure), but also, through its very institutionalization of social reform, as a means of defusing the demand for further class-based and/or more revolutionary political action.

Perhaps the clearest statement of this position is to be found in the work of T. H. Marshall. Addressing the specifically British experience, Marshall characterizes the process of modernization over

---

2 Typically, Flora and Heidenheimer insist that 'up to 1914, and to a large extent through the inter-war period, the social forces most relevant to welfare state development were those of the working class' (Flora and Heidenheimer, 1981a, p. 28).

**Table 1.2** The growth of citizenship

|  | Civil rights | Political rights | Social rights |
|---|---|---|---|
| Characteristic period | 18th century | 19th century | 20th century |
| Defining principle | Individual freedom | Political freedom | Social welfare |
| Typical measures | Habeas corpus, freedom of speech, thought and faith; freedom to enter into legal contracts | Right to vote, parliamentary reform, payment for MPs | Free education, pensions, healthcare, (the welfare state) |
| | ————————→ | Cumulative | ————————→ |

*Source*: Marshall (1963) pp. 70–4

the past 300 years as one of the general expansion of citizenship. It is a history of the expansion of the rights of the citizen and a growth in the numbers of those entitled to citizen status.

Marshall identifies three species of rights (see table 1.2) – civil, political and social – each with its own 'typical' historical epoch, which have been cumulatively secured over the last 300 years. The macro-history of the period since 1688 in the UK is seen as one of progress from the securing of a body of civil rights – the rights of the freely contracting individual, sometimes identified with the structure of a capitalist market economy – which, in turn, made possible the expansion of political rights (principally, the expansion of voting rights), which meant in its turn the enfranchisement of the working class and the rise of mass social democratic parties. The winning of civil rights (in the eighteenth century) and of political rights (in the nineteenth century) made possible the securing in the twentieth century of an epoch of social rights. Such rights, which Marshall describes as embracing 'the whole range from the right to a modicum of economic welfare and security to the right to share to the full in the social heritage and to live the life of a civilized being according to the standards prevailing in the society', are frequently identified with a broadly based definition of the welfare state. Upon such an account, the coming of the welfare state is indeed an historical process, but one which is part of a broader progressive history of expanding citizenship. The coming of the welfare state in the early twentieth century is thus the product of the exercise of the expanded political citizenship of the late nineteenth century, broadly under social democratic auspices (Marshall, 1963).[3]

---

**Thesis 2**

The welfare state is a product of successful political mobilization to attain full citizenship, in the context of industrialization.

---

## Traditional Social Democracy and the Welfare State

Very similar assumptions underlie much traditional social democratic thinking on the development of the welfare state. Here again there is an emphasis upon the process of modernization (associated with the rise of an industrial civilization), and once more an acknowledgement of the importance of the capitalist organization of the economy. Also repeated is the belief that political changes effected under the rubric of extended citizenship (and under the pressure of working class political mobilization) may, in fact, have *undermined* the conditions for further class-based political mobilization.

The distinctiveness of the traditional social democratic position may be established around three key points. First, while social democrats recognize that the birth of capitalism had severe and oppressive consequences for the formative working class, they insist that its further development has not, as Marxist critics have insisted, seen an inexorable worsening of the relative position of the working class. The situation of the urban-industrial working class (often through their own mobilization and agitation first in trades unions and then in social democratic political parties) has improved not worsened. Thus, capitalism has proven capable of reform. The excesses of liberal capitalism have been checked by an increasingly interventionist 'social state' which has counteracted the inequitable outcomes of liberal capitalism through legislative interference.

Secondly, the class structure of capitalism, again in defiance of Marxist expectations, has not been increasingly polarized but has, in practice, grown to be ever more diffuse and differentiated. Significantly, the development of capitalism has been accompanied by the

---

3   In fact, Marshall's was not a straightforwardly evolutionary view. He repeatedly stressed the potential clash between citizenship equality and class/economic inequality (Marshall, 1963). For a critical commentary, see Barbalet (1988). See also below, pp. 196–207.

secular growth of the middle class. In the twentieth century, the growing division between the legal ownership of capital and its effective control (the 'managerial revolution') is seen to have weakened the power of capital as a class. At the same time, the expansion of the interventionist state not only ameliorates the position of the working class, but, in creating an expanding public employment sector, increasingly unseats the logic of the market and further complicates and differentiates class structure.

Thirdly, since a (reformed) capitalism is capable of growth without crises, and furnishes an increasingly complex class structure, the social democrats argue that further social progress (towards conceptually rather indistinct 'socialist' ends) is best effected, indeed is only possible, through the continued promotion of (capitalist) economic growth.[4]

All of these strategic claims and conclusions rely upon a fourth and decisive element in the social democrats' position. This is their belief in the definitive importance of the winning of mass parliamentary democracy and the changing balance of social forces this occasions between the attenuated economic power of the owners of industry and the enhanced political power of elected governments. The expansion of the franchise within the core societies of developed capitalism in the late nineteenth and early twentieth centuries – which generally corresponded with the rise of social democratic parties – is afforded an unchallenged primacy in social democratic accounts as the key to subsequent social development. Such social development is best explained not by concentrating upon patterns of capitalist development alone, but rather by considering the impact of the expansion of democratic institutions and political rights against a background of economic growth. Of decisive importance is the winning of democracy which brings a new social and political order under which it is *political* authority which exercises effective control over the *economic* seats of power.[5] Buttressed by the increased power of organized labour and the diffusion of the capitalist interest through the 'managerial revolution', the state emerges as

---

4  According to the leading turn-of-the-century revisionist Eduard Bernstein, 'the prospects of socialism depend not on the decrease but on the increase of social wealth' (Bernstein, 1909, p. 142).

5  According to Sidney Webb, 'collectivism is the obverse of democracy'; if the working man is given the vote, 'he will not forever be satisfied with exercising that vote over such matters as the appointment of the Ambassador to Paris, or even the position of the franchise ... he will more and more seek to convert his political democracy into what one may roughly term an industrial democracy, so that he may obtain some kind of control as a voter over the conditions under which he lives' (Webb, cited in Hay, 1975, p. 14).

the principal directing authority within the advanced capitalist societies. Increasingly, outmoded and irrational direction by the market, responsible to no-one, gives way to the planning and administrative logic of an accountable political authority.

Further, the securing of democratic institutions allows for the *gradual* transformation of both state and society. Before the coming of mass democracy, the exclusion of the mass of the people from within 'the pale of the constitution' justified, indeed necessitated, the call for the revolutionary overthrow of capitalism. However, the winning of parliamentary democracy transformed this relationship, allowing (indeed requiring) that the now legal mass political and industrial organizations of the working class should effect the gradual transformation of capitalism into socialism by first securing democratic control of the state and then using such state power to effect social and economic transformation. The 'social state' or welfare state – the state which intervenes within the processes of economic production and exchange to redistribute life chances between individuals and classes – was the principal mechanism for prosecuting such a transformative political strategy.

## Social Democracy and the Coming of the Keynesian Welfare State

However, this perspective still left practising social democrats with the theoretical 'problem' of the long-term socialization of the economy. As we have seen, early social democrats were distinguished from their more radical socialist opponents not by rejection of the final *aim* of socialization of the economy (which formally, at least, they endorsed), but by their differing (gradualist or evolutionary) *method* for achieving such an end. Neo-classical economics insisted that capitalism required the free play of untrammelled market forces. It seemed that for its socialist (including social democratic) opponents, socialism must by contrast be premised upon some form of centralized and directive planning and investment. However, the social, political and economic costs of transition to such a socialized/ planned economy were great, perhaps insurmountable, for social democrats pledged to the introduction of socialism through the medium of liberal parliamentary democracy.[6] The 'solution' to this

---

6   On the costs and difficulties of revolutionary transition, see Emmanuel, (1979); Offe (1985); Przeworski (1985); Przeworski and Sprague (1986).

social democratic dilemma was to be found in the development of Keynesian economic policy in association with the promotion of an expanded welfare state – the so-called *Keynesian Welfare State*. It is in this way that the welfare state comes to assume its familiar centrality in social democratic thinking.

For social democracy, the vital importance of Keynesianism resided in its status as 'a system of political control over economic life' (Skidelsky, 1979, p. 55). Its great strategic beauty lay in its promise of effective political control of economic life without the dreadful social, economic and political costs that social democrats feared 'expropriation of the expropriators' would bring. Though Keynes was not a socialist, he was an opponent of the belief that capitalism was a self-regulating economic system. Above all, it was the neo-classical belief in a self-regulating market mechanism securing full employment that Keynes sought to subvert, indeed to invert.

Say's Law – that under capitalism supply created its own sufficient demand – held true, Keynes claimed, only under the peculiar conditions of full employment. It did not however itself *guarantee* equilibrium at full employment. Such a balance could only be secured outside the market, by the state's manipulation of 'those variables which can be deliberately controlled or managed by central authority' (Keynes, 1973). The key variables which governments could manipulate were the propensity to consume and the incentive to invest. It was the duty of governments to intervene within the market to generate an enhanced level of 'effective demand', promoting both the propensity to consume and to invest, so as to ensure sufficient economic activity to utilize all available labour and thus to secure equilibrium at full employment. To achieve this, a whole range of indirect measures – including taxation policy, public works, monetary policy and the manipulation of interest rates – were available to the interventionist government.

Keynes' advocacy of a 'managed capitalism' offered a neat solution to the social democratic dilemma of how to furnish reforms for its extended constituency and maintain its long-term commitment to socialism without challenging the hegemony of private capital. It was Keynesian economics that provided the rationale for social democracy's abandonment of the traditional socialist aspiration for socialization of the economy. Keynes himself had famously insisted:

It is not the ownership of the instruments of production which it is important for the state to assume. If the state is able to determine the aggregate amount of resources devoted to augmenting the instruments and the basic rate of reward to those who own them, it will have accomplished all that is necessary. (Keynes, 1973, p. 378)

In this way, it was possible for social democrats to represent formal ownership of the economy (and the traditional strategy of socialization/nationalization) as (largely) irrelevant. Economic control could be exercised through the manipulation of major economic variables in the hands of the government. The owners of capital could be *induced* to act in ways which would promote the interests of social democracy's wide constituency. At the same time, social democratic governments could shape the propensity to consume, through taxation and monetary policy, as well as through adjusting the level of public spending. They could also rectify the disutilities of the continuing play of market forces through the income transfers and social services that came to be identified with the welfare state. Happily, the raising of workers' wages and income transfers to the poor, a 'vice' in classical economics, suddenly became, given the tendency of lower income groups to consume the greater part of their incomes, a Keynesian 'virtue'. Social democracy was thus able simultaneously to secure the 'national interest' and to service its own constituency.

For traditional social democrats, then, the development of the welfare state institutionalized the successes of social democratic politics. The Keynesian revolution made possible the transition from the (zero-sum) politics of production to what, under conditions of economic growth, were the (positive-sum) politics of (re-)distribution. As Berthil Ohlin described it in the 1930s, 'the tendency is in the direction of a "nationalization of consumption" as opposed to the nationalization of the "means of production" of Marxian socialism' (Ohlin, 1938, p. 5). It was a two-fold strategy built upon active government intervention through (1) the macro-management of the economy to ensure economic growth under conditions of full employment and (2) a range of social policies dealing with 'the redistribution of the fruits of economic growth, the management of its human effects, and the compensation of those who suffered from them' (Donnison, 1979, pp. 146–50).

---

### Thesis 3

The welfare state is a product of industrial and political mobilization. It embodies the successes of the social democratic political project for the gradual transformation of capitalism.

---

# The Power Resources Model

The power resources model offers a distinctive variant of the social democratic approach. At its heart is a perceived division within the advanced capitalist societies between the exercise of economic and political power, often presented as a contrast between markets and politics. It is insisted that 'the types of power resources that can be mobilized and used in politics and on markets differ *in class-related ways*' (Korpi, 1989, p. 312; emphasis added). Thus, in the *economic* sphere, the decisive power resource is control over capital assets, the mechanism for its exercise is the (wage labour) contract and its principal beneficiary the capitalist class. However, in the *political* sphere, power flows from the strength of numbers, mobilized through the democratic process and tends to favour 'numerically large collectivities', especially the organized working class.

Institutionalized power struggles under advanced capitalism are then best understood as a struggle between the logic of the market and the logic of politics and 'this tension between markets and politics is likely to be reflected in the development of social citizenship and the welfare state' (Korpi, 1989, p. 312). The more successful are the forces of the organized working class, the more entrenched and institutionalized will the welfare state become and the more marginalized will be the principle of allocation through the market (Korpi, 1989; Esping-Andersen, 1985; Shalev, 1983; Esping-Andersen and Korpi, 1984; Esping-Andersen and Korpi, 1987).

In the face of recent criticism, Korpi has insisted that the power resources model is not to be understood as a 'one-factor theory claiming to explain welfare state development more or less exclusively in terms of working class or left strength' (Korpi, 1989, p. 312n.). A more complex position – including, for example, the role of confessional parties, party coalitions and pre-emptive conservative reforms – may be developed through the application of a 'games theoretical perspective' to a range of protagonists in the struggle over the welfare state (Korpi, 1989, p. 313). However, to date, the principal application of the power resources model has been to underwrite a distinctive left social democratic account of the welfare state as an entrenchment of the power of organized labour and as an avenue of gradual transition towards socialism.

The two core claims of this left social democratic position are succinctly summarized by John Stephens: first, 'the welfare state is a product of labour organization and political rule by labour parties' and secondly, it 'thus represents a first step towards socialism' (Stephens, 1979, p. 72). While recognizing that the welfare state is not universally an expression of the strength of the organized working class, these left social democrats insist that, under the right circumstances, the inauguration and promotion of welfare state policies and institutions has been and can be an effective strategy for the gradual transition from capitalism to socialism. However, their position differs decisively from traditional social democracy in its belief that the coming of democracy, social democratic parties and the welfare state do not transform the social and political nature of the advanced capitalist societies. The logic of Marx's analysis of the contradictions of capitalism and the centrality of class struggle still holds but parliamentary democracy and the interventionist state are seen to provide new media for the prosecution of the class politics of socialism.[7]

Generally, the inception of welfare state policies is seen to follow upon the universalization of the franchise, itself seen as a victory for the organized working class. Initially, social policy may represent an attempt to pre-empt political reform or else to disorganize or demobilize the organized working class. But it is insisted that under wise and far-sighted social democratic governance, welfare state policies can be used both to counteract the dominance of capital that market relationships entail and to reinforce the effective solidarity of organized labour. The left social democrats afford much greater independent importance to political power than do many others in the Marxist tradition and social democratic governments elected under universal franchise are seen to constitute an effective counter to the power exercised by capital within the privately owned economy. Where social democratic governments become more or less permanently entrenched in office (and this is an essential precondition), an effective balance or at least stalemate may be established between the political powers of social democracy and the economic powers of capital. Under these circumstances, some sort of working compromise between capital and labour is likely to emerge, characteristically under the rubric of the welfare state.

But the left social democrats insist that, however long-standing, such a compromise is in essence temporary. Indeed, if the social democrats govern wisely and make the right strategic choices, it is argued that the (Marxian) logic of continuing capitalist development will increasingly tilt the balance of power in favour of organized

---

7   In fact, Marxism has always embraced such a radical social democratic wing (with a strategy for socialism built upon incrementalism and parliamentary democracy), perhaps best represented by Karl Kautsky and the Austro-Marxists (Kautsky, 1909; Kautsky, 1910; Kautsky, 1983; Pierson, 1986, pp. 58–83; Bottomore and Goode, 1978).

labour and against private capital. Thus it is suggested that continuing capitalist development will tend to produce an expanding and homogeneous broad working class. Social democratic governments that mobilize this constituency and promote its internal solidarity (through, for example, nationally agreed and uniform salary increases, the support of 'full employment' and the provision of generous unemployment and sickness benefits) can undermine the effectiveness of traditional market disciplines and further entrench their own political power. At a certain point in the strengthening of the powers of organized labour, conditions of balance/stalemate with capital no longer apply. At this point, it is possible for the social democratic movement to advance beyond the 'political' welfare state, with its indirect (Keynesian) influence upon the management of the economy, and to engage directly the traditional socialist issue of socialization of the economy.

This process is seen to be most advanced in Sweden. Here, where 'the welfare state has been developed by a strongly organized and highly centralized trades union movement ... in co-operation with a social democratic government that remained in office for 44 years ... the welfare state is characterized by high levels of expenditure and progressive financing and thus represents a transformation of capitalism towards socialism' (Stephens, 1979, p. 129). To summarize, this suggests that the most 'successful' social democratic welfare states will be associated with:

1 the extension of the franchise
2 the rise of social democratic parties
3 a strong (and centralized) trades union movement
4 weak parties of the right
5 sustained social democratic governmental incumbency
6 sustained economic growth
7 strong class identity and correspondingly weak cleavages of religion, language and ethnicity

---

**Thesis 4**

The welfare state is the product of a struggle between the political powers of social democracy and the economic powers of capital. Its further development, under social democratic hegemony, makes possible the gradual transition from capitalism to socialism.

---

## Commentary: Modernization, Social Democracy and Working-Class Power

Some of the weaknesses identified in the industrialism thesis are at least addressed in the literature of modernization and traditional social democracy and in the 'power resources' model of welfare state development. In fact, there has sometimes been a tendency to elide explanations in terms of modernization with those premised upon industrialization. However, Hage, Hanneman and Gargan insist upon the need 'to separate the independent effects of modernization from those of industrialization' and argue that 'the modernization process has much more impact than the industrialization process on the expansion in social welfare expenditures'. Specifically, they isolate urbanization and the increasing density of communication (measured by quantities of mail and electronic/telegraphic communications) rather than industrialization or economic growth as decisive indicators of welfare state growth (Hage, Hanneman and Gargan, 1989, pp. 100–10). Similarly, Peter Flora and Jens Alber prefer the 'vague and ambiguous' but 'multi-dimensional' concept of modernization to either industrialization or democratization as the key to explaining the development of European welfare states (Flora and Alber, 1981, pp. 37–8).

However, the major issue that has divided advocates of modernization and social democratic theses on the welfare state from the claims of industrialism is the independent importance that they attribute to *political* forces in shaping the development of the welfare state. Often, this advocacy of the political causes of welfare state development is simply an inversion of the claims of industrialism. Thus, for example, the burden of Stephens' refutation of Wilensky was to buttress his belief 'that the welfare state is a product of labour organization and political rule by labour parties and thus represents a first step towards socialism' (Stephens, 1979, p. 72; see p. 17 above). Similarly, the purpose of Furniss and Tilton's comparative history of welfare state experience in the US, the UK and Sweden is to demonstrate 'that a democratic majority, backed by a committed labor movement, can capture and employ political power to create a more decent society along the lines of a social welfare state' (Furniss and Tilton, 1979, p. 93). Christopher Hewitt has also argued that social democratic parties can have a profound influence upon the narrowing of income inequality in advanced capitalist societies largely through the mechanism of government redistribution through the welfare state (Hewitt, 1977, pp. 450, 460; see also Hicks, 1988).

In the 1980s, Walter Korpi was an influential advocate of the view that (social democratic) politics makes a difference. Writing of the post-war experience of Germany, Austria and Sweden, he and Gosta Esping-Andersen argue that 'the relative power position of wage-earners has been of central significance for the development towards an institutional type of social policy' (Esping-Andersen and Korpi, 1984). More recently, assessing survey evidence on the emergence of social rights during sickness in eighteen OECD countries since 1930, Korpi finds 'rather unequivocal support for the assumption of the significance of left government participation in the development of social policy'. By contrast, 'while it appears reasonable to assume that the rate of growth of economic resources is of relevance for the opportunities to enact social reforms', he finds 'limited support for this hypothesis'. He concludes cautiously that 'class-based left parties appear to have played a significant role in the development of social rights' (Korpi, 1989, pp. 323–5). Julia O'Connor also claims to have isolated a strong association between left power (in both parties and trades unions) and levels of civil consumption expenditure (O'Connor, 1988).

There is then some (contested) evidence that 'politics makes a difference'. However, we need also to consider *how* it is that 'politics makes a difference'. Much as we found in discussing the evidence brought to support the industrialism thesis, evaluating data in support of modernization and traditional social democratic theses is problematic. Many of the differences in outcomes result from the use of differing indices of welfare effort and comparison across differing time periods. In his recent magisterial review, Esping-Andersen, for example, argues that very little difference can be found in the impact of politics upon *levels* of welfare expenditure (a commonly used indicator of welfare effort) but that political forces are crucial in determining differing welfare *policy regimes* (Esping-Andersen, 1990, pp. 35–54; see below, pp. 186–7).

Furthermore, some empirical surveys have found that if politics does matter, it is not necessarily the political impact of social democratic forces that matters most. Castles, for example, identifies the weakness of parties of the right as decisive for the emergence of 'generous' welfare states, while Hicks and Swank argue that '*all* less business-oriented parties, Christian democratic as well as social democratic, centrist as well as labor, prove about equally supportive of welfare expansion' (Castles, 1978; Castles, 1982; Castles, 1985; Hicks and Swank, 1984, p. 104: emphasis added). Wilensky identifies Catholic rather than left party incumbency as the strongest indicator of welfare expenditure and suggests that the intensity of party competition (notably between left and Catholic parties) may itself tend to increase welfare spending effort.[8]

Nonetheless, we can identify some analytic advances in the modernization and social democratic approaches. Most significantly, they do allow that the processes of transformation that create the modern world are simultaneously industrial/technological and political. Correspondingly, weight is given to the expansion of citizenship and the extension of democracy and attention is also directed to the ways in which the specifically capitalist organization of the production process shapes the circumstances of welfare state emergence. Unfortunately, among advocates of modernization and the more traditional variants of the social democratic thesis, these analytic advances are substantially vitiated by the form that this revised assessment takes. Thus they have tended to share with industrialism a Panglossian celebration of progress and the imposition of assumptions of 'inevitable' development. Inasmuch as they deal with both historical actors (most notably, the organized working class) and the importance of capitalism, they may be accused of misunderstanding both. Thus, for example, in the influential work of Tom Marshall, the working class is often seen to struggle historically to ensure full political citizenship and to use democracy once achieved to secure social rights under the welfare state. But the very achievement of democracy (and associated welfare state rights) is seen to resolve or at least to accommodate the differences of interest between capital and labour out of which such political struggle might have been seen to arise. The spectre of capitalism, and the deep-seated division of interests it is seen to generate, is raised only to argue that it has been 'tamed' or 'subverted' by the rise of the welfare state.

There are a number of historical objections to this account. First, it is far from clear that the coming of parliamentary democracy does bring the irreversible cessation of class hostilities and a uniform social democratic consensus on the welfare state and the mixed economy. Even where the formal concession of democracy has led to the more or less successful incorporation of the working class within the political apparatus of the existing state, this has not led to the permanent reconciliation of class differences and class hostilities in capitalist societies. Thus it is very uncertain that the spectre of 'the class politics that undermines the need for class politics' is justified by actual welfare state experience.

---

8 Wilensky (1981) pp. 356–8, 368–70; for differential spending effort related to party competition among the individual United States, see Jennings (1979).

Secondly, whatever the role of the working class in the later *development* of the welfare state, the earliest welfare state measures were generally introduced by liberal and/or conservative elites and not by the representatives of organized labour. Even, for example, in the Scandinavian social democracies, in which the working-class welfare state is often seen to be most effectively entrenched, the origins of the welfare state lay with conservative or liberal political forces (a process that is especially clear in the early development of the Danish welfare state). Similarly, there is plenty of historical evidence of organized labour opposition to welfare state measures, often because these were seen as (1) an attack upon the autonomy and integrity of trades unions' own forms of mutual support, (2) as a way of depressing wages through welfare subsidization (a repeated argument against family allowances/child benefit) and (3) as a form of state control over the work-force (see below, p. 37).

Thirdly, historical experience suggests that the class analysis of social democracy/modernization theorists is not only too optimistic and uniform but also too crude. Early welfare state measures (of social insurance) were generally limited to particular, very suitable or very vulnerable trades. Disputes over contributory and non-contributory pension schemes exacerbated differences of interest between the independent/skilled/'respectable' working class (who made limited provision for death and sickness through friendly societies) and the residuum of unskilled (and uninsured) workers. Similarly, there have been differences of interest among employers of labour, between large capital-intensive employers with an interest in a healthy, well-educated and 'regular' work-force, and those in the most keenly competitive, labour-intensive markets whose interest was in securing a mass of unskilled labour at the cheapest possible price (De Swaan, 1988). Such differences of interest among both labour and capital continue down to the present.

The historical record also shows that the state may have its own interest in the promotion of social policy, not least in the securing of a citizenry fit and able to staff its armies. For example, the concern with 'national efficiency' and the physical incapacity of the UK working class to defend the empire against the challenge of the Boers has long been cited as a source of UK welfare reforms at the turn of the twentieth century (Thane, 1982, pp. 60–1; Fraser, 1973, p. 133; Hay, 1975). This view was echoed by Lloyd George, who argued in 1917 that 'you can not maintain an A-1 empire with a C-3 population' (cited in Gilbert, 1970, p. 15).

Advocates of the traditional social democratic position certainly have good grounds for stressing the importance of citizenship. The idea of a shared status of all members of the community and especially the *right* to varying forms of provision from the state is seemingly a definitive element of the welfare state and Esping-Andersen insists that 'few can disagree with T. H. Marshall's (1950) proposition that social citizenship constitutes the core idea of a welfare state' (Esping-Andersen, 1990, p. 21). Yet Marshall's un-ilinear model of expanding citizenship, his qualifications notwith-standing, is unsatisfactory (see pp. 22–4 above). In fact, the nature of citizenship has been, and continues to be, much more consistent-ly contested than Marshall allows. The question of who counts as a citizen, whether full citizenship is gender-specific, what is to count as a citizen's entitlement and under what circumstances welfare rights will be granted and by whom continue to be daily concerns of contemporary political life. Only the very general process of overall social expenditure growth (often under very varying rules of citizen entitlement) has concealed this continuing struggle over the status of citizenship (Turner, 1986; Turner, 1990; Held, 1989).

The 'Keynesian revolution' occupies a similarly problematic place in the traditional social democratic account. Even more explicitly than the winning of citizenship, the emergence of Keynesian forms of economic management, which we have seen to occupy a central place in the justification of the social democratic theory of gradual social transformation, has not been a once-and-for-all change in the governance of capitalist economies. In a number of developed wel-fare states, perhaps most triumphally in the UK, the formal commit-ment to full employment and government macro-management of demand has been abandoned, and with it goes a substantial part of the theoretical justification of the social democratic position.

These observations on citizenship and the fate of Keynesianism may suggest a need to re-orient our understanding of the elements of bipartisanship, consensus and shared citizenship which have been so frequently identified in the post-war period. Certainly, post-war social policy was often institutionally bipartisan and apparently consensual. However, this bipartisanship may have depended in substantial part upon the favourable economic climate that made positive-sum resolutions of distributional conflicts a viable policy. Accordingly, this policy may be better understood in terms of the capacity simultaneously to satisfy a number of differing constitu-encies rather than in terms of a straightforward universalization of citizenship or the coming of consensus. Where reforms did not satisfy these several constituencies, political conflict over social po-licy could still be acute. Just such an argument has been made about the post-war period in the UK and both phenomena may also be seen in the violent conflict over the Swedish social democrats' pen-sions reform of 1958 (see, on Sweden, Esping-Andersen, 1985; on the UK, Taylor-Gooby, 1985; Pimlott, 1988; Deakin, 1987). Thus it is possible that the universal citizenship *form* may have been the medium for promoting interests with a much more traditional class-based political and economic *content*.

Finally, as Esping-Andersen has pointed out, welfare state measures may only properly be seen as securing the overall interests of social democracy's natural constituency in the (broad) working class inasmuch as they are *market-usurping* – that is to the extent that they insulate workers from the discipline of the market.[9] But clearly many welfare state measures, and especially early welfare state social policy, was not market-usurping but *market-supporting*. Trades unions were, for example, extremely suspicious of the way in which labour exchanges would be used to recruit strike-breakers or generally to service employers with non-unionized labour. Social welfare provision was, and still is, criticized as a mechanism for depressing wages and Pat Thane writes of 'widespread suspicion' towards Liberal welfare reforms in the UK from a working class which found them to be 'too limited, too "intrusive", and a threat to working-class independence both collective and individual' (Thane, 1984, p. 899; see also Marwick, 1967; Pelling, 1968; Hay, 1978a, pp. 16–21). Many early recommendations on work/farm colonies, even those supported by social democratic politicians, were explicitly coercive in intent (Harris, 1977; Gilbert, 1966, pp. 253–65). Terms of entitlement continue to reflect labour market status and often explicitly 'encourage' labour market participation. Thus, any straightforward claim that the welfare state is an imposition of working class interests through the medium of parliamentary democracy, which accordingly attenuates the conflict of (class) interests, 'tames' the excesses of capitalism and promotes a national unity based around common citizenship is unsustainable.[10]

Several of these weaknesses are confronted by the 'power resources' model. Whilst this approach is still broadly social democratic (premised upon the pursuit of a reformist path through legal-parliamentary means), the benign assumptions of an end

---

9 The issue of whether such market-usurpation will prove to be in the *long-term* interests of the working class will depend upon the place of the national welfare state within the world economy and other political developments.

10 There is a case for insisting that it is the capacity of the organized working class to continue to pursue class-based politics that is the basis for the continued capacity of the welfare state to represent a practice that is in the interests of that class.

to class conflict and an irreversible progress towards an ever-enhanced citizenship is rejected. This is a social democratic strategy premised upon the historical strength of working-class forces in continuing struggle with the powers of capital. A very considerable effort is made to show empirically that the effective strength of working-class forces (articulated through labour parties and trades union organizations) has made a real difference to the patterns of promotion of the welfare state under advanced capitalism.

However, there remain a number of problems with this model. First, while the more naïve evolutionism of traditional social democracy is rejected, elements of a Marxist evolutionism persist. Presumptions about the uniformity of workers' interests, the necessary growth in the proportion of the working class, and the weakening of the powers of capitalism in the face of the collective action of the workers underpin several of the strategic claims in the 'power resources' model. However there are good grounds for doubting that these presumptions about a majoritarian working class with unified interests are true (Pierson, 1986, pp. 7–30, 58–83; Przeworski, 1985; Przeworski and Sprague, 1986).

It may also be that the political focus of the 'power resources' model is too narrow. Middle-class support has been crucial to the pattern of welfare state development, particularly in the post-war period, and at strategic times in the historical emergence of the European welfare states the attitudes of the rural classes have also been a decisive element. Similarly, parties other than the social democrats (especially the confessional parties of continental Europe) have also played an important historical role in the expansion of the welfare state and their position has not always been one of seeking to minimize levels of social expenditure. This suggests that any understanding of the class politics of the welfare state must be one that considers the positions of a number of classes (not just capital and labour) and of a number of parties (not just the social democrats) and that the decisive element in the success of the social democratic welfare state project may lie in the capacity of the working class and social democratic parties to forge long-term, majoritarian *alliances* in support of its decommodifying form of social policy.

A second criticism of the 'power resources' model is that some of its favourable assumptions about the possibilities for successful social democratic strategies arise from its concentration upon particularly favourable examples drawn from Scandinavia and, especially, from Sweden. As Lash and Urry have pointed out, all of the favourable corporatist/welfare state examples generally cited in support of the social democratic model are numerically swamped by the single counter-example of the US.[11] Even within the Scandinavian heart-land of the welfare state, Esping-Andersen has challenged the claim that the disposition of class and political forces favours a gradual and linear progression towards an ever more extensive and market-usurping welfare state. Indeed, he argues that contemporary changes in the class structure of advanced capitalism render the 'old' social democratic politics of the welfare state redundant and threaten an unreconstituted social democracy with the prospect of early 'decomposition' (Esping-Andersen, 1985; Esping-Andersen, 1990).

Three further general criticisms have been raised against the social democratic perspective. First, there are those who insist that the social democrats' exclusive concentration on the politics of class neglects the decisive impact of interest or 'ascribed status' groups or, indeed, of the state apparatus itself. Secondly, there are those who maintain that all the social democratic approaches fail to recognize that the most important aspects of power under the welfare state lie in its gender-specific consequences for women and its 'race'-specific consequences for ethnic minorities. The claims underlying these first two criticisms will be addressed in chapter 3. A third objection to the social democratic approach is that it underplays the extent to which the welfare state, *even under social democratic auspices*, continues to be, in essence, an instrument of social control of the working population in the interests of capital. This perspective of 'social control' will be considered in chapter 2, in which we turn to criticisms of the social democratic welfare state informed by 'the new political economy'.

---

11 They observe that 'over 40% of the population living in advanced capitalist societies in fact live in the US. The size of the American population living under *non*-corporatist, low-welfare state disorganized capitalist relations is more than *three times* larger than the combined population of Austria, Switzerland, Denmark, New Zealand, Holland, Belgium, Finland, Norway and Australia; that is more than three times the size of those small countries most often cited as proofs of high levels of corporatization and organization of contemporary capitalism'. (Lash and Urry, 1987, p. 10).

# 2
# Capitalism, Social Democracy and the Welfare State II: Political Economy and the Welfare State

In the twenty-five years following the Second World War, it was largely the traditional social democratic outlook that defined the prevailing orthodoxy on advanced capitalism and the welfare state. Buttressed by empirical and programmatic work in social adminis- tration, sanctioned by bi-partisan support for the expansion of state services and underpinned by continuous economic growth, the social democratic prescription for managed capitalism and social amelioration dominated throughout the advanced industrial world. But from the late 1960s onwards, both the social democratic post-war settlement and its comforting assumptions about the reconcilability of advanced capitalism and the welfare state came under increasing challenge from both right and left. In this chapter, we begin to consider the range of critical responses to the post-war social demo- cratic orthodoxy.

## The New Right and the Welfare State

Perhaps the most prominent (and successful) opponent of the post- war orthodoxy has been the New Right, which has argued for a strong identity between social democracy and the welfare state, while insisting that both are inconsistent with the moral, political and economic freedom that only liberal capitalism can guarantee. In common with the other theoretical positions outlined in this study, the New Right does not define a unique set of prescriptions for the welfare state. In fact, it is possible to identify at least two distinct 'strands' in New Right thinking: 'a liberal tendency which argues the case for a freer, more open, and more competitive economy, and a conservative tendency which is more interested in restoring social and political authority throughout society' (Gamble, 1988, p. 29; King, 1987, pp. 7–27). In brief, both elements of the New Right are hostile to welfare state intervention because (1) its administrative and bureaucratic methods of allocation are inferior to those of the market, (2) it is morally objectionable (for both the sponsors and the recipients of state welfare), (3) it denies the consumers of welfare services any real choice and (4) despite the enormous resources devoted to it, it has failed either to eliminate poverty or to eradicate unjust inequalities of opportunity (Gamble, 1988, pp. 27–60). Indeed, the New Right almost invert the common sense of industrialism, modernization and social democratic approaches to insist that the origins of the present social, economic and political problems of advanced capitalist societies lie not in the failure of markets but in the mistaken pursuit of those market-usurping policies identified with the welfare state.

The more interesting and the more important intellectual challenge of the New Right probably comes from its neo-liberal rather than its neo-conservative wing. However, those political movements and ideologies of the 1980s which identified themselves with the New Right, most notably 'Thatcherism' in the UK and 'Reaganism' in the US, were in practice a potent, if not entirely consistent, mixture of economic liberalization and renascent conservatism. In defiance of the libertarian conclusions drawn by some on the New Right, in the UK and still more prominently in the US, the 'freeing up' of the economy was associated with the traditionally conservative imperatives of strengthening the 'law and order' state, a more aggressively nationalistic foreign policy, the reversal of minority rights, the glorification of 'traditional family life' and an endorsement of the religious and moral crusade of the moral majority (Nozick, 1974; Gilder, 1982; Stockman, 1986; King, 1987). Some of these conservative elements on the New Right receive fuller attention in chapter 5. Here our attention is more closely focused upon its neo-liberal aspect.

Underlying most neo liberal assessments of the relationship between capitalism, social democracy and the welfare state is a rehearsal of the sentiments of Adam Smith's advocacy of liberal capitalism (see p. 8 above). It is recognized that Smith wrote under very different circumstances and for a quite different agenda and audience than his latter-day admirers. Yet his was a critique of the interventionist (albeit in his time mercantilist) state and a call for limited government, whether or not democratic. He advocated the spontaneously arising market economy as the means of securing both optimum individual and social welfare and as the surest guarantee of individual liberty. It is just these prescriptions, and the ways in which social democracy and the welfare state countermand them, that lie at the heart of the contemporary neo-liberal view.

In essence, the argument of the New Right is that the impact of social democracy and the associated welfare state represent a usurpation of the sound principles of liberal capitalism. Its political ideal is to achieve a return to what is understood to have been the social and political *status quo ante*. Thus Milton Friedman insists that

> The scope of government must be limited. Its major function must be to protect our freedom both from the enemies outside our gates and from our fellow-citizens: to preserve law and order, to enforce private contracts, to foster competitive markets. (Friedman, 1962, p. 2)

Though government intervention beyond this minimum might sometimes be justified, according to Friedman, it is 'fraught with danger', (Friedman, 1962, pp. 2–3; see also Minford, 1987). Certainly, where we have had economic progress, this has been the 'product of the initiative and drive of individuals cooperating through the free market. Government measures have hampered not helped this development' (Friedman, 1962, p. 200; King, 1987, pp. 83–4). Correspondingly, Friedman's advocacy of monetarism is at least in part directed at curtailing the counter-productive interventions of social democratic governments (Friedman, 1980; Bosanquet, 1983, pp. 5–10, 22–4, 43–61).

Perhaps the most sophisticated philosophical statement of the neo-liberal view is that developed by Friedrich Hayek in the three volumes of *Law, Legislation and Liberty* (Hayek, 1982). For Hayek, the liberal 'Great Society' championed by Smith can only be secured on the basis of 'catallaxy', the neologism Hayek uses to describe 'the special kind of spontaneous order produced by the market through people acting within the rules of the laws of property, tort and contract' (Hayek, 1982, vol. 2, p. 109). Both social democracy and the welfare state seek to undermine this order based on the interlocking of spontaneously emerging markets and are thus inconsistent with the principles of a free and just society.

In fact, Hayek's Smithian liberalism is tempered by a good measure of Burkean conservatism. As in Burke's critique of the French Revolution, Hayek condemns the *'constructivist rationalism'* of all those, from 1789 onwards, who have sought to recast society in accord with some understanding of the principles of Reason (Hayek, 1982, vol. 1, pp. 5, 29–34). Order (and tradition) certainly appeal to Hayek's conservatism but this is the spontaneously generated and in principle unknowable order created by innumerable interactions within a number of interlocking markets – the catallaxy. Indeed, 'it is because it was not dependent on organization but grew up as a spontaneous order that the structure of modern society has attained that degree of complexity which it possesses and which far exceeds any that could have been achieved by deliberate organization' (Hayek, 1982, vol. 1, p. 50). In part, this is an issue of philosophical principle, namely, Hayek's belief that every individual should be, insofar as is possible, self-directing. But it also embodies a seemingly compelling sociological argument. As Hayek himself makes plain, in even the most centralized and state-dominated societies, the central political authorities can have only a very tenuous control over the many millions of social decisions made every day within its domain. By contrast, the individual may have a very intimate control as well as an irreducible/irrepressible interest in that much smaller range of *salient* decisions he or she must make in organizing his or her own life. Hayek combines this with something like Smith's own faith in the benevolence of 'the invisible hand' to sustain a distinctive account of the promotion of welfare. Thus, he argues,

> a condition of liberty in which all are allowed to use their knowledge for their purposes, restrained only by rules of just conduct of universal application, is likely to produce for them the best condition for achieving their aims. (Hayek, 1982, vol. 1, p. 55)

Hayek ascribes a correspondingly limited role to the state. The duty of the public authority is not to pursue its own ends but rather to provide the framework within which 'catallaxy' may develop. Those functions for which the state may properly raise taxation are limited to these:

1 provision of collective security against the threat of external assault
2 preservation of the rule of law where law is in essence confined to the impartial application of general rules of property, contract and tort
3 provision for (though not necessarily the administration of) those collective or public goods which the market cannot efficiently provide; for example, protection against (internal) violence, regulation of public health and the building and maintenance of roads

To these duties of the minimal state, Hayek adds the following:

4 provision of 'a certain minimum income for everyone', more precisely for 'those who for various reasons cannot make their

living in the market, such as the sick, the old, the physically or mentally defective, the widows and orphans – that is all people suffering from adverse conditions which may affect anyone and against which most individuals cannot alone make adequate provision but in which a society that has reached a certain level of wealth can afford to provide for all' (Hayek, 1982, vol. 3, p. 55)

However, Hayek is insistent that this last duty to relieve destitution is not to be identified with the welfare state. Relief is not a statutory right of citizenship, but needs-based and discretionary. Least of all is such relief to be understood as part of an attempt to manufacture 'social justice'.

Hayek's model may be completed by a brief consideration of his views on democracy. Although Hayek would doubtless consider himself a democrat, he is perhaps still more an advocate of individual freedom, and certainly he is an opponent of the ideas of sovereignty and unlimited government frequently associated with the rise of democracy. 'Only limited government can be decent government', he insisted, 'because there does not exist (and cannot exist) general moral rules for the assignment of particular benefits' (Hayek, 1982, vol. 2, p. 102). Where parliament is sovereign, governments become the plaything of organized sectional interests. Principles and 'the national interest' are abandoned in the attempt to mobilize a majority-creating coalition of particular interests against the genuinely common or public interest.

The welfare state and the political agenda of social democracy are seen by Hayek to be at odds with almost every aspect of this model of the liberal capitalist ideal. First, social democrats set out to adjust the spontaneous order of catallaxy, a project which Hayek has depicted as hopeless given the impossibility of adequate centrally organized knowledge of the infinity of market-like decisions. Interventions in the market will *always* have suboptimal outcomes and *always* lessen general social welfare. Secondly, the welfare state represents a break with Hayek's insistence that the law must be confined to rules of 'just conduct of universal application'. Social democracy prescribes particularistic legislation, most notably to confer privileges upon its allies in the organized labour movement, and governments under its auspices seek not only to negotiate general and market-usurping agreements between labour and capital but even to intervene on a day-to-day basis in the conduct of particular transactions within the marketplace. Not only is this an invasion of individual freedom and a usurpation of the proper role of the law, it is also bound to fail, given the opacity of the spontaneously generated catallaxy.

Thirdly, the welfare state is also the principal institutional vehicle of the misconceived aspiration for 'social justice' (Hayek, 1982, vol. 2, p. 1). Justice, Hayek insists, is strictly *procedural* and can only refer to the proper enforcement of general rules of universal application without regard to its particular results. No set of human arrangements, no cumulation of particular actions (however unequal its outcomes) can be described as just or unjust. 'The mirage of social justice' which the social democratic welfare state pursues is, at best, a nonsense and, at worst, pernicious and itself unjust. It means undermining the justice of the market, confiscating the wealth of the more successful, prolonging the dependency of the needy, entrenching the special powers of organized interests and overriding individual freedom. Indeed, 'distributive justice [is] irreconcilable with the rule of law' and in seeking to press state intervention beyond its legitimate minimum, the social democrats have been the principle offenders in 'giving democracy a bad name' (Hayek, 1982, vol. 2, p. 86).

## Public Choice Theory

Hayek's writings may be newly prominent but they are certainly not new. His arguments against the welfare state date back at least half a century. But in recent years, this long-standing (and largely philosophical) case has been supplemented with arguments drawn from social science sources and particularly from work in public choice theory. The latter is often seen to give enhanced empirical and logical rigour to the moral and philosophical case against the welfare state.

Public choice theory, located on the boundaries between economics and political science, has traditionally been concerned with collective or non-market forms of decision-making. In the hands of the New Right, it is taken to show that under liberal democratic procedures, collective choice through state actions, beyond that necessary minimum advocated by both Smith and Hayek, will always tend to yield outcomes that are less efficient or desirable than outcomes determined by private choice through markets. Public choice writers sympathetic to the New Right seek to show that the welfare state project is flawed both logically and sociologically.

The great weakness of decision-making procedures under the liberal democratic arrangements within which the welfare state has developed is that it encourages both governments and voters to be fiscally irresponsible. The individual making a private economic choice within the market has always to weigh costs against benefits in making a decision. Public choice theorists argue that in the political 'market' both voters and governments are able to avoid or at least to deflect the consequences of spending decisions and thus to seek benefits without taking due account of costs. Within the rules of the liberal democratic game, it is then possible for both governments and voters to act rationally but through their collective action to produce suboptimal or even positively harmful consequences. This, it is suggested, may be shown in a number of ways.

First, it may not be rational for individual voters carefully to consider the full range of a prospective government's public policy, still less to consider the overall consequences of such policies for the 'national interest'. The marginal impact of a single voter's decision is so limited that the opportunity costs of a well-considered decision would be unreasonable (Downs, 1957; Olson, 1982). Under these circumstances, no rational actor will normally press his or her consideration beyond a crude calculation of how the incumbent government has benefited the voter. Given this, it is in the interests of a government seeking re-election to ensure that the pre-election period is one in which as many voters as possible feel that they are prospering under the current regime. Government will then, it is suggested, seek to manage the economy in the run-up to an election so as to lower inflation and unemployment and to maximize incomes (perhaps through lowering personal rates of taxation). In this way, a political business cycle may be established, with governments manipulating economic variables in the prelude to an election. Not only will this give misleading signs to the electors, but it will also undermine the long-term stability of the economy and will tend to increase the state's indebtedness (through an imbalance of spending and taxation). Under circumstances of adversary politics, such fiscal irresponsibility is unlikely to be challenged by the opposition who are more likely to 'bid up' the electorate's expectations, promising 'more for less' in the attempt to unseat the existing government (Downs, 1957; Alt and Chrystal, 1983).

Clearly in a private economic market such over-bidding would be constrained by the threat of bankruptcy. A corporation that sold goods and services at less than their cost of production would soon be forced out of business. But governments do not face this same constraint (at least in the short and medium term). By increasing the public debt, governments may defer the costs of their present spending upon future governments (and generations). This may have a damaging effect on the medium-term prospects for the economy – by encouraging inflation, squeezing out private sector investment or whatever – but although this runs against the overall public interest, it is not rational for either particular governments or particular voters to seek to stop it. Indeed, Olson argues that economic growth becomes a 'public good' for most interest groups. It is more rational to seek to extract a greater proportion of the national budget (through political pressure) than to seek to enhance the overall growth of the economy (Olson, 1965; Olson, 1982; Rose and Peters, 1978).

In a number of other ways, this logic of collective action can be seen to furnish suboptimal outcomes. Governments that are seeking to maximize their electoral appeal are driven to support the particularistic claims of well-organized interest groups and to satisfy the claims of special interests. The costs of meeting the claims of the well organized are discharged upon the unorganized generality of the population. The politics of voter-trading and political activism tend to lead to an expansion of government beyond that which is either necessary or desirable (Tullock, 1976).

This oversupply of public services is further exacerbated by the nature of the public bureaucracy. First, the public bureaucracy is itself a powerful interest group and public bureaucrats have a rational interest in maximizing their own budgets and departments. Secondly, the public bureaucracy does not normally face competition, nor indeed any of the economic constraints of acting within a marketplace. Where costs are not weighed against benefits and where the utility maximization of bureaucrats is dependent upon the maximization of their budgets, the public choice theorists insist that there will be a chronic tendency for the public bureaucracy to over-supply goods and services (Niskanen, 1971; Niskanen, 1973; Tullock, 1976). This problem becomes still more acute when the monopolistic powers of the public bureaucracy are strengthened by an expansion of white collar trades unionism, as happened, for example, in the much expanded UK civil service in the period after the Second World War (Bacon and Eltis, 1978).

This complex is seen broadly to describe the political circumstances of the modern welfare state. Under liberal democratic and adversarial political arrangements, and without some sort of constitutional constraint upon the action (and spending) of governments, politicians, bureaucrats and voters *acting rationally* will tend to generate welfare state policies which are suboptimal, indeed, in the long run, unsustainable.

## The New Right and the Welfare State: A Summary

The case of the New Right against the welfare state, which, in the hands of its academic advocates, often took an abstract and technical form, achieved its present polemical status largely as a response to a series of social and political problems in the advanced capitalist world of the 1970s. Accordingly, further comment upon these New Right theses is deferred to the more appropriate context of chapter 5. Here we can conclude our consideration of the general New Right case, by briefly summarizing the main substantive claims to which it has given rise:

1  **The welfare state is uneconomic.** It displaces the necessary disciplines and incentives of the marketplace, undermining the incentive (of capital) to invest and the incentive (of labour) to work.
2  **The welfare state is unproductive.** It encourages the rapid growth of the (unproductive) public bureaucracy and forces capital and human resources out of the (productive) private sector of the economy. Monopoly of state provision enables workers within the public sector to command inflationary wage increases.
3  **The welfare state is inefficient.** Its monopoly of welfare provision and its creation and sponsorship of special/sectional interests lead to the inefficient delivery of services and a system which, denuded of the discipline of the market, is geared to the interests of (organized) producers rather than (disaggregated) consumers. Generally, as governments extend the areas of social life in which they intervene, so policy failures mount.
4  **The welfare state is ineffective.** Despite the huge resources dedicated to it, welfare state measures fail to eliminate poverty and deprivation. Indeed, they worsen the position of the poorest by displacing traditional community- and family-based forms of support and entrap the deprived in a 'cycle of dependence'.
5  **The welfare state is despotic.** It constitutes a growth in, at best, the enervating hand of bureaucracy and, at worst, social control of individual citizens and, in some cases, whole communities, by an overweening state. In many such cases the victims of state control and manipulation are those same deprived citizens that it is claimed the welfare state exists to assist.
6  **The welfare state is a denial of freedom.** Its compulsory provision of services denies the individual freedom of choice within the welfare sector, while its heavy and progressive tax regime can be represented as 'confiscatory'.

---

**Thesis 5**

The welfare state is an ill-conceived and unprincipled intrusion upon the welfare- and liberty-maximizing imperatives of a liberal market society. It is inconsistent with the preservation of freedom, justice and real long-term welfare

# Marxism, Neo-Marxism and the Welfare State

A second general account of the irreconcilability of capitalist and welfare state imperatives, and thus a rejection of the social democratic orthodoxy, has come from the Marxist and neo-Marxist left. It is a much-cited paradox of this Marxist analysis of the welfare state and welfare capitalism that it seems to share much in common with the politically quite opposed New Right. This is not perhaps so surprising, given the status of Marx's definitive study of *Capital* as 'a critique of political economy'. Just as Marx took the work of the classical political economists and sought to press their premises to radically new conclusions, so do contemporary Marxist writers find much to endorse in the New Right's morphology of the problems of welfare capitalism, while seeking quite different explanations pressed to very different conclusions. What they share is a common belief that the 'steady-state' welfare capitalism of traditional social democratic analysis is untenable. Both have sought out contradictions within the welfare state/welfare capitalism, the one to label them 'the excesses of democracy/socialism', the other to style them 'the contradictions of capitalism'. In essence, the impasse of social democracy and the welfare state is seen to lie in the impossibility of reconciling the imperatives of capitalism with the requirements of authentically democratic arrangements or the furnishing of 'genuine' social welfare.

# Twentieth-century Marxism and the Welfare State

In chapter 1, we saw that the essence of Marx's view was that even if limited social reform could be forced by organized labour, the securing of widespread state welfare for the majority of the population was inconsistent with the demands of capital accumulation. Down to the Second World War, mainstream classical Marxists saw little reason to amend this account of welfare provision under capitalism. Though these were the years in which many formative welfare states emerged, provision was seen to be minimal and in the 1930s rising unemployment and falling benefits were seen to express the dominance of the (crisis) logic of capital over the wishful thinking of welfarist social democrats. By contrast, in the halcyon years of social democracy after 1945, it was the social democrats who had little time for 'outmoded' Marxist analyses of (a now transformed) capitalism. Marxism, with its outdated appeal to the class war, belonged to a bygone era of working-class poverty, mass unemployment and class privilege. While post-war societies were not egalitarian, under the impact of Keynesian economics and extensive social welfare provision, systematic differences of class no longer carried their pre-war resonances. Meanwhile the Marxist left, demoralized by the experience of the Hungarian uprising, the (limited) exposure of Stalinism and the seemingly uninterrupted growth of the post-war economy, increasingly directed its attention towards alienation and the cultural consequences of capitalism. Marcuse's *One-Dimensional Man* depicted organized capitalism as a system of total administration in which the working class was lost as the revolutionary agent of social change. Even opposition was now co-opted within an all-embracing system of structured irrationality (of which the welfare state was an important component). Consciousness of the need for radical change was confined to marginal groups on the periphery of society – students, ethnic minorities and *déclassé* elements. The provision of welfare to the working class became not an avenue for their gradual advance towards socialism but the means by which workers were controlled, demoralized and deradicalized. According to Marcuse, 'the prospects of containment of change ... depend on the prospects of the welfare State ... [as the embodiment of] a state of unfreedom' (Marcuse, 1972, pp. 51–2).

However, by the end of the 1960s – especially under the impact of the events loosely and graphically associated with 1968 – the image of unproblematic post-war social democratic consensus began to crack. A period of uninterrupted political and industrial unrest also saw a re-emergence of academic interest in Marxist and other radical/socialist thinking. It is from this period that we can date the emergence, or possibly the renaissance, of Marxist theories of the (welfare) state.

## Neo-Marxist Analysis of the Welfare State

Although others, and most notably Antonio Gramsci, might claim to have initiated Marxist study of the welfare state, the origins of this renaissance are widely seen to reside in the much-rehearsed Miliband–Poulantzas debate (Gramsci, 1971; Miliband, 1969; Poulantzas, 1973; Poulantzas, 1978). These more recent accounts have instituted a number of changes from classical Marxist thinking on the state. Without entering upon this extended debate here, we may note the following significant amendments in more recent accounts:

### Proposition 1

That the state enjoys *relative autonomy* from the capitalist class; the possibility of the state acting in the general interests of capital is dependent upon its distance from particular capitals.

## Proposition 2

That the state articulates the general needs of capital accumulation – and this may involve paying an *economic* price for securing the *political* compliance of non-ruling class interests.

## Proposition 3

That the state is not straightforwardly unitary; it is, as Poulantzas has it, 'constituted-divided' by the same divisions that characterize capitalist society more generally.

# Neo-Marxism I: The Welfare State as Social Control

In fact, (neo-)Marxist responses to the welfare state have been remarkably varied. We have already seen that advocates of the power resources model have interpreted the welfare state (under specified conditions) as a strategic element in the transition to socialism. Others, drawing on Propositions 1 and 2 above, continue to regard the welfare state as predominantly an instrument for the social control of the working class, acting in the long-term interests of capital accumulation. Within the broadly neo-Marxist camp, this is the view that is perhaps closest to the classical Marxism of Marx, Engels and Lenin. It confronts quite explicitly the traditional social democratic perspective of a benign and progressive welfare state but also challenges the claims of the 'revisionist' power resources model.

We have seen that one of the core claims of the classical Marxist position was that in any epoch, the state mobilizes exclusively the interests of a single ruling class. Thus, in contrast to the social democratic view (and Proposition 3 above), it is insisted that, under capitalism, 'the functioning and management of state welfare remains part of a *capitalist* state which is fundamentally concerned with the maintenance and reproduction of capitalist social relations' (Ginsburg, 1979, p. 2). Above all else, the welfare state is involved in securing the production and reproduction of labour power under capitalist forms. The benefits of the welfare state to the working class are not generally denied, but they are seen to be largely the adventitious by-product of securing the interests of capital. Here there is characteristically an echo of Marx's commentary on an earlier series of reforms, the UK Factory Acts, which, while a gain for the working classes thus protected, arose from the 'same necessity as forced the manuring of English fields with guano' – that is the need to preserve from total exhaustion the sole source of future surplus value (Marx, 1973a, p. 348).

Thus, Norman Ginsburg maintains

> From the capitalist point of view state welfare has contributed to
> the continual struggle to accumulate capital by materially assisting
> in bringing labour and capital together profitably and containing
> the inevitable resistance and revolutionary potential of the work-
> ing class ... the social security system is concerned with repro-
> ducing a reserve army of labour, the patriarchal family and the
> disciplining of the labour force. Only secondarily and contingently
> does it function as a means of mitigating poverty or providing
> 'income maintenance'. (Ginsburg, 1979, p. 2)

This principal thesis is defended through a number of more specific
rebuttals of the social democratic position:

1  Social provision under the welfare state is characteristically
   geared to the requirements of capital not the real needs of the
   working population.
2  Many welfare policies were originated not by socialists or social
   democrats but by conservative or liberal elites. Their intention
   was to manage/regulate capitalism and to discipline its work-
   force, not to mitigate the social hardship of the working class.
3  Social policy has long been recognized by these elites as the
   'antidote' to socialism. As UK Conservative Prime Minister
   Arthur Balfour insisted in the 1930s, 'social legislation ... is not
   merely to be distinguished from Socialist legislation, but it is its
   most direct opposite and its most effective antidote' (cited in
   Marshall, 1975, p. 40).
4  Changes in social welfare regimes reflect the changing accumulation needs of capital: for example (1) the shift from extensive to
   intensive exploitation of labour (and the correspondingly greater
   need of a healthy, docile, disciplined and educated work-force),
   (2) the need for fit men to staff the armies of the imperialist
   capitalist nation states (and of women to replace them in the
   sphere of industrial production); and (3) the rise (and perhaps
   the fall) of mass production and scientific management.
5  The funding of welfare state measures has often been regressive
   and/or associated with an extension of the tax base; at best,
   welfare state spending has been redistributive within the working class or across the life cycle of the average worker.
6  The compulsory state management of welfare has deprived the
   working class of the self-management of its own welfare
   (through friendly societies and trades unions); the *form* of
   welfare services has characteristically been bureaucratic and
   antidemocratic.

7  Social legislation has often enhanced the intrusive powers of state professionals within the everyday life of individual citizens and concentrated surveillance and discretionary power in the hands of agents of the state.

8  The ameliorative impact of state relief and the ideology of a welfare state in which each member of the community is guaranteed a certain minimum of welfare provision has demobilized working class agitation for more radical economic and political change.

---

**Thesis 6**

The welfare state is a particular form of the developed capitalist state. It functions to secure the long-term circumstances for the continued accumulation of capital.

---

## Commentary: Neo-Marxism I: The Welfare State as Social Control

A number of commentators have complained that it is extremely difficult to 'operationalize' Marxist theses on the welfare state (Pampel and Williamson, 1988, p. 1450; Korpi, 1989, pp. 315–17). However, there is a good deal of historical evidence to support the social control thesis. Firstly, welfare state measures often developed in tandem with a traditional Poor Law whose intent was explicitly coercive (as in the UK down to 1948). Secondly, the conditions that are placed upon state benefits (a record of regular employment, 'willingness to work' clauses, a qualifying period and cut-off points for payment of benefits), are often oriented not to the meeting of recipients' needs but rather to the requirement not to undermine the dynamics of the labour market. Thirdly, the administration of benefits by the state has placed considerable discretionary, investigative and directive powers in the hands of (middle-class) state officials. Thus, Piven and Cloward argue that the intent of welfare provision in the US has always been one of 'regulating the poor', allowing for more generous provision at times when mass mobilization (rather than mass need) pressed upon the prevailing order, but then reimposing tighter labour market disciplines upon recipients (by moving them off welfare rolls) once the immediate threat of disorder has been demobilized. This, for example, was their verdict on the New Deal social security reforms:

The first major relief crisis in the US occurred during the Great Depression. By 1935, upwards of twenty million people were on the dole. But it would be wrong to assume that this unprecedented volume of relief-giving was a response to widespread economic distress, for millions had been unemployed for several years before obtaining aid. What led government to proffer aid ... was the rising surge of political unrest that accompanied this economic catastrophe. Moreover, once relief-giving had expanded, unrest rapidly subsided, and then aid was cut back – which meant, among other things, that large numbers of people were put off the rolls and thrust into a labour market still glutted with unemployment. But with stability restored, the continued suffering of these millions had little political force.(Piven and Cloward, 1971, p. 45).

Further support for the social control thesis may be found in the evidence of early working class hostility to the state provision of welfare. Such hostility (from trades unions and friendly societies) can be understood not simply as 'respectable' working class conservatism but rather as a fear that the state would replace working-class self-administration with forms of social welfare that would serve the interests of capital. There is further historical evidence that many early social work/public health initiatives – for example, the activities of Charitable Organization Societies on both sides of the Atlantic or the introduction of schools' medical services – were immediately concerned with the production of a literate, docile, 'regular' and 'fighting fit' work-force. According to Elizabeth Wilson, 'the literature of social work *is* the ideology of welfare capitalism' (Wilson, 1977, p. 28; Ginsburg, 1979; Taylor-Gooby and Dale, 1981; Langan and Lee, 1989). Again, much of the earliest US welfare legislation was concerned with rehabilitation which would bring the economically inactive off benefits and into work. Often states' welfare legislation was commended precisely because of the financial benefits which would accrue to business and taxpayers. Meanwhile, the severest punitive measures were reserved for those who could not or would not respond to their 're-education' and remained unemployable (see, for example, Katz, 1986).

Yet, despite all this evidence, it is difficult to sustain the argument that the growth of the welfare state was exclusively or even preponderantly in the interests of the capitalist class. It is certainly true that early public welfare measures were parsimonious, often introduced under conservative/dual monarchy regimes and with an explicitly anti-social democratic or anti-trades union intent. Yet, the more liberal reforming regimes were often driven by a radical/social democratic wing, they were a response to new working-class electors and they frequently sought to outmanoeuvre the electoral appeal of social democratic parties by offering public welfare for the working classes. Similarly, while early public welfare measures often had a coercive and disciplinary element, they still represented an improvement in the basic circumstances of many members of the working class. Thus, for example, even though early pensions were minimal and means-tested, this represented an improvement upon reliance on the Poor Law and the workhouse. Again, while there were, for example, attempts to restrict welfare to non-unionized labour, state management of welfare was probably less antagonistic to labour than was the administration of welfare by employers (though less in the working-class interest than self-management through trades unions or friendly societies). Where such measures were introduced on a social insurance rather than a public assistance basis, an (albeit circumscribed) *right* to public welfare was also established. While such early gains were often extremely limited, they were not generally conceded without a struggle. While parliamentary democracy and the welfare state might have come to constitute part of the apparatus for the political incorporation of the working class and the deradicalization of labour, the view that accordingly such measures were willingly embraced by enlightened and sophisticated conservative elites proves to be historically quite exceptional.

Contemporary fears among elites (and the pattern of early take-up of social insurance) also suggest that social insurance might indeed lessen the stranglehold of the market upon the working class. Even very limited compensation for unemployment or sickness did lessen the drive for workers to return to the market to undergo the disutility of labour. Thus although public welfare has often been fiscally regressive (based on a payroll tax and (re)distributing benefits to the better-off and longer-lived), inasmuch as programmes were based on (or subsidized by) general tax revenues this could be expected to have a mildly redistributive effect. Similarly, fears that the expenditure incurred could lead to a fiscal crisis of the state can, in fact, be retraced to the very origins of the public welfare system. Indeed, the escalating cost of earlier systems of public assistance was one of the major spurs to welfare reform – in the UK, for example, both in the 1840s and again in the 1900s.

One response to this evidence is to suggest that such improvements as the working class did enjoy under the welfare state were simply the adventitious benefits of capital's interests in a more productive source of surplus value. In this sense, the evidence is but a vindication of Marx's understanding of the contradictory logic of capitalism. The capitalist class could not have a healthier, better educated, reliable (and thus more profitable) source of surplus value without improving the health, education and housing of the working class. It may also reflect the importance of the working class as a source of consumption under difficult circumstances for the valorization of capital. Yet this does not lessen the material improvements secured by the working class and it was the case that these services were generally being provided by the state rather than in a potentially more coercive and partisan way by the owners of industry themselves. Furthermore, the *unintended* consequences of welfare state legislation might significantly strengthen the defensive powers of the working class. The experience of the early introduction of sickness insurance in the UK was of a greater than expected take-up and of a lower return to work by recuperating workers (Gilbert, 1966). As we shall see in chapter 5, the ways in which social insurance (even if self-financed) would distort the labour market was to become a very major concern of those who argued that the post-war welfare state was undermining the very bases of the capitalist economy.

## Neo-Marxism II: Contradictions of the Welfare State

This view of the welfare state as primarily the instrument of capitalist social control continues to attract significant political support. However, more typically, the renaissance in neo-Marxist thinking has followed Proposition 3 above and concentrated upon contradictions within the welfare state itself. It has also become increasingly oriented around the apparent crisis experienced in the welfare state following twenty-five years of seemingly unproblematic growth in the post-war period. Indeed, it is difficult to isolate a general statement of this (neo-)Marxist view from the context of a perceived crisis of the welfare state. This is most clearly the case with James O'Connor's path-breaking work on the *Fiscal Crisis of the State*, which is considered in some detail in chapter 5 (O'Connor, 1973; O' Connor, 1987). It is also a concern of Ian Gough's classic study *The Political Economy of the Welfare State* (1979).

Locating the welfare state in terms of the overall structure of welfare capitalism, Gough is profoundly critical of those social democratic accounts of welfare which have sought to isolate economy and polity or to reduce welfare to the study of discrete social problems and particular institutions. He himself defines the welfare state 'as the use of state power to modify the reproduction of labour power and to maintain the non-working population in capitalist societies' (Gough, 1979, pp. 44–5). Such modification is effected through the taxation and social security systems, regulation of the provision of certain 'essentials' (for example, food and housing) and the provision of certain services in kind (most notably, health and education). He views the development of this welfare state as essentially *contradictory*. Thus, it 'simultaneously embodies tendencies to enhance social welfare, to develop the powers of individuals, to exert social control over the blind play of market forces; and tendencies to repress and control people, to adapt them to the requirements of the capitalist economy' (Gough, 1979, p. 12). On the one hand, welfare state institutions are seen to be consonant with the interests of capital. They represent a response to changes undergone in capitalist development – for example, periodic unemployment, technological change, the need of a skilled and literate work-force – and to the new requirements these changes generate in the area of social policy. On the other hand, the origins of the welfare state lie in organized working-class struggle – and the ameliorating response of organizations of the ruling class to the threat this was seen to pose. This means that the welfare state cannot be seen as straightforwardly 'functional for capital' – as simply a means of exercising social control over the working class and subsidizing capital's profit-making. At least a part of the prodigious growth of the post-war welfare state may be seen as a response to the defensive economic strength of the organized working class and the labour movement. Yet, at the same time, 'paradoxically . . . it would appear that labour indirectly aids the long-term accumulation of capital and strengthens capitalist social relations by struggling for its own interests within the state' (Gough, 1979, p. 55).

The welfare state, then, is a 'contradictory unity', exhibiting both positive and negative features for both capital and labour. Correspondingly, the long-term consequences of the welfare state for the continued accumulation of capital are themselves ambivalent. Although the welfare state may serve to subsidize some of the costs of capital, its strengthening of the defensive powers of the working class may in the long run undermine the reproduction of suitable conditions for profitable capital accumulation. The welfare state's institutionalization of income support and full employment will tend to strengthen the defensive power of the organized working class and thus the capacity of labour to protect real wage levels and to resist attempts to raise productivity. Under the (perhaps consequent) circumstances of sluggish economic growth, it will prove ever more difficult to finance the growing state budget without increasing inflation or further weakening growth or both. For the funding of the welfare state could be neutral for capital accumulation only if the whole of the tax burden of funding it could be met within the household sector and thus preponderantly by the broad working class. However, in reality, the distribution of the burden of taxation between capital and labour – and indeed the scale and distribution of welfare services themselves – is itself a matter of class struggle and reflects the prevailing balance of social forces. Under these conditions, the circumstances for long-term capital accumulation may be imperilled. The outcome is likely to be inflation, a slow-down in economic growth and, for developed welfare states operating within a world market, the potential loss of international competitiveness.

## The Welfare State as the 'Crisis of Crisis Management': Offe

Perhaps the most developed account of the welfare state as the contradictory and contested product of continuing capitalist development within the neo-Marxist or, more properly, 'post-Marxist' literature is that developed by Claus Offe. Offe follows classical Marxism in arguing that the '"privately regulated" capitalist economy' is innately crisis-prone. However, this is not best understood as a predominantly *economic* crisis. In fact, the welfare state emerges as an institutional/administrative form which seeks to 'harmonize the "privately regulated" capitalist economy with the [contradictory] processes of socialization this economy triggers' (Offe , 1984, p. 51). The welfare state is that set of political arrangements which seeks to compromise or 'save from crisis' what classical Marxism had ident- ified as the central contradiction of capitalism – that between social forces and private relations of production. The welfare state arises then as a form of systemic crisis management.

For Offe, borrowing here upon Niklas Luhmann's analysis of the functioning of society's interacting 'subsystems' (Luhmann, 1990, pp. 30, 73–8), the structure of welfare capitalism can be character- ized in terms of three subsystems as in figure 2.1.

According to Offe, the economic subsystem of capitalism is not self-regulating and has dysfunctional consequences for the legitima- tion subsystem. The state has to intervene in and mediate between the other two subsystems to secure, on the one hand, continued accumulation, and on the other, continued legitimation. Correspon- dingly, the state under welfare capitalism is to be seen as a form of crisis management – and for twenty-five years following the Second World War a remarkably successful one. But this process of recon- ciliation under the welfare state proves in the long run to be im- possible as the welfare state is subject to a particular crisis logic of its own. Three manifestations of this underlying contradiction of the welfare state are of particular importance:

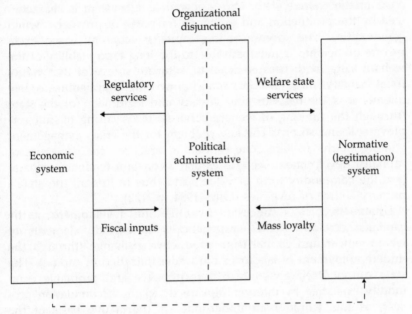

**Figure 2.1** Three subsystems and their interrelationship
*Source*: Offe (1984) p. 52

1 **The fiscal crisis of the welfare state.** The state budget required to fund strategies of recommodification tends to grow uncontrollably and to become increasingly self-defeating, occasioning (through high taxation and welfare provision) both a 'disincentive to invest' and a 'disincentive to work'.
2 **Administrative shortfall.** The welfare state repeatedly fails to live up to its own inflated programmatic-administrative claims, a failure variously attributed to the ineffectiveness of the indirect instruments of public policy, to struggles *within* the state and to the external imperatives of public accountability, democratic representation and short-term political expediency.
3 **Legitimation shortfall.** Under these circumstances of fiscal crisis and administrative shortfall, state intervention is seen to be increasingly particularistic and *ad hoc* and this undermines the political norms of 'equality under the rule of law', leading to a short-fall of mass loyalty/legitimacy.

This makes the focus of Offe's analysis *the crisis of crisis management* (Offe, 1984, pp. 57–61).

Under advanced capitalism, Offe argues, *economic* contradictions of capital accumulation increasingly express themselves in a *political* crisis of the welfare state. Offe's economic subsystem is characterized by the production and exchange for profit of privately owned commodities. The success of this capitalist economy based upon private ownership is indispensable to the long-term viability of the welfare state, both because it is the ultimate source of that state's fiscal viability (through taxation and borrowing) and because consequently it is the basis of mass loyalty and legitimacy for the state (through the funding of welfare services, the securing of 'full employment' and so on). The key problem for the crisis management strategy of the welfare state is that, in practice, 'the dynamics of capitalist development seem to exhibit a constant tendency to paralyse the commodity form of value', and thus to imperil the state's primary source of revenues (Offe, 1984, p. 122).

Unregulated, it is suggested by Offe, the development of the capitalist economy tends systematically to exclude elements of labour power and capital from productive exchange (through the underemployment of labour or the underutilization of capital). The state cannot itself generally restore effective and profitable commodity exchange by intervening directly in the accumulation process, as this would both undermine the normative basis of the private-exchange capitalist economy and engender the risk of an (anti-nationalization) capital investment strike.[1] Since the state is prevented from intervening directly in the economy, it has to proceed indirectly, through essentially Keynesian means, to re-establish the conditions under which capital and labour will be drawn into profitable commodity exchange, through regulations and financial incentives (corporate tax concessions, special development areas, interest-free industrial loans, subsidizing energy costs), public infrastructural investment (training and re-training, recruitment services, subsidized transport facilities), and the sponsoring of neo-corporatist arrangements (between trades unions and employers). Offe calls this strategy 'administrative recommodification'. The intention is to promote the fuller utilization or *commodification* of both capital and labour through indirect, administrative means. Its vitiating weakness is that, in practice, it promotes a process of *decommodification* – that is, it undermines the circumstances for the fuller utilization of capital and labour. Thus the strategies which are supposed to encourage more effective commodity exchange in fact place ever greater areas of social life outside of the commodity form and outside the sphere of market exchange. The principal contradic-

---

1   Corporatism may represent a partial attempt to realise such a policy. Elsewhere Offe discusses the nature of state interventions of this kind (Offe and Wiesenthal, 1985).

tion of the welfare state then is that strategies of *re*commodification effect a widespread process of *de*commodification (Offe, 1984).

---

**Thesis 7**

The welfare state is a particular form of the developed capitalist state. It embodies the essentially contradictory nature of developed capitalism and is chronically liable to the logic of fiscal crisis.

---

## Disorganized Capitalism and the Decline of the Keynesian Welfare State

It is also possible to isolate a further approach which, while broadly sympathetic to the historical achievements of the welfare state, insists that the accommodation between capitalism and social democracy which it expressed has now been exhausted by a series of profound changes in the economic structure and accumulation strategies of advanced capitalism. This perspective is developed in Lash and Urry's analysis of *The End of Organized Capitalism* and in Claus Offe's more recent work, in which the welfare state is seen to face a 'structural disintegration process', which 'can neither be fully explained by economic and fiscal crisis arguments, nor by political arguments emphasizing the rise of neo-conservative elites and ideologies' (Lash and Urry, 1987; Offe, 1985; Offe, 1987, p. 528). In essence, the Keynesian welfare state is identified with the epoch of organized capitalism or Fordism which dominated the world economy from the early twentieth century until the last twenty years. Very broadly, this was a period based upon the economic dominance of mass production and semi-skilled labour, the centralized organization of both large-scale capital and labour and an enhanced social and economic role for the interventionist state. The welfare state was one of the most characteristic national organizations corresponding to this period of state-managed and organized capitalism. However, under a range of social, economic and political pressures, these formations are now seen to be yielding to a new period of *dis*organized capitalism or post-Fordism and correspondingly to a decline in the traditional welfare state. These new circumstances will not see the wholesale withdrawal of the state from intervention in the organization and reproduction of labour power. Indeed, the role of the state in training and the movement in and

**Table 2.1**   Organized and disorganized capitalism

| *Organized capitalism* | *Disorganized capitalism* |
|---|---|
| The dominance of mass production in large-scale factories with predominantly semi-skilled labour | Batch production; transfer towards smaller production sites; growth in office work; growing division of work-force into skilled, flexible and permanent core and unskilled, insecure periphery |
| The mass consumption of mass-produced goods | 'Niche marketing', targeted products and short production runs |
| Concentration and centralization of industrial, banking and commercial capital | Division between financial, industrial and commercial capital; growing division between banks and industry |
| Cartelization; the control of markets and monopolistic pricing | Breakdown of cartels and monopolistic pricing; declining national control over markets |
| The emergence of national labour market organizations of both labour and capital. Growing importance of national collective bargaining | Decline in power of national labour market organizations – especially TUs – and displacement of national collective bargaining by local/firm-based agreements |
| Capitalist relations concentrated in a few manufacturing sectors employing huge numbers of male workers in a few key nation-states | Diffusion of capitalism into most Third World countries; transfer of extractive and manufacturing jobs from the First World |
| The social and economic dominance of large-scale industrial cities within regional economies | Decline in economic importance of industrial cities; transfer of economic activity to smaller towns and semi-rural areas |
| Enhanced role for nation state in economic management, intermediation with capital and labour | Declining capacity of the nation state for effective economic intervention |
| Politics organized around social classes, collective identities and work-defined relations | Class politics of declining importance: emergence of new issues and new political actors |
| Development of the Keynesian welfare state | Growing structural challenges to the welfare state |

*Sources*:   Lash and Urry (1987); Offe (1985); Offe (1987); Jessop (1988) out of paid work may be enhanced. But it will herald the end of the 'citizens'' welfare state premised upon full employment and welfare *rights'* (Offe, 1987).

Such a prognosis relies very heavily upon the contrast between organized and disorganized capitalism.[2] The most important changes are summarized in table 2.1.

The welfare state under organized capitalism arose in response to both the accumulation needs of capital (including mass consumption as an important component in the valorization of capital) and the defensive strength of the organized working class. It facilitated not only the class basis for mobilization behind the welfare state (the massification of collective labour), but also the corporate basis (in the rise of organized labour and organized capital) and the institutional basis (with the rise of the interventionist state). However, the compromise of the interests of capital and labour which it allowed could only be temporary. In the longer run, the structure of organized capitalism/Fordism (in part through its institutionalization of the defensive powers of the working class) tended to *undermine* the conditions for long-term capital accumulation. The disorganized capitalist formation which increasingly displaces it in the attempt to restore long-term profitability is one which characteristically undermines those very conditions that made the rise of the welfare state possible.

According to Bob Jessop,

> Whereas Fordism facilitated a policy of full employment and welfare rights to secure demand and thereby created the basis for a class compromise between capital and labour, the new post-Fordist regime poses serious problems for full employment and the class alliances which this entails. (Jessop, 1988, p. 9)

Thus, disorganized capitalism moves towards (1) the de-massification of labour and the decline of a clear and collective working-class interest, (2) a decline in the institutions of organized capital and, more especially, of organized labour and (3) the undermining of the authority and capacity of the interventionist state.

For Offe, it is, above all, the disorganization of traditional classes and established class alliances which explains the 'exhaustion' of the welfare state settlement. Thus

---

2  The analysis here focuses upon the contrast between organized and disorganized capitalism, rather than upon Fordism and post-Fordism. Though these perspectives are different in a number of important respects, their analyses of the welfare state and its transformation are sufficiently similar to allow of this elision.

The disorganization of broad, relatively stable, and encompassing commonalities of economic interest, associational affiliations, or cultural values and life-styles ... lead[s] to the virtual evaporation of classes and other self-conscious collectivities of political will, economic interest, and cultural values whose existence [is a] necessary condition for solidary and collectivist attitudes and ideologies. (Offe, 1987, pp. 527–8).

He isolates a number of tendencies in disorganized capitalism which are destructive of 'self-conscious interest communities in advanced industrial societies, and *hence* of the cultural and normative under-pinnings of the welfare state'. The most important of these are:

1 **De-massification of the work-force.** Disorganized capitalism pre-scribes increasing disparities of life-chances among the totality of wage workers. Most significantly, the division in the work-force between a skilled employed core and an unskilled and partially employed periphery and the prospect of 'jobless growth' means that those 'who are most desperately dependent on the welfare state's provision of transfers and services are, however, politi-cally most vulnerable'. The 'core' working class no longer has any reason to adopt the material interests of this disadvantaged 'surplus class' as its own.

2 **Self-interest in 'hard times'.** Pro-welfare state alliances are a product of 'good times' of economic growth and full employ-ment. 'In that sense, the economic crisis of the welfare state generates individualistic political attitudes and orientations and thus translates ... into a political crisis of the welfare state.'

3 **Declining faith in the state.** The means by which welfare state policies have traditionally been prosecuted – that is, bureaucratic and professional interventions – are 'increasingly seen in the corrosive light of a distributional and exploitative game'. Public faith in the capacity of the state to achieve 'public goods' is replaced by hostility to the welfare state as (1) an entrenchment of the interests of middle-class bureaucrats and (2) ineffective or counterproductive ('dependency-creating') as a response to the needs of its clients.

4 **Middle-class defection from the welfare state.** The middle class has consistently been the principal beneficiary of the welfare state, both through state services – for example, higher education and graduated pensions – and in the take-up of secure employ-ment opportunities. Yet the more secure and prosperous does the middle class (and increasingly the skilled and prosperous core of the working class) become, the greater is the temptation facing its members to defect from collective forms of provision.

Thus 'the higher the status and income that the welfare state provides you with, the *lesser* your rational motivation to have your privileges tied to (foreseeably precarious) collectivist arrangements, and the greater accordingly the inclination to look for – and to support parties that propose designs for – private market alternatives.' This tendency is the more pronounced given the growing political attention of middle-class actors to non-class, non-redistributive issues (the politics of the new social movements), to the neglect of traditional conflicts over social security, distributional justice and solidarity. (Offe, 1987, pp. 529–34)

Under disorganized capitalism, then, Offe identifies 'a self-reinforcing and self-propelling dynamic' of defection from all forms of support for the welfare state and he concludes 'that the welfare state as we know it as a major accomplishment of postwar West European societies is rapidly losing its political support' (Offe, 1987, p. 534).

Similar conclusions are drawn by Lash and Urry. With the decline of its mass basis in a massified working class, the continuing protection of the welfare state 'will depend upon a variety of social movements supporting and protecting state expenditures'.

And yet because of the salient division between the people and the state much potential support will be diverted into generating less bureaucratized, more decentralized and in cases more privatized forms as the welfare state of organized capitalism makes way for a much more varied and less centrally organized form of welfare provision in disorganized capitalism. (Lash and Urry, 1987, pp. 230–1)

Their expectation, echoing that of Offe, is that 'depending on the balance of characteristically disorganized capitalist social and political forces', the European welfare states will increasingly move towards a two-tier structure, much closer to the experience of 'America's incomplete welfare state' (Lash and Urry, 1987, p. 231; Skocpol, 1987).

Rather more abstractly, the same issues are raised by Offe's distinguished countryman, Jurgen Habermas. Writing in the early 1970s, his argument was that under organized capitalism, crises that are endemic in all capitalist forms of organization (given the central contradiction between social production and private appropriation) become displaced from the immediately economic to the political-administrative sphere. Here again, the state has to intervene to secure the process of successful capital accumulation but must also secure mass loyalty (legitimacy). This is a contradictory demand upon the state, generating conflicting demands that cannot all be met and undermining the traditional ideology of a neutral state securing 'freedom under the rule of law'. The tendency for the state's interventions to be increasingly particularistic and ineffective in turn displaces the state's rationality crisis towards a legitimation crisis, manifest in the deficit of citizen support for state institutions. At the individual level, this may express itself as a motivational crisis, producing individuals whose motivational make-up is not based upon that possessive individualism which the capitalist economy requires. Such a crisis may only be resolved through the transformation of organized capitalism or through the much intensified manipulation of individuals under a system of 'total administration' (Habermas, 1976).

More recently, Habermas has taken up the issue of the nature of this crisis in the developed capitalist state as a crisis not so much of capitalism as of the reactive aspirations and strategies of its opponents. Sociologists of all persuasions have tended to present *abstract labour* as the key explanatory variable in industrial societies and the Utopia that has inspired most socialists is that of 'a labor-based social organization of free and equal producers'. But, Habermas insists, within the advanced capitalist societies, labour no longer enjoys this definitive centrality nor can production and growth any longer provide the basis for a Utopian view of a future society. Thus, the 'Utopian idea of a society based on social labor has lost its persuasive power'. The great import of this discovery is that, for Habermas, it was precisely this Utopia of 'free and equal producers' which inspired the development of the welfare state. Since the mid–1970s such a model has been rapidly losing its authority. What Habermas calls the 'new obscurity' (the incapacity of progressive forces to decide how or whither we should progress) 'is part of a situation in which a welfare state program . . . is losing its power to project future possibilities for a collectively better and less endangered way of life' (Habermas, 1989a; pp. 53–4).

'The welfare-state compromise and the pacification of class antagonisms' were to be achieved by 'using democratically legitimated state power to protect and restrain the quasi-natural process of capitalist growth'. The status of employee was to be complemented by social and political citizenship, on the presupposition 'that peaceful coexistence between democracy and capitalism can be ensured through state intervention' (Habermas, 1989a, p. 55). For a period following the war this strategy was successful within the expanding economies of advanced capitalism, but from the early 1970s it became increasingly problematic, not least because of contradictory elements within the welfare state itself.[3]

The first of these contradictions turned upon the familiar question of the reconcilability of capitalism and democracy and the incapacity of the state to intervene directly to organize the accumulation process. Accordingly, Habermas argues, the more successful is the welfare state in securing the interests of labour the more will it come to undermine the conditions for its own continuing success and the conditions for its long-term viability. For those voters on whom the social democrats or 'welfare state parties' relied in the post-war years, and who benefited most from the development of the welfare state, may increasingly move to protect themselves against the more underprivileged and excluded.[4]

Habermas also identifies a second and less familiar contradictory principle within the welfare state project. The pioneers of the welfare state directed themselves almost exclusively towards the taming of capitalism, as if the state power they used to effect such control was itself neutral or 'innocent'. But while their interest lay in the emancipation of labour, the day-to-day practice of the welfare state has increased state control over the individual worker. In the promotion of welfare legislation programmes, 'an ever denser net of legal norms, and of governmental and para-governmental bureaucracies is spread over the daily life of its potential and actual clients'. Habermas concludes:

> In short, a contradiction between its goal and its method is inherent in the welfare state project as such. Its goal is the establishment of forms of life that are structured in an egalitarian way and that at the same time open up arenas for individual self-realization and spontaneity. But evidently this goal cannot be reached via the direct route of putting political programs into legal and administrative form. (Habermas, 1989a, pp. 58–9)

In part because of its former successes in securing the basic needs of the mass of the population, the welfare state is subject to increasing discontent and defections among a more affluent population dissatisfied with the bureaucratic and alienating way in which its 'services' are delivered.

---

3 Though Habermas does recognize other extrinsic sources of difficulty for the welfare state from the mid–1970s (Habermas, 1989a).
4 A similar logic applies to trades unions whose very success in terms of full employment and wage militancy may eventually lead to their losing power and membership (Habermas, 1989a).

> **Thesis 8**
>
> The accommodation of capitalism, social democracy and the welfare state represents the 'exhausted compromise' of the passing phase of 'organized capitalism'.

For the most part, the 'political economy' approaches which have been discussed in this chapter are concerned with the fortunes of the welfare state in the widely identified period of 'crisis' of the last fifteen to twenty years. Accordingly, further commentary upon them is delayed until we have had an opportunity to review some of the evidence for this 'crisis of the welfare state' in chapter 5. We have also though to consider criticisms of the social democratic orthodoxy that have their origins in the political theory of the 'new social movements' and it is to these that we turn in chapter 3.

# 3
# Capitalism, Social Democracy and the Welfare State III: New Social Movements and the Welfare State

In the Introduction, I indicated that recent years have seen the emergence of a distinctive critique of the social democratic welfare state from the perspective of several new social movements. These have generally been concerned with those costs and consequences of welfare provision which have escaped the vision of the political economists. In this chapter, we consider the distinctive contributions of the feminist, anti-racist and green critiques of welfare state arrangements. In the final section of the chapter, we consider the claims of those who are sceptical about *all* of those generalizing theories of welfare state development which we have so far considered and who insist upon a much closer examination of the individual historical records of a range of quite differing welfare states.

## Feminism and the Welfare State

The burgeoning of distinctively feminist writing on social policy in the last ten to fifteen years cannot be seen to define a single and unified perspective on the welfare state (see Barrett, 1980; Dale and Foster, 1986; Pascall, 1986; Acker, 1988; Pateman, 1988; Shaver, 1989; Williams, 1989). There are, however, a number of shared features of feminist accounts of welfare state development which help to distinguish them from all of the 'mainstream' approaches so far considered. First, feminist writers concentrate upon the gender-specific consequences of the welfare state. Secondly, they broaden their evaluation of welfare beyond the formal or monetarized economy, to consider production and reproduction within the domestic sphere. Thirdly, they register that the welfare state is largely *produced* and *consumed* by women, though typically under the control of, and in the interests of, men. There is disagreement as to whether the welfare state is primarily to be explained in terms of *patriarchy* (the systemic oppression of women by men) or *capitalism* (the systemic oppression of labour by capital), but generally feminist approaches represent the welfare state as organized in the interests of men and of capital, at the expense of women. While there have been those who have understood the welfare state as overwhelmingly explicable in terms of the dominance of men or of capital, perhaps the best-developed account has been that Marxist-feminist view which represents the welfare state as an expression of *both* patriarchal and capitalist oppression.[1]

Such analyses begin from the recognition that, left to themselves, markets are unable to secure the circumstances for the successful long-term accumulation of capital. Particularly within advanced capitalism, the state must intervene within the economy and society to guarantee conditions for sustained capital accumulation. It is in this context that the development of the welfare state must be understood. For the welfare state describes all those state interventions which are required to ensure the production and reproduction of labour power in forms which will sustain capitalism's profitability. However, given the (ideological) imperatives of maintaining the family, in which labour power is reproduced, as a 'private' sphere, the state typically intervenes 'not directly but through its support for a specific form of household: the family household dependent largely upon a male wage and upon female domestic servicing' (McIntosh, 1978, pp. 255–6). Thus, the profitability of capitalism is sustained not just through the state-sanctioned oppression of labour under the wage contract but also through the oppression of women within the state-supported form of the 'dependent-woman family' (Weir, 1974).

This state-sponsored family form is promoted through a range of taxation and benefit provisions (differential arrangements for men and women, and for single and married women) and omissions (the absence of statutory nursery places or collective cooking/laundry facilities). It secures the interests of capital in three main ways:

1   It lowers the costs of the reproduction of labour power. A major determinant of the wage costs of capital is the reproduction (on a

---

1   Among those who see the principal opponent/beneficiary as men are Firestone (1979) and Delphy (1984). For a classification of feminist approaches to the welfare state, see Williams (1989) pp. 41–86.

day-to-day and generation-to-generation basis) of labour power. These costs are substantially cut where they can be displaced upon either the state (public education, public healthcare), or upon women's unpaid domestic labour (cooking, washing, child-care, care of dependent relatives).

2  It provides employers with a 'latent reserve army of labour'. Married women are a source of potential cheap labour (given the prioritization of the male 'family wage'), to be drawn into employment in times of labour scarcity and to be re-deployed towards their 'natural' role in the home when jobs are scarce.

3  Where 'caring'/reproduction services are performed within the waged sector of the economy, the definition of such employment as 'women's work' enables it to be provided at comparatively low cost.

In recent years, a number of important qualifications have been appended to this briefly outlined position. First, it has been suggested that such accounts tend to underestimate the specific impact of *patriarchy*. It is argued that greater weight must be given to the way in which the welfare state serves the interests of (especially white and skilled) working-class men. Some commentators suggest that the welfare state has an *economic* cost for capital (in privileging male wages) but that this is outweighed by the *political* benefits of the gender division of interests within the general category of wage labour which it sustains (Barrett, 1980, p. 230). Secondly, greater attention has been directed towards the ideological construction of women's subordination under welfare state capitalism. The capacity of the welfare state to organize the interests of capital in the ways indicated relies upon pre-existing forms of oppression of women by men which the state is able to shape and exploit but not to create. More weight is given to the deep-seated ideology of men and women's 'natural' roles, which are seen to be crucial in underpinning the structures of patriarchal capitalism. Greater attention is thus directed towards the specifically patriarchal aspects of women's oppression under the welfare state. Thirdly, there has been a re-evaluation of the nature of women's work in the welfare state. Women do not function straightforwardly as a reserve army of labour. In fact, the dependent-female, male-waged household is increasingly untypical within modern economies, while labour markets are heavily sex-segregated, so that expanding women's employment does not typically mean supplementing or replacing a male work-force.

Finally, it is argued that while the expansion of the welfare state has often meant the replacement of women's unpaid labour in the home with women's underpaid 'caring' work in the public sector, state provision of such services can represent a strengthening of women's position (Quadagno, 1990, p. 27; see also Balbo, 1987, p. 204). It does, for example, represent the recognition of a public/state responsibility for those forms of care which were previously defined as exclusively a private (and woman's) responsibility. The welfare state has afforded an avenue of (otherwise blocked) career mobility for some women. It has offered (albeit very limited) childcare provision and healthcare services. These are not to be exhaustively understood as securing the long-term interests of capital, but rather as forms of provision which constitute a 'second-best' strategy for both women *and* capital. According to Brenner and Ramas, 'the welfare state is a major arena of class struggle, within the limits imposed by capitalist relations of production. Those limits can accommodate substantial reforms'. Yet this establishes a context in which women have to choose 'between a welfare state which assumes the male-breadwinner family and no state help at all' (Rein, 1985; Brenner and Ramas, 1984).

The precise configuration of the feminist view of the welfare state continues to be disputed. Sheila Shaver argues of the Marxist-feminist paradigm that it has tended to lapse into functionalist modes of explanation and that, in general, 'Marxism's categories were too little questioned, and feminism's too superficially applied'. She calls for a more historical approach grounded in 'the day-to-day legislative and bureaucratic politics of the welfare state', recognizing that the structure of the welfare state is simultaneously 'gendered' and 'classed' (see Shaver, 1989, pp. 91–3). However, what feminist work appears unquestionably to have established is (1) that the domestic sphere of production and reproduction in which most welfare is secured has been systematically ignored in traditional accounts, and (2) that the more public systems of formal economic and state welfare cannot be understood except in the context of their relation to welfare within the family household system.

---

### Thesis 9

The welfare state is a characteristic form of the developed capitalist state securing the interests of capital and of men, at the expense of women. It is heavily dependent upon arrangements outside the formal economy and/or public provision through which women provide unwaged/low-waged welfare services.

# Commentary: The Feminist Critique of the Welfare State

There is a good deal of evidence to support the broad bases of the feminist argument. Firstly, the welfare state is largely provided for, and by, women. Because they are poorer than men, live longer than them and generally have less access to market-provided services, women are much more reliant on welfare state provision. Thus, in the US, for example, more than 81 per cent of households receiving public assistance (Aid to Families with Dependent Children or AFDC) are headed by women; more than 60 per cent of families receiving food stamps or Medicaid are headed by women; and 70 per cent of all households in publicly owned or subsidized housing are headed by women (Fraser, 1989, p. 107). At the same time, in the UK, 'the state is the largest employer of women workers and most of these women work in the welfare services of health, education and the social services' (Williams, 1989, p. 181). Though this concentration of women in what Rein calls 'the social welfare industry' (SWI) varies between countries, he finds decisive evidence of (growing) segregation in employment between men and women. Looking at four developed capitalist countries, he found that the concentration of women in the SWI ranged from 66 per cent in Germany to over 80 per cent in Sweden. Furthermore, the SWI was the major area of women's increased labour force participation over the past 30 years and an especially important avenue of career mobility for professionally trained women (Rein, 1985, pp. 36–47). Despite this, women are still grossly underrepresented in the *decision-making* levels of the welfare apparatus.

One of the clearest indicators of the gendered structure of inequality under the welfare state is given by the differential vulnerability of men and women to poverty. While poverty has nowhere been eliminated under the welfare state, its incidence and distribution has altered. In preparing his Report for Britain in the 1940s, Beveridge found that the insufficiency of wages to support children explained up to a quarter of all poverty (Beveridge, 1942, p. 7). Thirty years later, over half of the lowest quintile group of income by family type were pensioner households. While low pay and pensioner status remain important sources of poverty (especially for women), these causes of poverty have been in part attenuated by economic and social policy changes. What these changes have in their turn exposed, particularly over the last 20 years, is a process of *the feminization of poverty*. While some commentators insist that 'it is not so much that women are more likely than before to be poor, but that their previously invisible poverty is becoming increasingly visible', it is possible to identify at least a *statistical* feminization of poverty (Glendinning and Millar, 1987, p. 15).

In the US, the basic facts of this 'new poverty' are these:

> Two out of three poor adults are women and one out of five children is poor. Women head half of all poor families and over half the children in female-headed household are poor: 50 per cent of white children; 68 per cent of black and Latin children. A woman over 60 years of age is almost twice as likely as her male counterpart to be impoverished. One-fifth of all elderly women are poor. (Stallard, Ehrenreich and Sklar, 1983, pp. 6–7)

Wilson cites similar evidence:

> Female-headed families comprise a growing proportion of the poverty population. Individuals in female-headed families made up fully a third of the poverty population in 1982. Forty-six per cent of all poor families and seventy-one per cent of all poor black families were female headed in 1982. . . . Female-headed families are not only more likely to be in poverty, they are also more likely than male-headed families to be persistently poor . . . 61 per cent of those who were persistently poor over a ten-year period were in female-headed families, a proportion far exceeding the prevalence of female-headed families in the general population. (Wilson, 1987, pp. 71–2; see also Bane, 1988)

In the UK, Millar notes that 'there are estimated to be almost one million lone parents caring for about one and a half million dependent children . . . Nine out of ten of these lone parents are women and well over ½ of these women and children are living in poverty' (Millar, 1989, p. 1; Millar, 1987, p. 159). In the US, Wilson observes that 'by 1983, almost one out of five families with children under eighteen were headed by women, including 14 per cent of white families, 24 per cent of Spanish-origin families, and 48 per cent of black families' (Wilson, 1987, p. 66; see also Bane, 1988). While the poverty and welfare status of these lone mothers has attracted particular attention in recent years, not least because of the 'explosive' growth in this family form especially among blacks in the US, elderly women, and particularly lone elderly women, have continued to be a group particularly vulnerable to poverty. In the UK, for example, Walker notes that in 1981

> nearly two in every five elderly women (38 per cent) were living on incomes on or below the poverty line compared with 28 per cent of elderly men. Over half of lone elderly women compared with just under two-fifths of single elderly men had incomes on or

below the poverty line. In all, more than two-thirds of elderly women were living in or on the margins of poverty. (Walker, 1987, p. 180)

Overall, the Equal Opportunities Commission in the UK records that 'four per cent of all households are headed by a single parent of which 89 per cent are women. At the other end of the life-cycle, 14 per cent of all households are single adults over the age of retirement and 80 per cent of these are women. Statistics for household income show that single pensioners are the lowest income group, the next lowest being single parents. Women therefore make up a higher proportion of low income households' (EOC, 1987, p. 44). In the US, Quadagno notes that while by 1980 over 80 per cent of the elderly population was covered by old age survivors and disability insurance, average monthly benefits ranged from $432 for white males, to $351 for black males, $279 for white females and $235 for black females. She concludes that 'women and minorities have been unable to share fully in the economic rights of citizenship' (Quadagno, 1988a, p. 2).

Thus in the most basic area of income maintenance, the welfare state has probably failed women more comprehensively than any other group. However such failure is not simply to be explained in terms of inadequate levels of benefits. Rather, it must be connected to the evidence supporting the several other claims of the feminist critique.

One aspect of this is the *formal* inequality of welfare rights for men and women. While welfare states have always treated the claims and needs of men and women differently, there has, in fact, been considerable progress in the last 25 years towards eroding formal differences of entitlement on the basis of gender. There has been some movement away from taxation and social security provision based on the (male-headed) *family* towards a system based on the individual (male or female). Some formal differences do remain: for example, in unequal pensionable ages, in the allocation of survivor's and dependant's benefits within public insurance schemes and in assessments of the availability for work (OECD, 1985b, p. 139). In practice, such differences in the formal provision of services and benefits, while significant, are probably less important than the consequences of applying 'gender-neutral' rules to social and economic institutions which are themselves strongly sex-segregated. However, as we shall see, the welfare state does more than simply 'reproduce' existing patterns of sexual (and racial) inequality. It also reconstitutes and reorganizes the process of impoverishment and patterns of inequality.

A second major element in the feminist critique concerns the ways in which women's unpaid domestic labour – both in the social reproduction of the work-force and in caring for unwaged dependents – subsidizes those economic costs which would have otherwise to be met by capital, through the direct provision of services, increased taxation or an increase in workers' wages. It has long been recognized that housework – principally 'cleaning, shopping, cooking, washing up, washing, and ironing' – has been work that is overwhelmingly unpaid and done by women. Though difficult to quantify, a number of studies have estimated housework to be in excess of fifty hours per week in an average household (Oakley, 1974; Hartmann, 1981; Piachaud, 1984). A second aspect of such unpaid domestic labour is the work of caring for dependents – the sick and disabled, the elderly and, perhaps above all, children. Because much of such care is informal and within the private or domestic sphere, it is difficult to establish how much care is being given by how many carers. Government statistics in the UK suggested that in 1985

> about one adult in 8 ... was looking after an elderly or disabled person ... Overall women are more likely to be carers than men but the difference is not very marked, 15 per cent compared with 11 per cent. About 4 per cent of all adults devote at least 20 hours per week to caring. (CSO, 1989, p. 134)

This is almost certainly the *lowest* available estimate of the preponderance of women over men as carers and it seems clear that such figures under-record both the volume of care given and the proportion of it contributed by women (Graham, 1987; Joshi, 1987; Finch and Groves, 1983; though see also Arber and Gilbert, 1989). Attempts to redirect welfare provision from the state to 'the community' may intensify demands upon women to provide unpaid care. According to Finch and Groves,

> Both demographic change and the 'restructuring' of the welfare state have been grafted on to a pre-existing situation in which women have been defined as the 'natural' carers and also as the dependents of men. These alleged characteristics of women make them especially attractive as potential providers of unpaid care, in the private domain to which they have traditionally been assigned. (Finch and Groves, 1983, p. 5)

State policy is particularly explicit in regarding the provision of childcare as 'women's work'. Drawing upon a series of presumptions about the 'natural' dispositions of motherhood, the welfare state is often quite explicit in affording differential status to mothers and fathers (for example, in rights to paid and unpaid leave from work, in the payment of children's allowances and in the right to claim unemployment benefits). The clearest, if indirect, measurement of the differential costs of childcare for men and women can be seen in their differing patterns of participation in paid employment. As Graham observes, 'caring for young children is typically a full-time and unpaid job and most women withdraw from full-time paid work to do it' (Graham, 1987, p. 223). Throughout the developed capitalist economies, male labour force participation rates have fallen over the past twenty to thirty years, while female participation rates have increased (OECD, 1985b, pp. 12–13). Yet labour force participation rates of women (though not men) with (especially young) dependent children are low. In the UK, in 1985, while 47 per cent of women with no dependent children were in full-time employment, just 6 per cent of women with children under 5 were full-time employees. Overall, while 65 per cent of women with no dependent children were working, among those with children under five the comparable figure was 28 per cent.

For most women then, child-rearing implies economic dependency, whether upon a male partner's income or, failing this, upon the state. Lone parenthood and dependence upon state benefits is, as we have seen, a major and growing source of poverty. Figures for the UK in 1985 show that around half of all lone parents with children were in receipt of supplementary benefit (Millar, 1989, p. 31). Nor are the disadvantages to women of their responsibility for childcare confined solely to dependence and loss of present earnings. First, because of the characteristic break in career which child-rearing entails, most women who return to full-time employment do so on less advantageous terms than their male peers who have had no break in employment. Secondly, many forms of welfare provision, especially retirement pensions, are based on long-term contributions whilst in paid work. This includes not only public entitlements, but also, for example, rights under increasingly important private or company pension schemes, which are much less generally available to those with intermittent or part-time work records.[2] In summary:

---

2  Figures for membership of UK employers' pension schemes for 1987 show that among full-time workers, 62 per cent of men and 51 per cent of women were included. When coverage of both full-time and part-time workers is considered, the figures are 59 per cent for men and 33 per cent for women (General Household Survey, 1987, pp. 75 and 146).

the differential distribution of the rewards received from entitlement programs reflects their eligibility rules. Although these are
technically gender-neutral, they are modeled on male patterns of
labor force participation. By rewarding continuous attachment to
the labor force, long years of service, and high wages, these rules
disadvantage women whose shorter and more irregular work histories make it more difficult for them to obtain full benefits.
(Quadagno, 1990, p. 14)

These disadvantages are further exacerbated by the tendency of
women (especially those with continuing responsibility for dependants) to return to work on a part-time basis. The growth of
part-time work has been a secular trend in most OECD countries,
particularly pronounced over the last twenty years, though perhaps
showing some tendency to level out in the most recent period
(OECD, 1985b, p. 16; Ermisch, 1985, p. 64). Although there is significant international variation, part-time work is disproportionately
carried out by women. In 1985, the proportion of female workers
among part-time employees in the OECD ranged from 63 per cent in
Greece to more than 94 per cent in the UK (OECD, 1985b, p. 16).
Thus, much of women's enhanced involvement in paid work has
been on a part-time basis. So, for example, 53 per cent of working
women in Norway and 45 per cent in The Netherlands were part-
time employees, though in Finland, Greece, Ireland and Italy, the
figure remained below 10 per cent (OECD, 1985b, p. 16). While such
patterns of partial employment may enable women to reconcile their
caring and domestic responsibilities with paid employment, a number of disadvantages flow from part-time employment. Not only is
total remuneration lower, but part-time workers also tend to receive
lower rates of pay, enjoy less security of employment and less
prospect of promotion and have weaker welfare and employment
rights. It often means working antisocial hours (as, for example, in
much hospital-based nursing). It also helps to explain a pattern in
which women's average earnings continue to be about two-thirds
those of men (EOC, 1987, p. 39). Because of a lack of state provision
of childcare, many women wishing to return to work are forced to
make *ad hoc* arrangements, often with (female) relatives or friends.
Where such work is paid, especially within the 'informal' childcare
economy (for example, the work of unregistered childminders), it is
carried out by women on low wages with few welfare or employment rights (Jackson and Jackson, 1979).

This leads on to a final element in the feminist critique, that is, the
claim that women, in part because of their dependent status and
their domestic responsibilities, offer employers a potential pool of

cheap and adaptable labour. In fact, any straightforward version of the 'reserve army' thesis is probably unsustainable, because the very pronounced sex segregation of the labour market means that women's labour is not usually directly replacing the work of men. This does not however mean that women are not a source of cheap labour. Whatever its salience in the wider economy, in terms of employment *within* the welfare state, women are the principal and comparatively cheap source of labour power. Thus, the nursing profession, which is often seen to replicate women's 'natural' and 'caring' role in the home within paid employment, is almost 90 per cent female. Ancillary workers, responsible for much cleaning and catering work in the UK National Health Service, are predominantly female and disproportionately drawn from ethnic minority populations (Williams, 1989, pp. 170ff.; Cook and Watt, 1987, p. 60; Beechey and Perkins, 1987, pp. 86–90). Similarly, the teaching of young children is predominantly a female profession (with the partial exception of Germany). In both health and education, however, women are systematically under-represented in the more senior and decision-taking levels of the profession. In the UK, for example, while women make up more than 90 per cent of all staff nurses and auxiliary nurses, fewer than one in five senior managers are women (Steering Group on Equal Opportunities, 1988). In most advanced capitalist countries, this social welfare sector of employment has expanded rapidly over the last thirty years. Rein estimates that the social welfare industry (SWI) accounts for between 47 per cent (US) and 89 per cent (Sweden) of the growth in female non-agricultural labour force participation in the period 1960–1980 (Rein, 1985, p. 41). Much of this growth in social welfare employment has been in part-time work, (with all the attendant disadvantages which we have identified).

## The 'Anti-Racist' Critique of the Welfare State

In the non-institutional politics of the new social movements, a parallel has frequently been drawn between the disadvantaged position of women and the disadvantaged position of ethnic minorities. Such a parallel can and, to a very limited extent, has been applied to discussions of the welfare state (Williams, 1989). In fact, the anti-racist critique, as Williams' recent survey reveals, is less clearly delineated and less fully elaborated than the critical positions adopted by feminist writers. However, as Cloward and Piven make clear, in the US, at least, 'race' is crucial to any understanding of the politics of the welfare state (Block et al. 1987; see also Murray, 1984; Moynihan, 1965).

Few commentators deny that 'simple' racial prejudice amongst white people against black people is an important constituent of the latter's disadvantaged position within the welfare state. At the same time, very few suppose that individual racism can adequately explain the levels and persistence of such disadvantage. In seeking a more systemic explanation, and paralleling the discussion of 'patriarchy' and 'capitalism' in the feminist critique, there is some disagreement among commentators as to whether the disadvantages experienced by ethnic minorities under existing welfare state arrangements are primarily to be explained in terms of the interests of the majority community or else by the interests of international capital. However, there is widespread agreement with the core proposition that ethnic minorities face a 'double process' of disadvantage under the welfare state. First, their economically and socially less privileged position tends to make them more reliant upon provision through the welfare state. Secondly, this welfare state upon which they are peculiarly dependent treats them on systematically less favourable terms than members of the majority community. This core claim has been developed in a number of directions.

First, ever since its inception, the welfare state has been underpinned by a conception of nationhood and it has been counted as one of its strengths that it institutionalizes and strengthens claims based upon the equality of citizenship. However, not all those living within a given national territory have counted equally as 'members of the nation' or as citizens, and not everybody has enjoyed the same rights of access to the welfare state. In fact, some sort of residence qualification for relief is a commonplace of public welfare which long predates the coming of the welfare state (Webb and Webb, 1927; De Swaan, 1988; see pp. 104–5 below). Thus a whole series of disqualifications from access to the welfare state have been enacted against migrant workers, their families and their descendants. These divisions have been reinforced where the immigrant community can be further identified by differences of colour, language or religious background. Amongst those who see the welfare state as a form of class compromise, it is argued that this compromise represents a *rapprochement* between capital and a white, male, metropolitan and organized working class, secured largely at the expense of other groups of workers.

This dovetails with a second claim, that immigration has served as a source of cheap labour – to be employed (albeit intermittently) either by capital or indeed within the welfare state itself. Here again, ethnic minority and immigrant workers are seen to parallel the role

feminists attribute to women as a 'reserve army of labour', introduced in times of labour scarcity to do poorly paid work and to act
as a constraint upon rising wages. Similarly, and particularly for
black women, those areas of a highly segregated labour market to
which they most readily gain access are in low-skilled 'caring' or
'servicing' occupations. Indeed, Williams, writing of employment
within the National Health Service in the UK, insists 'that the racist
image of the *Black woman as servant* is as strong as that of *carer* in the
acceptance of Black women in domestic, nursing and cleaning roles'
(Williams, 1989, p. 72; Carby, 1982, p. 215). Because of their lower
levels of sanctioned skills and of unionization, and their lack of
accumulated employment rights and political clout, in periods of
economic downturn, ethnic minorities are subject to differentially
high levels of unemployment. Just as, for both state and employers,
the 'ideal' solution to the problem of unemployment in the case of
women was to define them out of the work-force, so the 'optimum'
solution in the case of migrant workers may be to repatriate them.
Where this is not possible, these displaced workers are still more
likely than others to find themselves dependent upon the residual
provision of state benefits.

A further parallel with the feminists' argument is to be found in
the role attributed to ethnic minority labour in reducing the costs of
the reproduction of labour power. First, immigrant workers may not
enjoy the same rights to housing, unemployment benefit and
healthcare as 'indigenous' workers. Secondly, immigration laws may
explicitly seek to exclude from citizenship, or indeed from residence,
dependent relatives of the immigrant worker. Thirdly, the costs of
education and training of the immigrant worker will generally have
been met by his or her country of origin, while the 'guest' worker
approaching retirement age may be 'encouraged' to 'go home'.

Critics also argue that the welfare state itself performs a role in the
reproduction of these disadvantages of ethnic minority labour. An
educational system in which ethnic minorities systematically under-
achieve or a system of housing allocation in which ethnic minorities
are confined to the poorest quality public stock are seen to reinforce
across generations disadvantages which were originally experienced
by an immigrant population. Finally, it is argued that access to more
generous forms of welfare provision – for example, Social Security in
the US or earnings-related pensions in the UK – is tied to an individual's previous employment record. This 'achievement'-oriented
welfare state is constructed around characteristically white and male
patterns of permanent, full-time and (more or less) continuous
employment. Even within a gender-blind and colour-blind welfare

system, characteristic differences in economic opportunities and rewards for women and blacks means unequal rewards from the welfare state.

Clearly, there are important similarities between the feminist and anti-racist critiques of the welfare state. But there are also substantial differences. For example, the ideology of 'promoting healthy family life' may have very different, if similarly unattractive consequences for white women and black men. Again, the patterns and consequences of exclusion of women and ethnic minority men from the employed work-force may be quite different. Perhaps the single most important issue raised in this context is the status of ethnic minority women. Thus, Williams writes of a black feminist critique of other schools of feminism arising from 'the use of the concept of 'patriarchy', from the omission of Black women's struggle against slavery, colonialism, imperialism and racism in the writing of feminist history (or "herstory"), and from the tendency to see racial oppression and sex oppression and the struggles against them as parallel but separate forms' (Williams, 1989, p. 70). Williams argues that 'Black women have a qualitatively different experience of the welfare state compared with white women' and if ethnic minority women are 'doubly disadvantaged' within the welfare state, this does not straightforwardly represent a process of *reinforcement*, but rather a *reconstitution* of their experience (Williams, 1989, pp. 78–9).

---

**Thesis 10**

The welfare state is a characteristic form of the developed capitalist state securing the interests of capital and of white people (and especially men) at the expense of ethnic minorities (and especially women).

---

## Commentary: The 'Anti-Racist' Critique of the Welfare State

Turning to the evidence which is cited in support of the 'anti-racist' perspective, we can again identify important similarities with (as well as some significant differences from) the feminist critique. The first point to note is that while ethnicity is seen as an appropriate way of describing people's differing and largely self-ascribed cultural identities, 'race' is widely rejected as a spurious and largely ideological term. Claims that 'races' and 'racial differences' have some biological basis, and often that they form some sort of evolutionary hierarchy, are denied. The rhetoric of race – of, for example, 'the British race' or 'the white races of South Africa' – is seen simply as a device for mobilizing prejudice in the interests of one (often ethnically diverse) group over others.

Characteristically, the idea of 'race' is associated with 'insiders' and 'outsiders' or members and non-members. Historically, it was perhaps most often used in the context of imperialism and colonialism to justify the dominance of a (generally white-skinned) minority over an (often brown- or black-skinned) majority. Within the welfare state, it is more typically a majority population that constitutes the 'insiders' and a minority or minorities that make up the 'outsiders'. Such accounts rest upon an extremely selective history. In fact, the whole of human history is marked by patterns of migration and many of the most developed industrial societies (and amongst them, some of the most developed welfare states) are largely immigrant societies (Australia, New Zealand, Canada and the US, for example).

The experience of these immigrant societies demonstrates that it is not always the indigenous population that successfully sustains the claim to constitute the 'true' basis of the nation. Thus in North America and Australasia the truly native population was effectively marginalized by more powerful incomers. The US, as is well known, was itself made up of successive waves of immigration. Following the English and other northern Europeans, the Irish, southern and eastern Europeans, and Hispanics found themselves to be successively and temporarily the newest and the most economically and socially disadvantaged sections of the US population. This history of successive waves of immigration was itself entwined with the forced importation of black Americans and their subsequent and continuing struggle for formal and substantive equality. The experience of the American blacks also illustrates the ways in which the dynamics of population in the welfare state have been affected by *internal* migration (as, for example, in their shift from southern agriculture to northern industrial cities). Though less dramatic and less long-distance, migration has been and continues to be an important element in the histories of the developed welfare states of Western Europe (Grammenos, 1982, pp. 30–2; Paine, 1974, pp. 5–36; Piore, 1979; Rosenblum, 1973). In the wake of recent developments in Eastern and Central Europe, it may be that (the aspiration for) large-scale immigration will present a renewed challenge for social policy in Western Europe in the 1990s.[3]

---

3 I am grateful to John Keane for drawing this likely development to my attention.

In practice, the experience of racism within the welfare state is not, of course, confined to immigrants or ex-immigrant populations (as the experience of Maoris, Aborigines and native Americans attests). Yet this has been the principal focus of the anti-racist critique and it is an experience which makes their claims particularly clear. Furthermore, it is a part of the disadvantaged experience of non-immigrant ethnic minorities to find themselves *treated like immigrants*. Correspondingly, the focus here is on the immigrant experience of the welfare state.

A crucial background condition for this immigrant experience is the fact that welfare states have always been *national* institutions based upon some conception of *national* citizenship. While we have seen that welfare as the right of a citizen has something to commend it as an alternative to welfare as the charitable relief of the destitute pauper, it clearly marginalizes the position of those resident within a national territory but not enjoying the full rights of citizenship. Exclusion from full citizenship is a frequent concomitant of immigrant status and exclusion from full citizenship will often mean exclusion from full participation in the welfare state (Freeman, 1986, p. 51). Correspondingly, formal differences in *legal* status are perhaps more important in the anti-racist than in the feminist critique. Of course, exclusions from access to the welfare state on the basis of citizenship are not necessarily racist, nor are they necessarily unjustified, if one understands the welfare state to be funded by the accumulated efforts and abstinence from immediate consumption of a given national population (see Carens, 1988). However, if the ways in which citizenship is granted and withheld, or the ways in which welfare rights are implemented, are themselves racist, this qualification is nullified.

In practice, different types of migrant, enjoying different legal status, are differentially excluded from rights of access to the welfare state (Hammar, 1990). The most disadvantaged group in this sense is likely to be made up of illegal immigrants. As workers, illegal immigrants tend to be almost wholly without employment rights. Normally, they have no rights to the provision of healthcare or to housing, no rights to welfare protection or pensions and no entitlement to social provision for their dependants. Living under constant threat of deportation, they remain largely on the sufferance of their employers and often find themselves 'super-exploited' in intermittent work on low wages, under poor and unregulated conditions, often, for example, in the building trade or in domestic service (Grammenos, 1982, pp. 17–8; OECD, 1985b, pp. 101–5). There are some indications that, as official migration to the developed countries has been increasingly restricted over the last twenty years, illegal immigration may have been rising (Maillat, 1987, p. 55).

Rather less marginal is the position of 'official' migrant workers. Facing a labour shortfall in a period of sustained economic growth in the 1950s and 1960s, a number of European countries sought to supplement their labour supply by 'inviting in' migrant workers from less developed countries. Those countries with an extensive colonial past (for example, The Netherlands and the UK) tended to turn to their former colonies, sometimes because such workers were seen to be cheaper to the host country than immigrants from extra-colonial sources (Joshi and Carter, 1984, p. 58). Others, such as West Germany, took workers from the less developed areas of southern Europe (initially from Italy, later from Yugoslavia and Turkey). While such migrant workers enjoyed certain welfare rights (for example, limited access to housing and healthcare, and the statutory protection of health and safety legislation), they did not enjoy the same rights as indigenous workers. They did not, for example, enjoy the same entitlement to unemployment benefit nor, very often, the right to bring in dependants with the same rights of access to housing, education and healthcare as the dependants of indigenous workers. Nor did they always enjoy the same rights upon *leaving* the workforce (Brubaker, 1989, pp. 155–60). As Grammenos points out, while migration before 1945 was largely 'one-way', in the post-war period, migration more commonly took the form of 'rotation' (Grammenos, 1982, pp. 30–1). Under such 'two-way migration', workers (ideally young, skilled, educated and free of dependants) work temporarily in the host economy, meeting pressing labour demands and leaving when the labour market slackens. West Germany's '*Gastarbeiter*' or 'guest worker' system, largely based on temporary Turkish migrant labour, is often seen as the archetypal expression of this system. The warmth of the welcome for such visiting workers, as for other 'guests', is contingent on the recognition that their stay will be temporary and, as Freeman points out, 'the problem with the guest-worker system from the point of view of the host state is that it tends to break down' (Cashmore and Troyna, 1983, p. 52; Grammenos, 1982, p. 30; Freeman, 1986, p. 60).

A third category of migrant worker is defined by those accepted for permanent settlement and/or incorporation into full citizenship. Formally, such a group may enjoy full equality with members of the indigenous population. However, where welfare practice is discriminatory, this formal equality of citizenship may not result in actual equality of treatment or of condition. Thus, as has been the experience of those with Afro-Caribbean and Asian backgrounds in both the US and the UK, formal equality of citizenship has not ended discriminatory practices in the provision of health, housing or personal social services. Perhaps most importantly, it has not ended discrimination in what is for most people the single most important source of welfare – that is, the labour market. Fully to appreciate this, we need to move on to consider how racism is seen to service the interests of the welfare state capitalist economies.

In discussing the feminist critique of the welfare state, we saw how women's subordinate position was said to serve the capitalist economy in three ways: (1) by providing a source of cheap labour, (2) by providing a 'reserve army' of labour to be drawn in and out of active participation in response to the changing needs of the labour market and (3) by reducing the costs of the reproduction of labour power. We can trace these same elements in considering the anti-racist critique of the economic consequences of existing welfare state arrangements.

Occasionally, the welfare state has been seen to be directly complicit in securing the supply of cheap labour within a racist regime. Writing of attempts at reform in the US in the 1970s, Jill Quadagno argues that for 'more than a century, blacks had been excluded from welfare in the South because the welfare system was an instrument of social control, a part of the local racial caste system' (Quadagno, 1990, p. 24). Both Alston and Ferrie (1985) and Quadagno (1988a; 1988b; 1990) argue that the structure of the welfare state in the American south from the 1930s to the 1970s was principally shaped by the interests of white southern planters in the preservation of a poor and dependent black population. When federally supported old age assistance was first introduced in the 1930s, the white Southern Democrats who controlled the southern political machine resisted all attempts to increase the levels of support to poor southern black families and thus the threat to the availability of the black population to perform low-paid and irregular work. In the cotton belt of the south, average monthly benefits were systematically lower than in the north and west (standing in 1938/9, for example, at $7.06 in Mississippi, $21.79 in New York and $30.54 in California). Rates were lower for blacks than whites throughout the cotton belt of the south, and within this region rates were lower within the cotton counties than in the non-cotton counties (Quadagno, 1988b, pp. 244–5). Through their control of the local welfare state, 'southern landholders .. were able to prevent the payment of significant benefits to their tenants, croppers, and wage workers under the Social Security Act, and thereby assured themselves a continued supply of cheap, loyal labor' (Alston and Ferrie, 1985, p. 117).

Although this particular form of the racial welfare state in the southern US was eventually to be rendered obsolete by changes in agricultural technology, black migration and black political empowerment, Quadagno identifies much the same process at work in the south in the 1970s. Reviewing President Nixon's unsuccessful welfare reform proposals aimed at securing a guaranteed annual income for the working poor (the Family Assistance Plan), a reform which promised significantly to raise the wages of black workers in the south and threaten its traditional low-wage economy, Quadagno found 'the Southern power elite' to be amongst its most vocal and committed opponents. As Georgia Representative Phillip Landrum protested: 'There's not going to be anybody left to roll these wheel-barrows and press these shirts' (Quadagno, 1990, pp. 23–5).

More usually, the 'complicity' of the welfare state in the supply of cheap labour is less direct. It is a process which is particularly well illustrated by the experience of immigrant labour. In fact, the long-term economic consequences of immigration for the receiving countries have been much discussed (see, for example, Paine, 1974, pp. 12–23). Some have suggested that, in the longer term, immigration may detract from capital accumulation by delaying technological innovation or increasing social infrastructural costs. Yet the predominant economic view, and certainly the motivation of those welfare states which encouraged migration in the 1950s and 1960s, was that the importation of migrant workers (especially on a temporary basis) would improve circumstances for capital accumulation. Under conditions of near full employment, there is likely to be a shortfall in the availability of indigenous labour, which will put upward pressure on wages and lead to difficulties in filling lower paid and unskilled jobs. Under these circumstances in the 1950s and 1960s, many of the Western European welfare states turned to migrants as a source of comparatively cheap labour to fill unskilled positions. For the migrants themselves, coming from less developed countries with high unemployment and much lower wages, there was clearly an economic incentive to take what were, by Western European standards, poorly paid and unattractive jobs. In the host countries, under conditions of near full employment, the use of such immigrant labour was not only in the interests of capital but also of native workers. Migrants were not competing with native workers, but, in fact, creating more skilled jobs for nationals by filling those unskilled positions which were needed to support higher levels of general economic activity. Thus migrant workers were generally introduced to perform unskilled jobs at low wages and were heavily concentrated in particular sectors of a highly segregated labour market (Maillat, 1987). In West Germany in 1968, for example, while the national average male wage was DM5.81 per hour, the average rate for male migrants from southern Europe was DM4.51 per hour (cited in Paine, 1974, p. 99). Such disadvantages are not confined to temporary migrants. In the UK, in 1984, median weekly earnings of full-time male employees were recorded as £129.00 for whites,

£110.70 for Asians and £109.20 for West Indians (Brown, 1984, p. 212). In the US, in 1985, 'the median annual income of families stood at $29,152 for whites, $19,027 for hispanics and $16,786 for blacks' (US Bureau of the Census, 1987, p. 436). From several countries there is evidence of 'an ethnic minority labour market which seems to be in some respects quite different from that of white workers' (Brown, 1984, p. 293). In France in 1980, 56 per cent of migrants were either manual workers or employed in the domestic service sector, compared with 26.5 per cent in the general population (cited in Grammenos, 1982, p. 19). In the UK in 1982, 42 per cent of white men were employed in non-manual occupations, compared with 26 per cent among Asians and 16 per cent among West Indians (Brown, 1984, p. 233). In the UK National Health Service, Doyal, Hunt and Mellor have estimated that half of the poorest paid ancillary staff are migrant workers. Their own survey of an acute non-teaching hospital in London found that 'in excess of 80 per cent of ancillary workers were from abroad' (Doyal, Hunt and Mellor, 1981, p. 54).

In turning to the status of migrants and ethnic minorities as a 'reserve army of labour', we again find a pattern of disadvantage which is rather different from that experienced by women. First, that migrant labour should act as a reserve pool of labour, to be taken up in times of heightened activity and stood down in periods of economic recession, is not seen as a regrettable economic 'accident'. It is entrenched as *an element of governments' economic policy*. The intention of bringing in temporary migrant labour is precisely to meet a temporary excess of labour demand. When demand no longer exceeds supply, the policy imperative is to shed labour by returning migrants to their countries of origin. This policy intention, however flawed its realization, was quite clear in the Western European welfare states following the economic downturn of the early 1970s.[4] In West Germany, new restrictions were placed on rights of entry for dependants of foreign workers; in France, family reunions were suspended for a time in the late 1970s (Grammenos, 1982, p. 29). In the UK, the 1971 Commonwealth Immigration Act changed the status of New Commonwealth citizens, effectively affording them the same status as workers from other overseas countries (Cashmore and Troyna, 1983, p. 65). In practice, the effects of recession on migration, integration and repatriation have often been very different from those that governments of the 1970s

---

4  Despite governments' policy intentions, the effects of recession in terms of migration, integration and repatriation have often been perverse (Hammar and Lithman, 1987).

had anticipated (Hammar and Lithman, 1987). But they have done little to improve the economic marginality of immigrant workers. Maillat concludes that

> In the final analysis, the differences in the unemployment rates of nationals and foreigners are indicative of the insecure nature of the jobs held by foreigners. Reasons for this vulnerability of foreign workers relate to their concentration in sectors in crisis, the high proportion of unskilled workers among them, their lack of any real negotiating power, and the fact that they are often the first in line in the event of redundancies. (Maillat, 1987, p. 51)

This disadvantage in terms of employment also extends to resident ethnic minority populations. In the UK in the mid-1980s (in a period of historically very high unemployment), levels of joblessness were twice as high among West Indians as among whites. Among those under 25, black unemployment was running at 33 per cent. West Indians and Asians were also over-represented among the long-term unemployed who had been out of work for a year or more (Brown, 1984, pp. 194–5). In the US in 1979, when the overall unemployment rate had fallen below 6 per cent, the rate for black male teenagers stood at 34.1 per cent. For Wilson, this signalled 'a problem of joblessness for young black men [of] catastrophic proportions' (Wilson, 1987, p. 43).

The problems of migrants and ethnic minorities are further aggravated by their generally low levels of formal qualifications and acquired skills, their lack of accumulated employment and welfare rights and, in the case of migrants, the unwillingness of state and employers to invest in a 'temporary' resource.

A third element indicated in the anti-racist critique is the role of immigrant and ethnic minority workers in lowering the reproduction costs of labour. Here again, for migrant labour at least, this is a conscious intention of various governments' economic policy. The preponderance of the young, single, healthy and economically active among migrants means that they make very limited demands on the most expensive elements of the welfare state – health, education and pensions. There are also elements of transfer income, for example, unemployment benefit, from which they may be effectively excluded. At the same time, migrants help to finance the welfare state through direct and indirect taxation. Although migrant and ethnic minority populations are often represented as a drain upon welfare state resources, Grammenos argues that they may be very substantial net contributors to the public exchequer. He cites evidence for West Germany, which shows 'that savings on child-rearing and education resulting from immigration come to at least 19 per cent of net investment for the period 1969 to 1973' (Grammenos, 1982, p. 31). Grammenos also argues that the fact that 'the host country receives young healthy workers without having to educate them or support them as children' led to savings in West Germany in the period 1957–73 which 'would have generated additional capital of 27.721 billion DM at 1973 prices' (Grammenos, 1982, p. 37; Blitz, 1977, p. 496). The economic consequences of a permanently-settled immigrant population are less clear-cut. The demographic make-up of this population will be different from that of the established population. In time, as the immigrant community aged, one would expect it to make greater demands on the social infrastructure. However, in the UK experience, the comparative growth of the (ex-)immigrant population and its historically high levels of labour force participation challenge the popular claim of the later 1970s that the ethnic minorities are a drain upon both the productive economy and the welfare state (see Golding and Middleton, 1982). In fact, a defraying of the costs of labour power may occur very directly through the dependence of the welfare state upon the low-paid labour of (especially female) workers from the ethnic minority population (see above, p. 81).

One final element in the anti-racist critique concerns the ways in which the welfare state itself reproduces the disadvantages of ethnic minority populations. In part, this simply echoes the observation made by the feminists (pp. 77–8) and by Jill Quadagno, that a welfare state which relates entitlements to previous labour market performance militates against all those, notably women and ethnic minorities, whose lifetime's earnings and employment are below the white male average. In part, it concerns racial discrimination on the part of those officials responsible for allocating public housing, adjudicating claims for benefits or making decisions about the educational destinations of children. Although patterns of welfare inequality are complex, and differ in important ways between different ethnic minority populations, evidence of unequal welfare outcomes is clear.

In the UK, the 1985 Committee of Inquiry into the Education of Children from Ethnic Minority Groups, established by the government under the chairmanship of Lord Swann, echoed earlier findings in identifying systematic educational underachievement among the West Indian school population (Swann, 1985; Brown and Madge, 1982).[5] The Swann committee cited evidence showing that

---

5  For varying reasons, Asian children were seen to achieve rough parity of educational outcome with their white peers (Swann, 1985; Brown and Madge, 1982).

low examination performance among sixteen-year-old working-class children stood at 20 per cent among white children and 21 per cent among Asians, but rose to 41 per cent among West Indians. It also noted that while 1 per cent of West Indian pupils went on to full-time degree courses in further education, this compared with a figure of 5 per cent amongst Asians and 'all other leavers' (Swann, 1985, pp. 60–2). The committee argued that

> A substantial part of ethnic minority underachievement ... is the result of racial prejudice and discrimination on the part of society at large, bearing on ethnic minority homes and families, and hence, *indirectly*, on children. [The rest] ... is due in large measure to prejudice and discrimination bearing *directly* on children, within the educational system, as well as outside it. (Swann, 1985, pp. 89–90)

The provision of housing is another area of the welfare state which reflects an ethnically divided access to resources and reveals a pattern of disproportionate disadvantage among ethnic minorities, as deprivations based upon social class and economic status are reinforced by patterns of discrimination. Patterns of household tenure among different ethnic groups are complex. Nonetheless, Brown insists that in the UK:

> The council property allocated to black tenants is generally worse than that allocated to white tenants ... Asian and West Indian families are on average larger than white families and more frequently have children. It is therefore a major source of disadvantage that they are housed in properties that are on average smaller, more likely to be flats than houses, and less likely to have access to gardens. (Brown, 1984, p. 320)

Similarly, and irrespective of tenure type, he found that 'black households have fewer rooms than white people, with the result that there is a much higher percentage of black people in every tenure with more than one person per room' (Brown, 1984, p. 74). In 1982, while 54 per cent of whites occupied detached or semi-detached houses, for blacks the comparable figure was just 18 per cent (p. 94).

Explanations of these patterns are very varied and not all support the claims of the anti-racist critique. Yet it is possible to identify a very broad agreement about the existence of *prima facie* evidence of discrimination and inequality along ethnic lines within the welfare state.

Finally, it is worth remarking upon the peculiar position of ethnic minority women. This population is seen to be disadvantaged in terms of both the feminist and the anti-racist critiques of the welfare state. Thus, Cook and Watt insist that 'Black women in Britain have to face ... the dual oppressions of racism and sexism which impinge on their opportunities and consign them to low-paid and lower-status jobs' (Cook and Watt, 1987, p. 69). A 1985 OECD study, *The Integration of Women into the Economy*, found that immigrant women were often the single most economically disadvantaged group within the population. Typically, they have 'more dependants but fewer family resources; they have a greater need for gainful employment but run a higher risk of unemployment' (OECD, 1985b, p. 92). However, this 'double disadvantage' is not simply cumulative. Thus, for example, while black women are disadvantaged economically both as blacks and as women, the nature of this disadvantage is also shaped by the fact that they are married to (economically disadvantaged and more marginally employed) black men or, particularly in the US, that they are disproportionately likely to be at the head of (frequently impoverished) single-parent families (Wilson, 1987). This may yield distinctive patterns of, for example, employment participation or welfare dependency. Correspondingly, the experience of black women under the welfare state is something other than the cumulative consequence of being black and being female.

## The Green Critique of the Welfare State

Insofar as we may speak of a single green perspective on the welfare state, it is principally to be derived from a characteristic concern with the harmful consequences of unsustainable economic growth and bureaucratized welfare services. While there is a conservative wing to the green perspective, which argues against the welfare state and in favour of traditional (and sometimes pre-democratic) forms of religious, community and family life, the mainstream green critique of the welfare state can be seen as an attack 'from the left'. Broadly, green commentators identify the welfare state with the political programme of traditional social democracy, and see both as inevitably implicated in the logic of advanced capitalism. In varying ways, they reject all three (Dobson, 1990).

We may summarize this green critique of the welfare state under two major headings: the welfare state and the logic of industrialism, and the welfare state as social control.

# The welfare state and the logic of industrialism

The welfare state is embedded in an industrial order which is itself premised upon economic growth. We have seen that such economic growth was a core component of social democratic strategy under the Keynesian welfare state. It was the engine of economic growth that was to fund the welfare state, which in turn would adjust patterns of distribution in society, so as to offset the inegalitarian consequences of growth under capitalist forms. For the greens, this perspective of open-ended economic growth is untenable. Theirs is a protest 'not against the failure of the state and society to provide for economic growth and material prosperity, but against their all-too-considerable success in having done so, and against the price of this success' (cited in Poguntke, 1987). The welfare state is not a viable long-term political arrangement because the costs of economic growth (upon which it relies) are too severe for the natural and human environment, and are eventually counter-productive.

Greens also insist that the welfare state is one of the most important sites of the dominance of technological rationality or technocracy in contemporary societies. Rejection of the attempt to subjugate all forms of human and social conduct to the logic of rational domination has a long history in the New Left/Western Marxism. Retraceable at least to the writings of Horkheimer and Adorno is the view that the attempt to dominate and exploit nature (which industrialism has represented) will always enjoin the subjugation and exploitation of humankind-in-nature. It was Marcuse who described the welfare state as a 'state of unfreedom' built upon 'technological rationality' and 'administered living' (Marcuse, 1972, pp. 51–2) For the greens, the welfare state is inextricably involved in surveillance, control and the creation of social capital, to the detriment of the human(e) development of the population it administers.

This subservience to both economic growth and technical rational domination are to be understood as a part of the logic of developed capitalism. Gorz, for example, follows more traditional Marxists in arguing that 'the two main functions of the institutions and policies of the welfare state [are] *the production of order and the production of the right type of demand* needed for capitalist development' (Gorz, 1985, p. 14). The welfare state, even if it emerges in response to the mobilization of the working class, is a way of discharging the social costs of capitalist development upon the general public. It also serves to represent collective problems and needs as individual ones, which may be responsive to marketable goods and services. For most greens, real social needs could be met more efficiently through greater public provision (preventative rather than curative healthcare, public rather than private transport), but this is not consonant with the interests of capital. The welfare state has also to respond to the surplus production of social need that is generated by capitalist forms of industrial organization (for example, nervous disorders and alcoholism generated by the stress of work under capitalist imperatives). The welfare state is a part of capitalism which is itself unavoidably tied to the corrupt logic of economic growth. Neither is consistent with the support of sustainable and humane forms of social life.

Green commentators also charge that the social democratic commitment to the welfare state as a compromise based on the encouragement of capitalist economic growth means 'bracketing out' a whole range of radical issues (including socialization of production, workers' control, quality of life, planning) which were a part of the traditional ideological baggage of pre-welfare state socialism. Its commitment to and association with the capitalist welfare state makes social democracy an impossible vehicle for radical social change. Finally, the welfare state represents a national rather than a global response to the problem of reconciling general social welfare with economic growth. As such, it depends upon displacing the dysfunctions of economic growth upon the Third World, offering a national political solution which makes global problems of welfare still more severe.

## The welfare state as social control

The greens' critique of the welfare state is also intimately concerned with its implications for the exercise of 'micro-power' or social control by the state over the individual. Thus, the history of the rise of the welfare state is simultaneously the history of the rise of the 'disabling professions' (Illich, 1977). In reducing the citizens of the democratic state to the clients of the welfare state, welfare institutions, under the guise of the 'helping' or 'caring' professions, exercise ever greater control over the personal lives of individuals. Far from 'enabling', welfare state professionals – doctors, social workers, teachers, housing administrators – much more characteristically 'disable' their clients, stripping them of the competence (and often the legal right) to make their own decisions and making them increasingly dependent upon the state and its paid professionals. For Lasch, 'the expansion of welfare services presupposed the reduction of the citizen to a consumer of expertise' (Lasch, 1978, p. 224). According to Illich, 'industrial welfare systems ... incapacitate people's autonomy through forcing them – via legal, environmental, and social changes – to become consumers of care' (Illich, 1978, p. 41). Pluralistic self-reliance, focused on communal and individual initiatives grounded in native knowledge and competences, is displaced by the legalized monopoly of standardized state management of state-defined needs in a subject and dependent clientele.

As a consequence, the welfare state is necessarily antidemocratic. What should properly be the subject of choices made by individuals or collectivities becomes the province of professionals, whose credentials are state-certified and whose interventions are state-legitimized. Choosing to give birth at home or without medical supervision, building one's own home to one's own specifications, educating one's own children at home are all choices or forms of self-help proscribed by the state. Furthermore, even the best-intentioned and 'enabling' of welfare state interventions are undermined by their bureaucratic form. Even where the welfare state is predominantly the product of working-class agitation to counterbalance the despotic control of capital, it cannot avoid itself becoming a form of domination over its subject population. Typically, the greens insist that 'the conflicts and contradictions of advanced industrial societies can no longer be resolved through etatism, political regulation and the proliferating inclusion of ever more claims and issues on the agenda of bureaucratic authorities' (Offe, 1985/6, p. 4). Insofar as social welfare is a response to real needs – and not simply to the 'false needs' created by the requirements of industrial capitalism – these can only be satisfactorily met by small scale, co-operative, 'bottom up' self-production and self-management.

---

### Thesis 11

The welfare state is a particular form of the industrial capitalist state. Even under social democratic auspices, it is vitiated by the logic of unsustainable economic growth and alienating bureaucratic forms.

---

We shall return to an evaluation of this green perspective in the closing chapter.

# The Historical Uniqueness of Welfare States' Development

All of those positions considered thus far have tended to identify one or more mobilizing principles underlying welfare state development. But I have already observed that not all commentators are persuaded that the development of welfare states can be most effectively explained in terms of these kinds of metatheoretical principles. In particular, and in response to the accounts of both left and right, criticism has increasingly been directed towards (1) the persistent functionalist or derivationist elements in such accounts, (2) the dominance of society-centred over state-centred explanations and (3) the dominance of class to the exclusion of other social forces in the generation of social policy. In a variety of ways, such critics have called for a greater concentration upon the *historical uniqueness* of particular welfare states' development and an emphasis upon multiple sources of social policy initiatives. In the final sections of this chapter, I turn to a brief assessment of this theoretically more sceptical approach.

# Interest-group Politics and the Welfare State

Given this theoretical scepticism, those who, for example, stress the importance of interest group activity in the emergence of welfare states do not represent this as the definitive guiding principle of welfare state development. Nor do they seek to isolate some particular social force or movement as the prevailing fact of such evolution. Indeed, in contrast to the major positions already outlined, they insist upon (1) the independent importance of the political processes through which welfare state policies emerge, (2) the importance of existing state formations for the structure of (early) welfare states and (3) the historically unique configurations of social and political forces which shaped welfare state development in different countries. Advocates of this position do not argue that the process of welfare state development is wholly indeterminate (and that industrialization, urbanization and democratization have no independent effect upon the emergence of welfare regimes), but they do maintain:[6]

---

6   Pampel and Williamson (1988); Pampel and Williamson (1989); Pampel and Stryker (1990); Weir, Orloff and Skocpol (1988b).

1 that prevailing accounts give too much weight to such determining societal prerequisites
2 that a more accurate understanding of the substantial differences between welfare states requires a closer investigation of their particular and peculiar historical circumstances
3 that many existing accounts overstress the salience of social class as a source of welfare state development, to the neglect of other social forces – based, for example, upon age or gender structures – and other social groups – for example, professional associations, civil servants and veterans' organizations
4 that the competing social forces at the fount of the welfare state must be understood to have been mobilized and accommodated within the comparatively new media of mass democratic political organization

The intent of the interest group politics approach is above all a procedural or methodological rather than a substantive one, calling for a clear interrogation of the historical record to be used to discipline the rather grander generalizations of some other approaches. However, a number of substantive claims can be identified with this perspective. Among the most important of these are:[7]

1 that economic and demographic change affect the structure of group resources and demands for welfare spending and that the existence of democratic institutions facilitates the realization of these group interests
2 that non-class, ascriptive groups (notably, the retired and the aged) are central to the growth of the welfare state
3 that democratic political procedures (voting participation and electoral competition) are important for explaining the translation of group demands into higher spending
4 that where (working) class organization is poorly developed, mobilization for public welfare measures is likely to be by other subaltern social forces, for example, by the unemployed or ethnic groups
5 that sectoral interests (for example, those of agriculture), professional interests (doctors), and business interests (private

---

7 Piven and Cloward (1971); Piven and Cloward (1977); Piven and Cloward (1985); Block et al., (1988); Ashford (1986a); Ashford (1988b); Ashford and Kelley (1986); Gilbert (1966); Gilbert (1970); Berkowitz and McQuaid (1980); Hay (1975); Hay (1977); Hay (1978a); Hay (1978b); Mommsen (1981); Ritter (1985); Lash and Urry (1987); De Swaan (1988); Hennock (1987); Skocpol (1980); Ullman (1981); Foot (1975); Klein (1983); Gale Research Company (1985).

insurance companies) may have a decisive effect in shaping the
particular character of welfare legislation

6   that within any given, broadly defined group, there may be a
diversity of interests for and against the welfare state. Thus, for
example, differing levels of the medical profession may have a
differing attitude to compulsory health insurance (UK: 1911);
differing groups of workers may have differing attitudes to state
provision of welfare (where, for example, trades unions offer
health insurance as a collectively bargained 'fringe benefit') (US:
1930s); employers in monopoly and competitive sectors of the
economy may also have quite differing approaches to, and interests in, the state provision of welfare (Germany: 1930s); or
their attitude may change through time (employers in UK and
Germany in the late nineteenth and early twentieth centuries).

## State-centered Approaches to the Welfare State

Again, what have been labelled 'state-centred' approaches to welfare
state development do not generally deny the salience of the sorts of
issues raised in the major theoretical positions outlined above. They
recognize the importance of industrialization, urbanization, democratization and class interests. However, they do insist that all these
influences are mediated in practice by the independent effects of
state organization. That is, the relationship between the 'macro'
causes of welfare state development and actual social policies and
practices is shaped by the differing configurations of historically
unique nation states. Characteristically, Theda Skocpol, one of the
leading advocates of 'bringing the state back in', criticizes both
pluralist and Marxist accounts of social change and welfare state
development as being too *society*-centred. What are required are
'state-centred accounts of comparative historical development'
(Skocpol, 1985; see also Nordlinger, 1981).

This point is pursued by Douglas Ashford in *The Emergence of the
Welfare States* (Ashford, 1986a). He insists that 'the many forms of
the contemporary welfare state are the manifestations of the complex and diverse compromises forged by political leaders and
administrative officials over many years' (Ashford, 1986a, p. 2).
Thus

> Political, institutional and even constitutional issues affected the
> transition from liberal to welfare state as much as economic and
> social realities. (Ashford, 1986a, pp. 3–4)

Abram De Swaan is still more explicit:

Social security was not the achievement of the organized working classes, nor the result of a capitalist conspiracy to pacify them ... The initiative for compulsory, nationwide and collective arrangements to insure workers against income loss came from reformist politicians and administrators in charge of state bureaucracies. (De Swaan, 1988, p. 9)

The perspective of the welfare state emerging fully formed and wholly determined from a set of pre-existing social prerequisites is a misconception based upon historical hindsight. The growth of the welfare state was 'a gradual and often uninformed process propelled as much by ambitious politicians and rather visionary civil servants as by an abstract notion of a crumbling social order or of fears of major social unrest' (Ashford, 1986a, pp. 3–4).

To see the (welfare) state as simply a response to the needs of capital or else as the product of industrialization is inadequate. What is required is an account of the process by which social issues move onto the policy agenda, what policy proposals are accepted, which rejected (and why), and how and by whom such policies are implemented. Correspondingly, state-centred accounts tend to stress *the growth of states' competence*. The growth of the state's capacity to act is a subtype of the more general evolution of bureaucratic forms of organized action. Thus, to an extent, the development of the welfare state is a product of the expanded techniques of information processing, communication and surveillance which make the nation state (and, especially important in the welfare field, the overcoming of localism) possible (Berkowitz and McQuaid, 1980).

Such accounts also stress the independent importance of *the state's 'learning' capacity*. This is an approach most fully developed by Hugh Heclo. Reviewing the varying sources of social policy development, he concludes that 'while parties and interest groups did occasionally play extremely important parts, it was the civil services that provided the most constant analysis and review underlying most courses of government action'. Furthermore, the politics of such social policy initiatives is not best understood as the exercise of power but rather through the idea of 'politics as learning'.

Governments not only 'power' ... they also puzzle. Policy-making is a form of collective puzzlement on society's behalf; it entails both deciding and knowing. The process of making pension, unemployment, and superannuation policies has extended beyond deciding what 'wants' to accommodate, to include problems of knowing who might want something, what is wanted, what should be wanted, and how to turn even the most sweet-tempered general agreement into concrete collective action. (Heclo, 1974, p. 305)

The principal agency and location of this political learning process has been the public bureaucracy.

The general tenor of the state-centred approach is effectively summarized by Skocpol and Ikenberry:

> the ideas for modern social insurance and welfare policies came from domestic experimentation and transnational communication, and they were put into effect by sets of political executives, civil administrators, and political party leaders who were looking for innovative ways to use existing or readily extendable government administrative capacities to deal with (initially key segments of) the emerging industrial working class. Pioneering social insurance innovations, especially, were not simply responses to the socioeconomic dislocations of industrialism; nor were they straightforward concessions to demands by trade unions or working-class based parties. Rather they are best understood ... as sophisticated efforts at anticipatory political incorporation of the industrial working class, coming earlier (on the average) in paternalist, monarchical-bureaucratic regimes that hoped to head off working-class radicalism, and coming slightly later (on the average) in gradually democratizing liberal parliamentary regimes, whose competing political parties hoped to mobilize new working-class voters into their existing political organizations and coalitions. (Skocpol and Ikenberry, 1983, pp. 89–90)

State-centred accounts of social policy development have tended to criticize prevailing explanations for their neglect of the (indeterminate) process of policy formulation and the (uncertain) practice of policy implementation. Correspondingly, they do not themselves produce a firm list of expectations to which the actual history of all welfare states can be expected to correspond. They do however recognize important similarities between actual welfare states and these tend to be addressed in terms of:

1  the international diffusion of social policy patterns (as part of the social policy 'learning' process)
2  the similarity of bureaucratic development
3  the ubiquity of the challenges to which social policy must respond

But a greater emphasis is placed upon the *uniqueness* of differing welfare states, particularly around:[8]

---

8  Orloff and Skocpol (1984); Quadagno (1984); Quadagno (1987); Quadagno (1988a); Skocpol (1980); Weir, Orloff and Skocpol (1988a); Orloff (1988); Skocpol and Amenta (1986); Amenta and Skocpol (1989); Amenta and Carruthers (1988).

1 the nature of state-building (federal/absolutist past, imperialism, period of state formation)
2 the nature of the civil service and its reform (period at which formed/reformed; meritocratic or appointed/nepotic)
3 the nature of the state (period at which democratized; federal or unitary)
4 the relationship of the state to powers in civil society (incorporation or isolation; attitude to organized labour and/or organized capital)

---

**Thesis 12**

The (partially indeterminate) development of welfare states must be understood in a comparative and historical context. Among the most important sources of this development are the actions of interest groups, nationally unique political configurations and varying patterns of state organization.

---

# Conclusion

Both interest group and state-centred approaches are concerned less with the generic development of the welfare state than with the historically unique development of differing welfare states. Indeed, if we are to make an informed evaluation of the multiplicity of theoretical claims outlined in these opening chapters and of the likely prospects for change in the future, it is essential to consider these historical patterns of welfare state development. It is to just such a consideration that we turn in chapter 4.

# 4
# Origins and Development of the Welfare State, 1880–1975

For many people, the welfare state is a product of the period immediately following the end of the Second World War. In the Anglo-Saxon world, it is widely identified with the (partial) implementation of the recommendations of Sir William Beveridge's celebrated Report on Social Insurance in the first years of the post-war UK Labour government (Beveridge, 1942). The very term 'welfare state' is widely associated with Archbishop Temple's wartime contrast between the *power state* of Nazi Germany and the *welfare state* which was to be the ambition and promise of post-war Allied reconstruction (Temple, 1941; Temple, 1942; Zimmern, 1934).[1] This common understanding may well be justified inasmuch as most of the developed capitalist world saw a quantitative and, at times, qualitative leap in the public provision of welfare in the twenty-five years following the war. Yet, while the world was profoundly altered by the experience of world war, after 1945 as after 1918, there were important elements of continuity with the pre-war order, not least in the provision of public welfare. In recent years, there has been a growing recognition that if we are to understand the experience of the 'Golden Age' of the welfare state after 1945 and the epoch of 'crisis' after 1970, we shall need to consider their common origins in a much earlier period of public welfare innovation. Correspondingly, this chapter offers a synoptic reconstruction of the history of the welfare state which

---

1 Ashford (1986a) attributes the first use of 'welfare state' to A. Zimmern (1934). It is sometimes suggested that the term 'welfare state' was already in common usage in the UK by the late 1930s. For a differing explanation, see Hayek (1960) p. 502.

runs from its origins in the last third of the nineteenth century through to the period of its much accelerated growth after 1945.

## Before the Welfare State

In fact, welfare states are scarcely a hundred years old and mass social democratic movements little older. Significantly, welfare states tended to emerge in societies in which capitalism and the nation state were both already well established and these pre-existing economic and state formations have themselves prescribed the limits of subsequent welfare state development. Capitalism in its many forms has a relatively long history, stretching across several centuries and touching upon, if not penetrating, almost every quarter of the globe. This longevity and ubiquity of capitalism has often been seen to predominate over the comparatively modern and (territorially limited) influence of welfare administered through the state. A similar logic applies to the relationship between the welfare state and pre-existing state forms. Normally, the welfare state was a product of already existing (nation) states, which were themselves intimately related to the rise of capitalism. Accordingly, prior elements of state formation (territoriality, monopoly over the legitimate use of violence, underwriting of the rule of law) have often been seen to predominate over the commitment to welfare even within the more highly developed welfare states.

While it is the case then that most welfare states emerged under (liberal) capitalism and its corresponding state forms, this does not define the first or original relationship between state, economy and welfare. Pre-capitalist (and, at least in their ideology, contemporary non-capitalist) societies have subscribed to quite different views of the responsibility for social welfare. In fact, the theorists of nascent liberal capitalism had considerable success in sustaining the belief that the laws of capitalism corresponded with the laws of nature and chimed with men's 'natural instincts'.[2] The brilliance of these accounts should not however blind us to the fact that liberal capitalism was not naturally given but historically created and often, if not universally, historically imposed. Taking up this argument, C. B. Macpherson insists that the pre-modern notions of 'fair prices', 'fair wages' and 'just distribution' – sustained by the external sanction of church or state – themselves arose as a defence of the pre-existing order against the novel encroachment of market relations. They

---

2  Definitively in Smith (1976a) Smith (1976b); though Smith famously had his reservations about this belief.

endorsed the subjugation of economic relations to social and political ends *under which all previous human societies had operated*. Similarly, the mediaeval idea of a 'Christian duty to charity', while more honoured in the breach than in the observance, reflected a view of the nature of welfare which was quite different from the maximizing individualism of the advocates of liberal capitalism. Furthermore, if we move forward to the early capitalist period itself, it was not the views of Adam Smith but those of the mercantilists, of whom he was so critical, that defined the prevailing view of state, economy and welfare. Under this mercantilist doctrine, the state was seen to have an active role to play in the promotion of national prosperity and a responsibility for the labouring poor, as the principal source of this national wealth. This, as seen, for example, in the Elizabethan reform and codification of the Poor Law, expressed itself in an almost modern disposition to coercion and control (Webb and Webb, 1927; Fowle, 1890; Fraser, 1981). Thus, the liberal capitalist view of an extremely limited entitlement to public welfare did not arise primordially from the state of nature but had, as Gaston Rimlinger and before him Karl Polanyi noted, itself to be created and sanctioned by the 'liberal break' in states' practice (Rimlinger, 1974; Polanyi, 1944). That is, the non-intervention of the state under liberal capitalism did not arise from a pre-ordained 'state of nature' but had consciously to be created by the state's *disengagement* from previous patterns of intervention in the securing of social welfare (albeit that the pre-modern state and its interventions were wholly different from those of its modern counterparts).

Nor did the 'minimal' nineteenth century state 'stand off' from involvement in the economy and the provision of welfare. Victorian Britain, sometimes depicted as the very essence of *laissez-faire* liberal capitalism and the 'nightwatchman' state, saw the implementation of a wide range of measures on the control of factory work, the quality of housing, the securing of public health, the provision of public education, the municipalization of basic services and compulsory workers' compensation following industrial accidents (Roberts, 1960; Mommsen, 1981; Ensor, 1936; Evans, 1978). Even the definitively liberal US made federal provision in the nineteenth-century not only for public education but also for the public support of the blind, dumb, insane and insane/indigent, as well as for public Boards of Health (Trattner, 1988; Katz, 1986). Other states, with a more paternalistic and activist state tradition, saw still more and more intrusive public regulation of welfare. Thus, the prelude to Bismarck's innovative welfare legislation in a newly unified Germany was a tradition of (sometimes compulsory) welfare and insurance legislation in nineteenth-century Prussia.[3] Again, states with a colonial background were often developmentally precocious in their welfare legislation. This in part explains the rapid and early development of the welfare state in Australia and New Zealand (Castles, 1985).

In practice, most of the developed capitalist countries considered here have institutional arrangements for the provision of public welfare dating back several centuries. Most had legislated some form of Poor Law, under which specified (generally local) public authorities were charged with the responsibility for raising and disbursing (often under pain of some civic penalty for the recipient) limited funds for the relief of destitution (Webb and Webb, 1910; Bruce, 1968; Henriques, 1979; Samuelsson, 1968, pp. 129–30; Axinn and Levin, 1975; Fowle, 1890). The concern of these earlier states was primarily with the maintenance of public order, the punishment of vagrancy and the management of the labour market rather than the well-being of the poor.[4] With the increasing spread of industrialization, a number of nineteenth-century states provided for the maintenance of public health, the regulation of conditions of employment and limited public education. These states also showed a growing interest in the day-to-day surveillance and management of their national populations (Giddens, 1985, pp. 172–97; Mitchell, 1975; Foucault, 1975).

## Origins of the Welfare State

Abram De Swaan has argued that 'the development of a public system of social insurance has been an administrative and political innovation of the first order, comparable in significance to the introduction of representative democracy' (De Swaan, 1988, p. 149). Yet for all its importance, it was an innovation that was both gradual and rather mundane, and there are considerable difficulties in defining with any precision the dates at which national welfare states

---

3  See Tampke (1981) pp. 72–5; Rimlinger (1974) pp. 102–15. Ritter (1985) argues that 'the 1854 law on miners' provident societies was of central importance in influencing the design of Germany's later social insurance legislation of the 1880s' (pp. 17–21).
4  Graphically, Fowle (1890) insisted that 'in England, France, Spain, and the German Empire, we read the same dismal tale of whipping, branding, the pillory, burning the ear, cropping the ear, couples chained together to cleanse sewers, long terms of imprisonment, and, finally, death itself, in hundreds every year in every country' (p. 43).

became established. The implementation of some measure of public control over welfare is hardly a sufficient criterion for such a definition and few would want to characterize even the most developed of these nineteenth-century capitalist states as welfare states. But identifying a point along a continuum of expanding public provision as the threshold of the welfare state is itself somewhat arbitrary. A substantial difficulty is that those traditional accounts through which 'the welfare state' moved into common usage have tended to describe it in terms of that state's intentions, that is, as a state principally concerned to realize the welfare aspirations of its subjects (see, for example, Hall, 1952). One obvious objection to this approach is that such an aspiration cannot be taken to define the intention or purpose of the welfare state. A still more fundamental objection is that attributing a global intentionality to the state and seeking to define it in terms of this intention is itself unsustainable (Weber, 1968, p. 55). At the same time, there is clearly a qualitative difference between a comparatively tiny nineteenth-century bureaucracy devoting a few hundred thousand pounds each year to the provision of poor relief and a modern state directing as much as half of its massively enhanced expenditure to the provision of social welfare. While offering no definitive resolution, in this study the origins of the welfare state are isolated around three sets of criteria:

1  **First introduction of social insurance.** This is a widely used indicator of welfare state development. Although very modest by contemporary standards, in both breadth and depth of coverage, these are the programmes which have developed into the major institutional (and financial) elements of the welfare state. They entail the recognition that the incapacity to earn a living through contingencies such as old age, sickness or unemployment is a normal condition in industrialized market societies and that it is legitimately the business of the state to organize for collective provision against the loss of income arising from these contingencies (Flora and Heidenheimer, 1981a; Flora, 1986; see also the reservations of Jones, 1985).

2  **The extension of citizenship and the de-pauperization of public welfare.** The legitimization of social insurance means also a change in the relationship of the state to the citizen and of both to the provision of public welfare. Firstly, the interest of the state in public welfare is extended beyond the traditional concerns with the relief of destitution and the maintenance of public order (albeit that these remain major elements within even the most developed welfare states). Secondly, the provision of social insurance is increasingly seen as a part of the assemblage of rights and duties which binds

the state and the (expanding) citizenry. Thirdly (and correspondingly), the receipt of public welfare becomes not a *barrier* to political
participation but a *benefit* of full citizenship.[5] Simple indices of this
extension of citizenship are the dates of the inauguration of male
and universal suffrage and the date at which the receipt of public
welfare ceases to be a bar to full citizenship (that is, no longer entails
disenfranchisement).

3 **Growth of social expenditure.** One of the most important
aspects of the developed welfare state is the sheer quantity of public
spending that it commands. Throughout the twentieth century (at
least until the 1970s), the welfare state has commanded a sometimes
rapidly growing proportion of a much enhanced national product.
Clearly there is no critical threshold figure at which the welfare state
may be said to have begun, but as an indicator of this important
quantitative aspect of welfare state development, we may take a
social expenditure of 3 per cent of GNP as a notional indicator of the
*origins* of the welfare state. It may be useful to compare this
threshold with the date at which social expenditure exceeds 5 per
cent of GNP.

## The Birth of the Welfare State: 1880–1914

Cross-national evidence of these developments is varyingly approximate. We may be reasonably certain about dates for the extension of
suffrage and for the first introduction of various measures of social
insurance. However, these last cover programmes with large varia-
tions in range, expenditure and funding criteria which may mask
important differences in the social and political impact of seemingly
similar initiatives. Of these differences, perhaps the most important
was whether provision was tax-funded or contributory. These
figures may also conceal the extent to which alternative policies (for
example, public works or retraining rather than unemployment
compensation) represent a society's commitment to the public re-
dress of the consequences of market disutilities by other means.
However, these cautions having been sounded, the figures do reveal
a striking historical pattern (see tables 4.1 and 4.2).

In the thirty years between Germany's initiation of health insurance in 1883 and the outbreak of war in 1914, all the countries cited
in tables 4.1 and 4.2, with the exception of Canada and the US, had
introduced some state-sponsored system of workmen's compensation. Even within the US, considerable advances were made towards

---

5  On the importance of claims to welfare as rights, see Goodin (1988).

**Table 4.1**  Introduction of social insurance (OECD countries)

| | Industrial Accident | Health | Pension | Unemployment | Family allowance |
|---|---|---|---|---|---|
| Belgium | 1903 | 1894 | 1900 | 1920 | 1930 |
| Netherlands | 1901 | 1929 | 1913 | 1916 | 1940 |
| France | 1898 | 1898 | 1895 | 1905 | 1932 |
| Italy | 1898 | 1886 | 1898 | 1919 | 1936 |
| Germany | 1871 | 1883 | 1889 | 1927 | 1954 |
| Ireland | 1897 | 1911 | 1908 | 1911 | 1944 |
| UK | 1897 | 1911 | 1908 | 1911 | 1945 |
| Denmark | 1898 | 1892 | 1891 | 1907 | 1952 |
| Norway | 1894 | 1909 | 1936 | 1906 | 1946 |
| Sweden | 1901 | 1891 | 1913 | 1934 | 1947 |
| Finland | 1895 | 1963 | 1937 | 1917 | 1948 |
| Austria | 1887 | 1888 | 1927 | 1920 | 1921 |
| Switzerland | 1881 | 1911 | 1946 | 1924 | 1952 |
| Australia | 1902 | 1945 | 1909 | 1945 | 1941 |
| New Zealand | 1900 | 1938 | 1898 | 1938 | 1926 |
| Canada | 1930 | 1971 | 1927 | 1940 | 1944 |
| US | 1930 | — | 1935 | 1935 | — |

*Note:*   These dates include schemes which were initially voluntary but state-aided as well as those that were compulsory.
*Sources:*   Flora (1987b) vol. 1, p. 454; Flora and Heidenheimer (1981a) p. 83; Dixon and Scheurell (1989) pp. 151, 245, 192; Flora (1987a) pp. 144, 210, 433, 559, 627, 777

the end of this period in individual *states'* provision (Axinn and Levin, 1975, p. 131; Reede, 1947; Kudrle and Marmor, 1981).[6] In the same period, eleven of the thirteen European countries had introduced measures to support health insurance and nine had legislated for old age pensions (as had Australia and New Zealand). Although compensation for unemployment was generally the last of the four initial measures of social insurance to be introduced, by 1920 ten of the European countries had acknowledged some form of state responsibility for protection against the consequences of unemployment. What table 4.1 also shows is that for most countries family allowances belong to a 'second generation' of welfare legislation. Only one-third of the states cited had legislated for family allowances by the outbreak of the Second World War.

---

6   Kudrle and Marmor (1981) cite evidence that about 30 per cent of the US work-force was covered by workmen's compensation legislation by 1915.

**Table 4.2** Welfare state innovators: first introduction of major welfare state programmes

|  | *First* | *Second* | *Third* |
|---|---|---|---|
| Industrial accident insurance | Germany (1871) | Switzerland (1881) | Austria (1887) |
| Health | Germany (1883) | Italy (1886) | Austria (1888) |
| Pensions | Germany (1889) | Denmark (1891) | France (1895) |
| Unemployment | France (1905) | Norway (1906) | Denmark (1907) |
| Family allowances | Austria (1921) | New Zealand (1926) | Belgium (1930) |
| Male suffrage | France (1848) | Switzerland (1848) | Denmark (1849) |
| Universal suffrage | New Zealand (1893) | Australia (1902) | Finland (1907) |

*Sources:* Flora (1987b) vol. 1, p. 454; Flora and Heidenheimer (1981a); Dixon and Scheurell (1989)

Turning to the expansion of citizenship, there is a strong correspondence (though, as we shall see, no straightforward causal link) between the coming of male universal suffrage and the earliest development of social insurance. In the quarter-century between 1894 and 1920, eleven of the seventeen countries shown in table 4.3 achieved (more or less) universal male suffrage. Notably, those that had achieved full male suffrage earlier (including Germany, France, Denmark and New Zealand) were also among the most precocious of welfare innovators. We might also note that New Zealand, which was 'a generation early' in extending the vote to women (while restricting this right to Europeans), was also 'a generation early' in introducing family allowances. It is also towards the end of this period that we see the abolition of rules disenfranchising those who had been in receipt of public welfare. As late as 1894, universalization of the suffrage in Belgium explicitly excluded 'les mendiants et vagabonds internés dans une maison de refuge ... par décision des juges de paix' (Orban, 1908 p. 24). However many countries extending their suffrage in the early twentieth century reversed this disqualification of paupers from voting. The enfranchisement of

**Table 4.3**   The expansion of citizenship

| | Universal male suffrage | Universal adult suffrage |
|---|---|---|
| Belgium | 1894 | 1948 |
| Netherlands | 1918 | 1922 |
| France | 1848 | 1945 |
| Italy | 1913 | 1946 |
| Germany | 1871 | 1919 |
| Ireland | 1918 | 1923 |
| UK | 1918 | 1928 |
| Denmark | 1849[a] | 1918 |
| Norway | 1900 | 1915 |
| Sweden | 1909 | 1921 |
| Finland | 1907 | 1907 |
| Austria | 1907 | 1919 |
| Switzerland | 1848 | 1971 |
| Australia | 1902[a] | 1902[a] |
| New Zealand | 1879[b] | 1893[b] |
| Canada | 1920 | 1920 |
| US | 1860[b] | 1920 |

[a]   With significant restrictions.
[b]   Largely restricted to Europeans/whites.
*Sources*:   Flora (1987b) vol. 1; Mackie and Rose (1982); Taylor and Hudson (1983)

paupers was effected during this period in, for example, the UK (1918), Norway (1919) and Sweden (1921) (Flora, 1987b, vol. 1; Rawlings, 1988, p. 98). This is an important indicator of the transition from public welfare as an *alternative* to citizenship to public welfare as one of the *rights* of citizenship. As we shall see later, this evidence does not however justify the unqualified claim that it was democratization that created the welfare state.

Figures for the growth of social expenditure in this early period (see table 4.4) must be approached with especial caution. Differing national criteria in defining 'social expenditure', differences in the calculation of national income, difficulties in aggregating national and sub-national expenditures and the unreliability and paucity of figures before 1945 mean that these expenditure thresholds must be seen to be very approximate. Certainly, they should not be taken to define some international sequence of rising expenditure. Yet the overall figures do give compelling expression to the modest but consistent growth in social expenditure throughout this period. With the possible exception of Germany and Switzerland, it appears

**Table 4.4**  The growth of social expenditure

| | Social expenditure ⩾3% GDP | Social expenditure ⩾5% GDP |
|---|---|---|
| Belgium | 1923 | 1933 |
| Netherlands | 1920 | 1934 |
| France | 1921 | 1931 |
| Italy | 1923 | 1940 |
| Germany | 1900 | 1915 |
| Ireland | 1905 | 1920 |
| UK | 1905 | 1920 |
| Denmark | 1908 | 1918 |
| Norway | 1917 | 1926 |
| Sweden | 1905 | 1921 |
| Finland | 1926 | 1947 |
| Austria | 1926 | 1932 |
| Switzerland | By 1900 | 1920 |
| Australia | 1922 | 1932 |
| New Zealand | 1911 | 1920 |
| Canada | 1921 | 1931 |
| US | 1920 | 1931 |

*Sources*:  Flora (1986); Flora (1987a); Flora (1987b); Mitchell (1975); Taylor and Hudson (1983); US Department of Commerce (1975) part 1, p. 340; Urquhart (1965); Commonwealth Bureau of Census and Statistics (Australia) (1910– ); New Zealand Official Year-Book (1902– )

that none of these countries had reached social expenditure levels of 3 per cent by 1900. Yet by 1920, more than half had reached this threshold and by 1930 all had passed it. Indeed, about a third of these states passed the 5 per cent threshold during the 1920s and most of the others were to follow in the early and middle years of the 1930s (years in which increasing demands upon social insurance funds had often to be met from a *falling* national product under circumstances of depression).

## Welfare States 1920–1975: The Epoch of Growth

In fact, this experience of the expansion of social budgets in the inter-war years helps to isolate the most consistent and remarkable feature of the welfare states in the whole of the period down to the mid-1970s – that is, the ubiquitous dynamic of *sustained growth*. By the 1970s, all of the welfare states we are considering were quite different from what they had been at the end of the First World

War. Much else in the advanced capitalist societies had changed with them, and sometimes because of them. Furthermore, the core institutions of the welfare state are now so commonplace that we are perhaps inclined to forget the sheer scale of the transformation wrought between 1920 and 1970. In fact, throughout this period, the pace of growth varied between differing phases, differing programmes and different countries. Here, as elsewhere, caution is required in talking about the generic experience of *the* welfare state. Yet so substantial and striking are the developments of this period that at least some generalizations are warranted.

## The growth of the social budget

First, there is the sheer scale and ubiquity of growth in the social budget. In 1914 only seven of the countries in table 4.4 had reached social expenditure levels of 3 per cent of GNP. By 1940, nearly all had reached social expenditure levels in excess of 5 per cent. In the early 1950s, this figure ranged between 10 and 20 per cent. By the mid-1970s, among the European welfare states, between one-quarter and something more than a third of GNP was devoted to social expenditure. Even the most 'reluctant' welfare states saw a wholesale transformation of their public budgets. In the US, total social expenditure rose from 2.4 per cent of GNP in 1890 to 20.2 per cent in 1981. Even in Japan, where an exceptional proportion of welfare is organized and delivered through private corporations, the social budget has expanded from 1.4 per cent of GDP in 1890 to 16.2 per cent in 1985 (Flora, 1986, vol. 1, p. xxii; Maddison, 1984; Minami, 1986, pp. 332ff; Oshima, 1965, pp. 368–371; OECD, 1985a; OECD, 1988; US Bureau of Statistics, 1975).

Much of the remarkable overall growth in public expenditure of the twentieth century can be attributed to the growth of the social budget, and this rapidly growing proportion of national wealth devoted to social welfare must be set against the background of a sevenfold increase in average per capita output in the cited countries over the past 100 years (Maddison, 1984, p. 59).

## Incremental growth and demographic change

A substantial source of this remarkable and general growth in the social budget was the maturing of rights and claims as pensions legislated in the 'take-off' period came 'on stream'. This was substantially an incremental and inertial development which was the more pronounced because of certain demographic changes which were common to most of the advanced capitalist societies. The most important of these changes were the continuing increase in life expectancy and the decline in mortality rates. For example, life expectancy of females at birth rose between 1900 and 1967 from 49.4 to 74.1 years in England and Wales, from 47 to 75 years in France and from 46.6 to 73.5 years in West Germany. Crude annual death rates fell in the same countries between 1900 and 1950 from 18.2 to 12.5 per thousand in England and Wales, from 21.9 to 12.7 per thousand in France and from 22.1 to 10.5 per thousand in West Germany (Winter, 1982; Mitchell, 1975, pp. 104–24). What did constitute an authentically *political* intervention was the common practice of introducing (contributory) pensions *before* sufficient premiums had been collected to fund these on an actuarially sound basis. The electoral call for 'pensions now' was a powerful one, even in the characteristically insurance-minded US (Quadagno, 1988b; Fraser, 1973, p. 213; Rimlinger, 1974, p. 234).

It is possible that the severest demographic challenge to the welfare state lies in the future, but the growing aged population in advanced capitalism has certainly hugely extended the costs of the welfare state not just in the provision of pensions, but in those other costly areas where the elderly are disproportionate users of services, as in public health provision. The proportion of the population aged 65 or over in the OECD countries has risen from 9.7 per cent in 1960 to 12.7 per cent in 1985, and is projected to increase further to 18.0 per cent by 2020 (OECD, 1988, p. 11). Meanwhile, Heikkinen notes that 'the use of [health and social] services among the aged is 3–4 times that expected on the basis of proportion of the population' (Heikkinen, 1984, p. 162).

In fact, the demographic structure of the several welfare states has varied. For example, the disproportionately youthful structure of the early twentieth-century New Zealand and Australian populations (as 'new', immigrant-based nations) afforded unusually favourable circumstances for their early expansion. In other countries, notably in France, social policy initiatives have been related to the demographic consequences of the First World War (especially in the number of war pensions and later in the structure of natalist policy).[7] But overall, the number of aged in the population has grown throughout the industrialized world as life expectancy has increased. In the 1880s, only 5 per cent of the population was over 65. One hundred years later, the elderly constitute some 13 per cent of the population

---

7   The First World War saw losses of approximately 1.3 million among the French population and an equally large 'birth deficit' (McEvedy and Jones, 1978, p. 56). See also McIntosh, 1983, esp. pp. 43–57; Ashford, 1986a, pp. 112–3; Dyer, 1978; Glass, 1940.

and a still higher proportion of the electorate. In Western Europe, the percentage of people aged 65 and over in the population is predicted to rise from 13.3 per cent in 1985 to 14.9 per cent in 2000 (Heikkinen, 1984, p. 162; OECD, 1984, pp. 3–6; OECD, 1986a, pp. 3–10). Still more importantly, the ratio of the economically inactive to the economically active section of the population (out of whose productive labour 'pay-as-you-go' pensions must be funded) is rising and set to continue to rise. Dependency ratios (the proportion of people aged 0–14 years plus the proportion of people aged 60 years and over as a ratio of the proportion aged 15–59 years) actually *fell* in Western and Northern Europe in the 1980s because of the declining numbers of young people. But they are set to rise from 59.2 per cent to 66.8 per cent in Western Europe and from 64.4 per cent to 66.2 per cent in Northern Europe between 1990 and 2000. The UK Treasury estimates that whereas there were 2.3 economic contributors to each pension claimant in the UK in 1985, by 2025 this number will have fallen to 1.8 contributors to each pensioner (Heikkinen, 1984, p. 169; DHSS, 1985, p. 15). Overall, the OECD estimates that the old-age dependency ratio will have doubled by 2040 (OECD, 1988, p. 35; this demographic challenge to the welfare state is extensively discussed in chapter 6).

## Sequential growth of welfare state programmes

Most of the welfare states considered here have also expanded their social welfare provision in terms of a broadly shared sequence. Certainly, there have been differences between 'early' and 'late' adopters in terms of the comparative stage of industrialization at which social welfare was introduced, the sorts of funding regimes established and the generosity of initial coverage. There is some disagreement as to whether the spread of the welfare state is best explained in terms of *prerequisites* (with state welfare initiatives being a response to endogenous national developments) or *diffusion* (a process of international imitation of welfare state innovators). In the period before 1908, the spread seems to have been from less industrially developed and more authoritarian regimes towards the more developed and democratic. In the period between 1908 and 1923, the principal determinant of innovation appears to have been geographical proximity to an existing welfare state rather than the level of industrial development. After 1923, there is a tendency for countries to adopt welfare state measures at a lower level of their own economic development (with the notable exception of the US). Paralleling the pattern of the spread of industrialization, 'late starters' have tended to develop welfare state institutions earlier in their own individual development and under more comprehensive terms of coverage (Collier and Messick, 1975, p. 1301; Schneider, 1982; Alber cited in Flora, 1986, vol. 1, p. xxiv; Alber, 1982; Kuhnle, 1981).

Wherever welfare states have emerged, the order of adoption and expansion of programmes has been broadly similar. We can identify three sequential patterns. In terms of *programmes*, workmen's compensation for industrial accidents was generally the first measure to be adopted. This was followed by sickness and invalidity insurance, old age pensions and finally unemployment insurance. Though some provision for maternity occurred quite early, family allowances were generally introduced rather later and were widely viewed as an 'endowment of motherhood' rather than as insurance against the contingency of having children. Secondly, *coverage* also followed a shared pattern. Initially, coverage was limited to workers in particularly strategic industries or in peculiarly dangerous occupations. Mining, for example, was often one of the first industries to be covered (Tampke, 1981, pp. 72–3). Legislation was subsequently extended to cover all industrial workers, thence to rural/agricultural workers and so to dependants and survivors of insured workers. In the later stages, coverage was extended to the self-employed and thence characteristically to the generality of the population (or at least to all those recognized as citizens) without further discriminating criteria.

Thirdly, there were broadly similar patterns in the *expansion* of programmes. Earlier extensions tended to be built upon a broadening of the criteria of eligibility (making for more beneficiaries) and the legislating of more generous benefits. Characteristically, later enhancements were built upon the less restrictive application of definitions of eligibility and, from the late 1950s and 1960s onwards, upon the transition from flat-rate to earnings-related benefits. There was also a general tendency for programmes to proceed from voluntary to compulsory provision.

## The Periodization of Welfare State Growth

In fact, it is possible to think not just of a sequential but indeed of a shared historical pattern in the development of the welfare states of advanced capitalism. Clearly this is not a uniform pattern. The US lacked basic federal provisions for social insurance down to 1935 and still lacks comprehensive measures for healthcare or family allowances. Some welfare states emerged early and then 'stagnated' (Australia), some developed early and expanded before 1940 (New Zealand), while others were marginal before the Second World War but expanded rapidly after 1945 (for example, Finland). Yet a significant historical pattern may be identified.

## 1918–1940: 'Consolidation' and Development

The period between the wars has often been described as a rather uneventful one for the welfare state, falling between the extensive innovations of the preceding twenty-five years and the period of remarkable growth immediately after 1945. Hamilton characteristically describes this period in the UK experience as one of 'steady and purposeful social advance' (Hamilton cited in Bruce, 1968, p. 255).

Yet more recent commentators have tended to see the 1920s and 1930s as the seed-bed of post-war welfare state development. For Douglas Ashford, this was the period in which serious obstacles to 'the complete nationalization of social policy' were removed, making the expansion of the welfare state after 1945 comparatively uncontentious:

> First, the liberal refuge of private or charitable assistance proved totally inadequate. Second, the private insurers learned ... that many serious social problems exceeded the capacity of actuarially sound insurance. Third ... professional groups were gradually co-opted into national social security programmes. Fourth, the agricultural sector first received the protection of the state ... before substantial aid went to urban dwellers. (Ashford, 1986b, p. 107)

In the UK, Sweden and the US, for example, this is seen as the decisive epoch in establishing the institutions and practices of that more interventionist form of government in which the post-war welfare state was grounded. It also saw governments facing new choices about the macro-management of the economy and the possibility of the active and interventionist pursuit of full employment. Thus Middlemas, in his study of *Politics in Industrial Society*, argues that it was in the inter-war years that a new system of 'managerial collective government', built upon the negotiation and compromise of the interests of the state, organized capital and organized labour, first emerged in the UK. This was a system oriented around the amelioration of class conflict and the avoidance of systemic crisis through, among other media, the promotion of social policy (Middlemas, 1979).[8] As we shall soon see, in both Sweden and the US,

---

8　Although primarily concerned with the UK, Middlemas comments that his 'propositions have an importance not only for modern Britain, but most western industrialized societies' (Middlemas, 1979, p. 23).

the Great Depression of the early 1930s triggered new forms of government intervention in social and economic life, new relationships between state, employers and trades unions and a process of political realignment which established new political forces at the heart of the state (Korpi, 1979; Korpi, 1983; Weir and Skocpol, 1985).

Certainly in terms of coverage and cost, the inter-war welfare state often dwarfs provision in the period of innovation. As the figures for social expenditure indicate, while the period between 1880 and 1920 is properly understood as the epoch of *legislative* innovation in the welfare state, it is only after 1920 that the *fiscal* consequences of these initiatives become clear. Many of the early systems of social insurance offered, like Lloyd George's old age pensions in the UK, extremely modest benefits to 'the very poor [and] the very respectable' (Thane, 1982, p. 83).[9] Many programmes, notably those in Germany, envisaged a strictly limited financial involvement by the state, expecting benefits to be drawn from the premiums of potential beneficiaries or their employers (Alber, 1986, pp. 40–1). However, the growth of social expenditure in the 1920s and the early 1930s is what we might have expected as the legislative innovations of the pre-1914 period yielded to the maturing of insurance and pension claims in the post-war age. In fact, this tendency for innate or incremental growth of social expenditure – growth not through legislative or executive initiative but through the maturing of pension rights or demographic change – has been a marked feature of the whole period of the welfare state.

In many countries, this process was accelerated by the consequences of the First World War. Firstly, it led to a major expansion of pension, health, housing and rehabilitation demands from those millions incapacitated or bereaved as a consequence of the armed conflict. In Australia in 1922, for example, war pensioners outnumbered old age and invalid pensioners in a proportion of nearly two to one.[10] Secondly, it conditioned politicians, bureaucrats and taxpayers to new levels of public expenditure, from which there was no wholesale retreat once the immediate demands of wartime had passed (the 'displacement effect' described by Peacock and Wiseman, 1961, pp. 52–61). Thirdly, it necessitated new forms of

---

9   New Zealand's innovative old age pensions, for example, cost £197,292 in 1900, rising to £362,496 in 1910 (*New Zealand Official Year-Book*, 1919).

10   In 1922, in Australia, there were 225,372 war pensioners, 110,278 claiming old age pensions and just 5,182 invalid pensioners. We shall see below (pp. 118–19) that the early American welfare state was largely made up of Civil War veterans. Germany, France and the UK lost a total of 3.75 million soldiers in the 1914–18 war. (*Official Year Book of the Commonwealth of Australia*, 1923; McEvedy and Jones, 1978, p. 34.)

governmental control and administration which were again not to be abandoned in the post-war epoch (Middlemas, 1979, p. 19).

The late 1920s and early 1930s also saw what might be described as the first 'fiscal crisis of the welfare state'.[11] The depth of the economic recession of the early 1930s occasioned the earliest major cuts in social welfare provision and demonstrated (1) that it was impossible to sustain actuarially sound social insurance under circumstances of profound economic recession, (2) that demand for social expenditure (especially unemployment compensation) was inversely related to the capacity of the economy to fund it and (3) that to respond to this problem by cutting social expenditure would simply intensify rather than alleviate these economic problems. The scale of the difficulties of the 1930s also probably dealt the final death blow to the belief among the governing classes that the provision of social welfare or even the relief of destitution could be satisfactorily met from voluntary or charitable sources.

## New Deal and Historic Compromise

The 1930s was also a decisive period in the development of two of the most widely differing and frequently contrasted welfare state regimes – those of Sweden and the US. In comparative typifications of welfare state development, these two examples are often recorded as the most developed (Sweden) and the least developed (US) welfare states, and, given the centrality of this opposition, it is worth developing this contrast in some detail.

Ironically, in much contemporary scholarship, the origins of the modern American and Swedish welfare states, as a response to the consequences of the Great Depression, are seen to be remarkably similar. Thus, Weir and Skocpol contrast the shared response of the US ('commercial Keynesianism') and Sweden ('social Keynesianism') to the traditionally deflationary policy of the UK government (Weir and Skocpol, 1985). Gosta Esping-Andersen has argued that 'at least in its early formulation, the New Deal was as social democratic as was contemporary Scandinavian social democracy' (Esping-Andersen, 1990, p. 28). In both countries, this period of welfare state enhancement also saw profound political realignment and the

---

11   In the UK, the 1931 May Committee Report 'compounded of prejudice, ignorance and panic' recommended a cut in public expenditure of £120m, including a 20 per cent cut in unemployment benefit. In Australia, old age, invalid and some war pensions were reduced under the terms of the Financial Emergency Act, 1931. (Taylor, 1965, pp. 287ff; *Official Year Book of the Commonwealth of Australia*, 1932, p. 30.)

installation of the Democrats and the Social Democrats, respectively, as 'the natural party of government'. Yet the contexts in which these 'similar' institutions were to be developed (and indeed the intentions of those who initiated and developed them) were profoundly different.

It is one of the many myths of the American welfare state that there was little or no public provision of welfare before the 1930s. In fact, 'American welfare practice has a very old history', but it is a practice that 'has always been mediated by the complex structure of American federalism'. Similarly, 'public welfare always has supported more dependent people than private relief'. Yet, in the 'protean mix' of public and private provision which characterizes every welfare state, the private and especially the corporate provision of welfare has always had an unusually prominent role (Katz, 1986, pp. xiii, x, 291).

At the turn of the twentieth century, such limited public relief as there was within the US was largely locally administered according to local poor-law customs (Quadagno, 1984, p. 635; Axinn and Levin, 1975; Katz, 1986). At the local level, public welfare rolls fluctuated wildly in response to changing social and political regimes (Katz, 1986, pp. 3–109). Federal provision was substantially confined to pensions for (Northern) veterans of the Civil War. However by 1900 these federal veterans' pensions had come to constitute an extremely extensive system of surrogate social welfare. At this time, 'at least one of every two elderly, native-born, white Northern men and many of their widows received a pension from the federal government' and 'pensions were the largest expense in the federal budget after the national debt' (Katz, 1986, p. 200). In 1913, I. M. Rubinow, 'one of the nation's leading social insurance advocates', calculated that American pensions were costing three times as much as the supposedly advanced UK system of old age pensions and covering 'several hundred thousand' more people (cited in Skocpol and Ikenberry, 1983, p. 97; Katz, 1986, p. 163). It is little wonder that Skocpol concludes that 'in terms of the proportional effort devoted to public pensions, the American federal government was hardly a 'welfare laggard'; it was a precocious social-spending state' (Orloff and Skocpol, 1984, pp. 728–9). However, as the number of veteran claimants and their dependents declined in the early years of the twentieth century, and despite the mobilization of pensions advocates such as Rubinow, Seager and the American Association for Labor Legislation, there was no attempt to replace the veterans' programmes with a more universal system of old age pensions (see Orloff and Skocpol, 1984, p. 735; Skocpol and Ikenberry, 1983, pp. 95–100; Katz, 1986, p. 128). There was some advance in other areas of welfare provision by the individual states in the years immediately prior to the First World War. Between 1909 and 1920, forty-three states enacted legislation on workmen's compensation and within two years of Illinois' 'Funds to Parents Act' of 1911, twenty states had provided similar cash relief programmes for widows and dependent children. Yet the financial impact of such measures was severely limited and although there was some programme enhancement in the 1920s, the prevalent welfare trend in the post-war New Era was away from the European model of social insurance towards a reliance on occupational welfare (employee representation, workers' shares, company welfare and pensions) under the rubric of welfare capitalism. However, this welfare capitalism was always largely confined to the 'progressive' corporate sector of American capital (to large companies such as Proctor and Gamble, Eastman Kodak and General Electric). It was more important as a legitimating ideology than as an effective social practice and certainly wholly unable to respond to the scale of social need generated by the Great Depression (Axinn and Levin, 1975, pp. 130–4; Brody, 1980; Skocpol and Ikenberry, 1983).

Opinions as to which social, economic and political forces shaped and were served by the expanded social policy of the New Deal are vigorously divided. So are judgements as to whether it was the 'social' or the 'economic' side of the New Deal that had the most lastingly influential impact. However, there is near universal agreement that the 'social' side of the New Deal, embodied in the 1935 Social Security Act, 'declared the birth of the [American] welfare state and established a basis for its growth and development' (Axinn and Levin, 1975, p. 195). It is also widely argued that this 'charter legislation for American social insurance and public assistance programs' set the parameters for virtually all further developments in America's 'semi-welfare state' (Skocpol, 1987, p. 35; Katz, 1986, pp. ix–xiv; Quadagno, 1988a).

The 1935 Act legislated for:[12]

1 a federal-state unemployment insurance programme
2 federal grants-in-aid to the states for assistance to:
    (a) needy dependent children
    (b) the blind
    (c) the elderly
3 matching federal funds for state spending on:

---

12 Berkowitz and McQuaid (1980) p. 103.

(a)   vocational rehabilitation
(b)   infant and maternal health
(c)   aid to crippled children
4   a federal old age insurance programme

Although the 1935 Act brought the US in some measure into align-
ment with the welfare states of Western Europe, it was still a quite
limited initiative. The provision of welfare was largely devolved to
the individual states, funded from (regressive) payroll taxation
rather than from general tax revenue and allowed for very considerable state 'discretion' and for very substantial 'exceptions'. (Initially,
one half of the employed work-force, notably black southern farm
workers, was excluded from participation in Old Age Insurance).
There was an emphasis upon actuarially sound insurance principles
and 'earned benefits' – the rhetoric of which long outlived its early
compromise in practice. Generally, where entitlement was not
earned through insurance payments, benefits were means-tested
and traditional relief of destitution (among the able-bodied poor)
remained a local responsibility. The legislation made no provision
for either health insurance or a family allowance.

The 1930s was also a decade of major change in the Swedish
welfare state and of a still more profound political realignment, the
nature of which is no less fiercely debated than that surrounding the
New Deal. In fact, the background of national public welfare was
already more extensive in Sweden than in its North American counterpart. Sweden had a more developed national bureaucracy and a
centralized state tradition dating back over several centuries. Schooling had been compulsory since 1842, state support of sickness and
occupational injury insurance had been legislated around the turn of
the twentieth century and Sweden had been the first state to introduce universal and compulsory (if minimal) old age pensions in
1913. At the start of the 1930s, her social expenditure as a proportion
of GDP stood at 7 per cent, compared with 4.2 per cent in the US
(Olsson, 1986, p. 5). However, Swedish provision, compared with
that of near neighbour Denmark, for example, was very modest. As
Esping-Andersen notes:

> the long era of conservative and liberal rule [prior to 1932] had
> produced remarkably few social reforms. There was no unemploy-
> ment insurance, except for financially weak union funds, and
> insurance coverage for sickness was marginal ... old age pension
> ... benefits were meager at best. In addition, no system of public
> job creation was in effect when the economic depression led to
> explosive unemployment. (Esping-Andersen, 1985, p. 153)

It was under these circumstances, with unemployment rising rapidly, that the first Scandinavian social democratic government was elected in 1932. In fact, the Social Democrats with 42 per cent of the popular vote were reliant upon the coalition support of the peasant-based Agrarian Party, and were consequently obliged to compromise the interests of their own core working-class constituency (in welfare reform and full employment) with policies for agricultural price support (in the interests of the rural peasantry). While 'social reform was a top priority [and] the party actually developed a long-range strategy for full social and industrial citizenship ... by and large, political energies were concentrated on the immediate problems of crisis management and economic relief' (Esping-Andersen and Korpi, 1987, pp. 46–7).

A still more important accommodation was that struck by the newly empowered Social Democrats and organized capital. Rather than pursuing the traditional (maximalist) socialist policy of pressing for immediate socialization of the ownership of capital, the Social Democrats, recognizing the stalemate between organized labour and organized capital that their election occasioned, pressed for a formalization of the division of economic and political control and the division of the spoils of continued and agreed capitalist growth. This celebrated 'historic compromise' ensured that capital would maintain intact its managerial prerogatives within the workplace, subject only to guarantees on rights to unionization, and capitalist economic growth would be encouraged. At the same time, the Social Democratic government would pursue Keynesian economic policies to sustain full employment and use progressive taxation to reduce economic inequality and promote provision for collective needs, such as education, health, and housing. When in the post-World War II period the defence of welfare institutions and full employment threatened inflation and the loss of international competitiveness, the compromise was complemented by the adoption of the 'Rehn' model, which entailed (1) an 'active manpower policy' – facilitating the redistribution and reallocation of labour and capital from less to more efficient enterprises – and (2) a 'solidaristic' wage policy, which would allow for the centralized negotiation of wages and the reduction of wage differentials, through a principle of equal pay for equal work, irrespective of a given company's capacity to pay. In this way, it was hoped that welfare provision and a rising standard of living for the working population could be reconciled with continuing non-inflationary economic growth.

Thus in the 1930s and beyond, the Swedish welfare state was secured as much by *economic* policy – the support of an active labour market policy, public works, solidaristic wage bargaining, deficit budgeting – as by social policy. Indeed, the Swedish social demo-crats have always shown an awareness of the intimate relationship between economic and social policy upon which the institutional or social democratic welfare state is dependent and which is recognized in the twin-termed Keynesian Welfare State.[13] Thus, job creation or full employment may be seen as a more desirable alternative to the payment of unemployment compensation. It may also be the indis-pensable basis of funding a 'generous' welfare system.

In Sweden in the 1930s, then, it was probably Keynesian *economic* policies, rather than innovations in *social* policy, that were the most important components in the nascent welfare state. Nonetheless, there were significant and complementary social policy initiatives. Perhaps the most important of these was the 1934 legislation that increased the state's involvement in what had previously been ex-clusively a union-managed system of unemployment insurance (Esping-Andersen and Korpi, 1987). In addition, between 1933 and 1938, the Social Democratic government also legislated:[14]

- new employment creation programmes
- a housing programme for families with many children including subsidies and interest-subsidized construction loans
- the indexation of pensions to regional differences in the cost of living
- maternity benefits to around 90 per cent of all mothers
- free maternity and childbirth services
- state loans to newly married couples
- the introduction of two weeks' holiday for all private and public employees

A number of other states saw major developments in their welfare states between the wars. Denmark's 'Great Social Reform' of 1933, if less radical than its advocates have claimed, 'nevertheless, remained the fundamental administrative framework of the Danish welfare state for a quarter century' (Johansen, 1986, pp. 299–300; Levine, 1983). New Zealand, which had introduced the first comprehensive pensions for the needy old aged in 1898 and been among the first to introduce family allowances in 1926, created, through its 1938 Social Security Act, 'what could be argued to be, in late 1930s terms, the

---

13   Ashford (1986b) stresses the general importance of the interrelationship between social and economic policy. He argues that historically this was recognized in France but not in the UK; this led to the French welfare state being the more effectively entrenched.

14   Olsson (1986) p. 5.

most comprehensive welfare state in the world' (Castles, 1985, p. 26). This unusually comprehensive measure was

> to provide for the payment of superannuation benefits and of other benefits designed to safeguard the people of New Zealand from disabilities arising from age, sickness, widowhood, orphan-hood, unemployment, or other exceptional conditions; to provide a system whereby medical and hospital treatment will be made available to persons requiring such treatment; and, further, to provide such other benefits as may be necessary to maintain and promote the health and general welfare of the community. (cited in Castles, 1985, p. 27)

Elsewhere, there were substantial if less spectacular advances. In Canada, (means-tested) old age pensions were introduced in 1927 and the 1930s saw a succession of federal–provincial unemployment compensation schemes culminating in the 1940 Federal Unemploy-ment Insurance Act (Bellamy and Irving, 1989; Leman, 1977). The UK, whose inter-war social policy was dominated by the spectre of unemployment, saw modest legislation on the social provision of housing and healthcare, education, contributory old age pensions, provision for widows and orphans and the steady 'break-up' of the Poor Law (Gilbert, 1970; Fraser, 1973; Thane, 1982). Yet, writing of the UK experience, Parry concludes that 'the creative impulse of the welfare state progressed little from the 1910s to the 1940s' (Parry, 1986, p. 159).

Even where initiatives of this period were very modest, some have argued that the *underlying* changes which permitted the flower-ing of the welfare state after 1945 were secured in the inter-war years. Such a view is sometimes taken in describing the Beveridge Report not as the founding charter of a radically new UK welfare state after 1945, but as a rationalization of existing pre-war legisla-tion. Addison, for example, suggests that Beveridge's 'background assumptions' – 'full' employment and a national health service – were much more radical and innovative than his 'fundamentally conservative' proposals on social insurance (Addison, 1977, p. 213). Similarly, Ashford argues that in France, where advances in pen-sions, health and accident insurance were limited and painfully slow between the wars, this was the period in which the political com-promises and coalitions upon which the developed post-war welfare state was built were themselves fought over and secured. Indeed, he suggests that the very slowness and difficulty of achieving welfare advances in France compared with the UK made these victories and the welfare state thus constructed more secure and entrenched than its less contested UK counterpart (Ashford, 1986a; Ashford, 1986b;

Ashford, 1982). As we have seen, what remains the single most important innovation in the US welfare state dates from the 1930s.

Other significant developments of this period included the evolution in Germany and Italy of a pattern of social policy interwoven with the corporatist institutions of Fascism. But everywhere, and particularly under the impact of the mass unemployment of the 1930s, the inter-war years were marked by growing welfare expenditures. Indeed, between 1920 and 1940, Flora and Alber's index of social insurance coverage in Western Europe more than doubled (see figure 4.1).

## 1945–1975: The 'Golden Age' of the Welfare State?

Just as the inter-war years have been seen as years of 'consolidation', so has the period after 1945 been widely characterized as ushering in a thirty years' 'Golden Age' of the welfare state. Upon such an account, the period between 1945 and the mid-1970s is seen as bringing (1) rapid initial reforms to create a much more comprehensive and universal welfare state based on the idea of shared citizenship, (2) a commitment to direct increasing resources towards the rapid expansion of benefits and coverage within this extended system, (3) a very broad-based political consensus in favour of a mixed economy and a system of extended social welfare, and (4) a (successful) commitment to economic growth and full employment.

In fact, this model of the post-war evolution of the welfare state has always been heavily dependent upon the (unique) UK experience, and indeed upon a particular, broadly social democratic and 'optimistic' understanding of this experience. Great emphasis is placed upon the consequences of the Second World War – its expansion of the powers and competence of government, the generation of new forms of collective provision and, above all, the broadly shared experience of austerity and mutual mortal danger generating a high degree of citizen solidarity in favour of radical reform. Also stressed is the 'messianic' quality of Beveridge and his proposed reforms, the radical break occasioned by the election of the post-war Labour government and the subsequent development of a broad cross-party consensus ('Butskellism') in favour of compromise of the interests of capital and labour, within which the welfare state was a crucial component.

Recently, this synoptic view of the post-war history of the (UK) welfare state has itself come under increasing challenge. First, claims about the impact of the Second World War on the development of social policy have been questioned. It has been argued: (1) that the

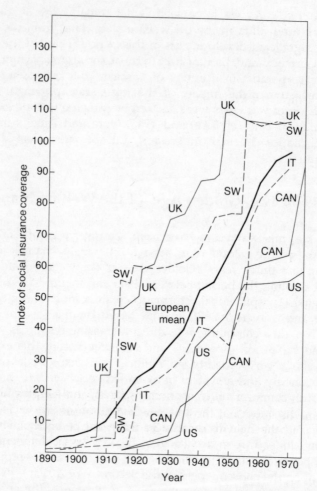

**Figure 4.1**   The growth of social insurance coverage in Western Europe
UK = United Kingdom, SW = Sweden, IT = Italy, CAN = Canada,
US = United States
*Source*:   Flora and Heidenheimer (1981a)

experience of government planning and state intervention in the wartime period was not an especially promising one, (2) that sympathy for collective provision arose not from the bonds of mutual citizenship but from the perceived threat of a commonly uncertain future and (3) that the pressure for social policy reform came less from a radicalized citizenry than from a trades union movement whose industrial muscle had been much strengthened by wartime full employment. Secondly, it is widely insisted that the social policy reforms proposed by Beveridge (and only partially enacted in the post-war period) represented not a radical charter for a new social order, but a tidying-up and codification of pre-war social legislation. Thirdly, it is argued that the consensus within which the post-war welfare state was said to have developed either never existed or else was much more limited than the traditional social democratic account has allowed (Barnett, 1986; Dryzek and Goodin, 1986; Addison, 1977; Taylor-Gooby, 1985; Deakin, 1987; Smith, 1986; Pimlott, 1988).

There are then serious doubts as to whether this model is fully applicable even to the UK experience.[15] Yet it retains a significant (if varying) element of truth. In 1948, Article 40 of the newly founded United Nations' *Universal Declaration of Human Rights* proclaimed that:

> Everyone has the right to a standard of living adequate for the health and well-being of himself and his family, including food, clothing, housing and medical care and the necessary social services, and the right to security in the event of unemployment, sickness, disability, widowhood, old age or other lack of livelihood in circumstances beyond his control. (United Nations, 1948)

Similarly, Article 38 of the Constitution of newly independent India declared that 'the State shall strive to promote the welfare of the people by securing and protecting ... a social order in which justice, social, economic and political shall inform all the institutions of national life' (cited in Brownlie, 1971, p. 43). Within the developed West, many countries other than the UK saw major social policy reforms immediately after 1945. In France and Ireland, for example, there was a period of rapid policy innovation in the late 1940s, and these policy changes had an immediate effect upon the proportion of GNP devoted to social welfare (Ashford, 1986a, pp. 255–65; Hage,

---

15  It has been very properly objected that 'intensive study of the British case' may not be 'the optimal way of starting to grasp the general characteristics of welfare state development' (Flora and Heidenheimer, 1981a, p. 21).

**Table 4.5** Growth in social expenditure (7 major OECD countries), 1960–1975, as a percentage of GDP (%)

|  | 1960 | 1975 |
|---|---|---|
| Canada | 11.2 | 20.1 |
| France | 14.4 | 26.3 |
| West Germany | 17.1 | 27.8 |
| Italy | 13.7 | 20.6 |
| Japan | 7.6 | 13.7 |
| UK | 12.4 | 19.6 |
| US | 9.9 | 18.7 |
| Average | 12.3 | 21.9 |

*Source*: OECD (1988) p. 10

Hanneman and Gargan, 1989; Maguire, 1986, pp. 246–7; Kennedy, 1975, p. 11). Indeed, throughout the developed capitalist world, the post-war period was one of unprecedented growth and prosperity, and of new and varied forms of government intervention in the economy.

By almost any criteria, these were years of rapid expansion in welfare state provision. Thus, for example, in Western Europe in the early 1930s, only about a half of the labour force was protected by accident, sickness, invalidity and old age insurance. Scarcely a fifth were insured against unemployment. However, by the mid-1970s, more than 90 per cent of the labour force enjoyed insurance against income loss due to old age, invalidity and sickness; over 80 per cent were covered by accident insurance and 60 per cent had coverage against unemployment. The average annual rate of growth in social security expenditure which stood at around 0.9 per cent in 1950–5 had accelerated to 3.4 per cent in the years 1970–4. Broadly defined, social expenditure which had in the early 1950s consumed some-thing between 10 and 20 per cent of GNP had grown to between a quarter and something more than a third of a rapidly enhanced GNP by the mid-1970s (Flora, 1986, vol. 1, p. xxii). A further indication of this rapid growth after 1960 is given in table 4.5. However we choose to explain this development, the sheer growth in social expenditure throughout this period is one of the more remarkable phenomena of post-war capitalist development.

For many commentators, these developments in social policy may only properly be understood in the much broader context of what in the US was styled the 'post-World War II capital labor accord' and is more familiarly described in the UK and Western Europe as the 'post-war consensus' (Bowles and Gintis, 1982). In this view, the new social, political and economic order of the post-war world was to be secured around (1) Keynesian economic policies to secure full employment and economic growth domestically, within the agreed parameters of an essentially liberal capitalist international market, (2) a more or less 'institutional' welfare state to deal with the dysfunctions arising from this market economy and (3) broad-based agreement between left and right, and between capital and labour, over these basic social institutions (a market economy and a welfare state) and the accommodation of their (legitimately) competing interests through elite-level negotiation (Bowles and Gintis, 1982, Taylor-Gooby, 1985; Kavanagh, 1987; Kavanagh and Morris, 1989). These liberal democratic or social democratic institutions were seen as the best guarantee of avoiding both the economic disasters and the concomitant political polarization of the inter-war years.

This post-war consensus may be thought of in two ways, as a consensus between *classes* or as a consensus between political *parties*. At the class level, consensus involved the abandonment by labour of its traditional aspiration for socialization of the economy and of the ideology and practices of 'class war'. For capital, it meant an acceptance of the commitment to full employment, to the public ownership of strategic utilities and support for the welfare state. Both labour and capital were to share in the common objectives (and rewards) of sustained economic growth. This compromise was to be managed by the overarching presence of the government, which would co-ordinate relations between unions and employers, secure the background conditions for economic growth and administer the welfare state. In its party form, consensus indicated broad agreement on the constitutional rules of the political game, the marginalization of the extremes of both left and right (both within and outside 'mainstream' parties), a political style of compromise and bargaining, the broad acceptance of predecessors' legislation and the 'mobilization of bias' in favour of certain interests and ideas, including organized capital, organized labour and Keynesian economics (Kavanagh, 1987, pp. 6–7).

In both formulations, there were certain core public policy elements around which the compromise was built. Internationally, there was an endorsement of the open international market and commitment to 'the collective defence of the Western world', (both under American leadership). Domestically, it meant a commitment to (1) the maintenance of a comprehensive welfare state, (2) support of the 'mixed economy' of private and public enterprise and (3) policies of full employment and sustained economic growth.[16]

For many commentators in the 1950s and 1960s, the coming of the post-war era of consensus politics seemed to herald 'an irreversible change'. Within the sphere of the welfare state, Tom Marshall argued in 1965 that there was now 'little difference of opinion as to the services that must be provided, and it is generally agreed that, whoever provides them, the overall responsibility for the welfare of the citizens must remain with the state' (Marshall, 1975, p. 97). Still more confidently, Charles Schottland proclaimed that 'whatever its beginnings, the welfare state is here to stay. Even its opponents argue only about its extension' (Schottland, 1969). Much more recently, Mishra comments that

> state commitment to maintaining full employment, providing a range of basic services for all citizens, and preventing or relieving poverty seemed so integral to post-war society as to be almost irreversible. (Mishra, 1984, p. 1)

We have already noted that recent scholarship has cast doubt upon the reality of the post-war consensus. Most sceptically, Ben Pimlott has written of 'the myth of consensus', while Deakin insists of the UK experience that while 'real convergences in policy between the major political parties and individuals within them certainly took place ... there was far less homogeneity than is usually believed' (Deakin, 1987; Pimlott, 1988; Taylor-Gooby, 1985). In Sweden, once identified by right-wing social democrats as the definitive terrain of the consensual 'middle way', there has been an attempt to redefine the historic accommodation of organized capital and organized labour as a temporary and strategic compromise of irreconcilable differences of interest which are now becoming increasingly manifest (Childs, 1961; Crosland, 1964; Tingsten, 1973; Tomasson, 1969; Tomasson, 1970; Scase, 1977a, 1977b; Korpi, 1979; Stephens, 1979; Himmelstrand et al., 1981; Korpi, 1983; Pierson, 1986; Pierson, 1991).

Yet even for its most enthusiastic supporters, the politics of consensus was always recognized to be a *positive-sum* game. Agreement rested upon the capacity to generate a growing economic surplus with which to satisfy simultaneously a multiplicity of disparate claims. In this way, it was reliant upon the fourth element we have identified in the post-war period, that is the commitment to economic growth and full employment.

---

16    On consensus, see Kavanagh and Morris (1989) and Deakin (1987); for a sceptical view see Pimlott (1988).

**Table 4.6** Annual percentage growth in GNP (7 major OECD countries), 1950–1981

|  | 1950–60 | 1960–73 | 1973–81 |
|---|---|---|---|
| Canada | 4.0 | 5.6 | 2.8 |
| France | 4.5 | 5.6 | 2.6 |
| West Germany | 7.8 | 4.5 | 2.0 |
| Italy | 5.8 | 5.2 | 2.4 |
| Japan | 10.9 | 10.4 | 3.6 |
| UK | 2.3 | 3.1 | 0.5 |
| US | 3.3 | 4.2 | 2.3 |
| Average | 4.4 | 5.5 | 2.3 |

*Sources:* OECD (1966) p. 20; Bruno and Sachs, (1985) p. 155

Economic growth was seemingly the irreplaceable foundation of the traditional welfare state. It was the basis of Keynesian policies to induce capital investment, the stimulus to support economic activity at levels securing full employment and the fount of resources for increased expenditure on health, education, welfare and social services. It was economic growth that made a reconciliation of the opposing interests of capital and labour viable and sustainable. Fittingly, what has been described as 'the "Golden Age" of the welfare state' was also a period of unprecedented and unparalleled growth in the international capitalist economy.

Table 4.6 gives some general indication of this growth. In the seven major OECD countries (which at the start of the 1950s accounted for 90 per cent of OECD output), annual growth in GNP stood at 4.4 per cent in the 1950s, rising to 5.5 per cent in the years between 1960 and 1973. There was substantial international variation in rates of growth. The UK struggled to achieve growth above 3 per cent even in the years of most rapid expansion, while Japan's remarkable growth exceeded 10 per cent per annum throughout the period. In the years after 1960, a number of previously 'underdeveloped' economies, (for example, Spain, Portugal, Greece and Turkey), achieved levels of growth in excess of 6 per cent per annum. Throughout the 1950s and 1960s average annual growth rates within the OECD economies as a whole stood close to 5 per cent while inflation, though rising slowly, stayed below 4 per cent until the late 1960s. This contrasts sharply with experience after 1973 when the average rate of economic growth was more than halved (falling as low as 0.5 per cent in the UK). At the same time, inflation became a persistent problem, peaking at 14 per cent in 1974.

**Table 4.7**  Unemployment rates as a percentage of total labour force in 6 major OECD countries, 1933–1983

|              | 1933  | 1959–67 | 1975 | 1983 |
|--------------|-------|---------|------|------|
| France       | —     | 0.7     | 4.1  | 8.0  |
| West Germany | 14.8  | 1.2     | 3.6  | 8.0  |
| Italy        | 5.9   | 6.2     | 5.8  | 9.7  |
| Japan        | —     | 1.4     | 1.9  | 2.6  |
| UK           | 13.9  | 1.8     | 4.7  | 13.1 |
| US           | 20.5  | 5.3     | 8.3  | 9.5  |
| Average      | 13.0  | 2.8     | 4.7  | 8.5  |

*Source*:   Godfrey (1986) p. 2

Table 4.7 reveals a parallel pattern in terms of employment. The years of sustained, low inflationary economic growth were also years of particularly low levels of unemployment. The period between 1950 and 1967 in which the average levels of unemployment in six major OECD countries stood at 2.8 per cent contrasts markedly with the experience in 1933 at the height of the depression, when unemployment reached 13 per cent. In fact, the figure for the 1960s is distorted by the persistently high levels of unemployment in Italy and the US, all the other countries showing averages significantly below 2 per cent. These figures from the 1960s also contrast sharply with the experience after 1970. Unemployment rose throughout the 1970s, peaking at about 8.5 per cent in 1983. This period also saw a particularly steep increase in youth unemployment and in long-term unemployment. In the UK, for example, youth unemployment reached 23.4 per cent in 1983 and the proportion of those unemployed for more than a year rose above 40 per cent in 1986, while overall unemployment rates in the early 1980s came close to the worst levels of the 1930s. Thus the 1950s and 1960s defined a period of sustained economic growth and full employment which contrasted not only with the pre-war years but also with experience after 1973.

Figure 4.2 illustrates the way in which this pattern of sustained economic growth was co-ordinated with an increase in the proportion of national product directed towards social expenditure.

## The Middle-Class Welfare State

Two further social and political consequences of this rapid growth of the welfare state in the post-war period are worthy of particular

**Figure 4.2** Real social expenditure and real GDP, 1965–1985 (1965 = 100)

*Source*:   OECD (1988) p. 13

attention. First, expansion of the social budget brought with it some 'universalization' of the constituency of the welfare state. Tomasson has written of three characteristic phases in the development of the welfare state:

> Social welfare before the First World War was a concern of the political Right for the poor. Between the World Wars social welfare was adopted as an issue by the political Left, still for the poor. After the Second World War social welfare became a concern of both right and left but ... "not for the poor alone". (Tomasson, 1983, p. ix)

Rarely has the post-war welfare state served simply the interests of society's poorest and most distressed. Almost everywhere, 'the non-poor play a crucial role of (variously) creating, expanding, sustain-

**Table 4.8** The distribution of public expenditure on the UK social services

| Service | Ratio of expenditure per person in top fifth to that per person in bottom fifth |
| --- | --- |
| Pro-poor | |
| Council housing | 0.3 |
| Equal | |
| Primary education | 0.9 |
| Secondary education | 0.9 |
| Pro-rich | |
| National Health Service | 1.4 |
| Secondary education (16+) | 1.8 |
| Non-university higher education | 3.5 |
| Bus subsidies | 3.7 |
| Universities | 5.4 |
| Tax subsidies to owner-occupiers | 6.8 |
| Rail subsidies | 9.8 |

*Source*: Goodin and Le Grand (1987) p. 92

ing, reforming and dismantling the welfare state' (Goodin and Le Grand, 1987, p. 3). Consequently, the nature of middle-class involvement has been one of the most important (if sometimes neglected) aspects of later welfare state evolution. In fact, the expansion of the welfare state in the post-war period has tended to benefit members of the middle class both (1) as *consumers*, giving rights of access to facilities in healthcare, education, housing, transport and so on which 'actually benefited the middle classes ... in many cases more than the poor' and (2) as *providers*, increasing professional employment opportunities within the public sector (Goodin and Le Grand, 1987, p. 91). As Le Grand's work on the UK welfare state suggests (table 4.8), perhaps counter-intuitively, it is often middle-class elements that have been the principal beneficiaries of such redistribution as the broad welfare state allows.

## The Growth of Welfare State Employment

A second general consequence of the rapid expansion of the welfare state in the post-war period is to be found in the radical changes in the composition of the work-force that it has effected. The state, and more especially the welfare state, is now a major employer in all advanced societies. The UK National Health Service is the single largest employer in Western Europe with an annual wages bill in excess of £13 billion (Department of Health, 1989). Within the more general shift in employment from manufacturing to the service sector, state welfare has had a peculiarly prominent role. Studying changes in employment patterns in West Germany, Sweden, the US and the UK, Martin Rein concludes that between the early 1960s and the 1980s social welfare and 'services to business' have been the only two areas of the service sector of the economy to experience real growth. By the latter period, the 'social welfare industry' accounted for between 11 per cent (West Germany) and 26 per cent (Sweden) of overall employment, and social welfare jobs accounted for between 20 and 40 per cent of all employment in the service sector (Rein, 1985, pp. 39–40).

OECD figures suggest that in Denmark by the mid-1980s, government employment (about two-thirds of which is in the social welfare sector) *exceeded* employment in manufacturing. In other countries (for example, Norway and Sweden), the two sectors were close to parity, while in *every* country reviewed, the gap between employment in manufacturing and government services had significantly narrowed since the early 1970s (OECD, 1989, pp. 120–2). Rein noted that the consequences of expanded welfare state employment were particularly pronounced for women, and especially for those women who had passed through higher education. In 1981, between 65 and 75 per cent of college-educated women in West Germany, Sweden and the US were employed in the 'social welfare industries'. The growth of the welfare state has clearly been a major area of growth in female labour force participation, especially for the growing number of professionally qualified women (Rein, 1985, pp. 43–5).

A number of profound (political) consequences have been seen to follow from this pattern of middle-class involvement and expanded employment within the welfare state. Therborn, for example, takes it as evidence of the 'creeping universalism' of the welfare state, which has rendered New Right attempts to dismantle it electorally impossible. For the New Right itself, the growth of a highly unionized, middle-class public sector work-force was a major source of economic and political crisis in the 1970s. Others have identified new lines of electoral cleavage developing around the welfare state (reliance on the public sector v. reliance upon the private sector), displacing traditional cleavages along the lines of social class (Therborn, 1987; Dunleavy, 1980). Claus Offe has argued that the secure employment and comparative affluence which first attached the middle classes to the 'welfare state project' is now increasingly threatening their defection to neo-liberalism and a consequent re-sidualization of state welfare. These themes are further developed in chapter 6. For now, we return to a more detailed assessment of social policy changes in the post-war period.

## 1945–1950: Reconstruction

Within the very broad parameters of the 'Golden Age' or, more soberly, the era of welfare state expansion between 1945 and 1975, it is both possible and useful to offer some further periodization. Thus we may think of the immediate post-war period down to 1951 as defining a period of *reconstruction* following the débâcle of World War Two. In this period, a number of countries created that broad and systematic platform upon which the developed welfare state was based. In the UK, even before the end of the war, the coalition government had passed legislation to reform secondary education and to introduce family allowances. In the immediate post-war period, the Labour government (partially) implemented Beveridge's reform proposals with the setting up of the National Health Service, the final abolition of the Poor Law and the reconstruction of national insurance and national assistance. The essentials of the post-war UK welfare state were in place by 1948.

In France, where social policy enhancement between the wars had been modest, there was a 'major commitment to social security in 1945 and 1946' (Ashford and Kelley, 1986, p. 257). This included a law providing sickness and disability insurance, pension legislation and a law providing for the aged poor. There was also an enhance-ment of the 1932 Family Allowances legislation, providing pre-natal payments, additional payments for the third child and a rising scale of benefits as families grew larger (Ashford, 1986a, pp. 183–4). In Finland, where pre-war provision had been still more limited, the years between 1945 and 1950 saw a spectacular average growth rate in social expenditure of 22.2 per cent. Social expenditure as a prop-ortion of central government spending rose from 3 to 13 per cent in the same period. Most of this increased effort was directed towards children and families, healthcare, the organization of social services, benefits for war victims and state-supported housing construction (Alestalo and Uusitalo, 1986, pp. 202–3, 246). Similarly in Ireland, 'the period from 1945 to the early 1950s was a time of heightened interest and activity in the area of social policy'. During these years, the share of social expenditure in GDP rose by almost six percentage points. The reforms included the enhancement of public health provision, the expansion of social insurance coverage and improved state aid for housing in both the public and private sectors (Maguire, 1986, pp. 246–8, 252; Kennedy, 1975, p. 5).

Not every developed capitalist country participated in this rapid enhancement of social legislation after 1945. In Italy, for example, proposals for a systematic reform of social insurance were rejected following the election of a Christian Democrat-dominated coalition government in 1948, which opted instead to restore the pre-war institutional framework (Ferrera, 1986, p. 390; Ferrera, 1989, p. 124). In New Zealand, the major period of welfare state expansion had *preceded* the Second World War, while it has been said that 'by the end of the Labour administration in 1949 Australia hardly possessed a welfare state' (Jones, 1980, p. 36). However, the single strategically most important nation in this period of international welfare state expansion was probably the 'laggardly' US. While Bowles and Gintis identify the emergence of a 'capital labor accord' in a number of legislative initiatives in the immediate post-war years, additions to the US's own 'semi-welfare state' were quite limited. It was, however, US military and economic power which underwrote the post-war reconstruction of Europe and the new political and economic order of which the welfare state was an essential feature. America was the guarantor and sponsor of Western Europe's 'embedded liberalism' (economic liberalism in a context of state intervention), and thus 'ironically, it was American hegemony that provided the basis for the development and expansion of the European welfare states' (Keohane, 1984, pp. 16–17).

## 1950–1960: Relative Stagnation

By contrast with the burst of legislative and executive action in the immediate post-war years, which for many commentators heralds the real coming of the welfare state, the 1950s was a decade of relative stagnation. In what was generally a period of sustained economic growth, the proportion of resources directed to social expenditure rose very slowly compared with both the years before 1950 and those after 1960. In Western Europe, the average growth in central government social expenditure as a percentage of GDP was something under 1 per cent for the whole decade (Flora, 1987b, vol. 1, pp. 345–449). Strong economic growth means that such figures often mask sustained growth in real social expenditure. Jens Alber writes of the period 1951–58 as the 'take-off' phase of the West German welfare state, but while average real growth in welfare expenditure rose over 10 per cent, its share in a rapidly growing

GDP rose by just three percentage points in the same period. Social expenditure commanded a very similar proportion of national wealth at the end of the decade as it had at its beginning (Alber, 1988b; Alber 1986, pp. 15–16; Maguire, 1986, pp. 321–30). However, there were some countries in which the proportion of social expenditure actually *fell* during the 1950s. In Ireland, for example, central government social expenditure as a proportion of GDP fell by 3.6 percentage points between 1951 and 1960. The share of social expenditure in GDP did not recover its 1951 level until 1964. In the period between 1952 and 1966, public social security expenditure in Australia rose by two percentage points, but this was from 6.1 per cent of GNP to a still modest 8.2 per cent. In New Zealand, growth in the same period was less than 1 per cent (Kaim-Caudle, 1973, p. 53). Of course, these figures for proportionate social expenditure do not give an exhaustive description of welfare state developments. Political disputes over welfare policy – the Swedish pension reforms of 1957 or the introduction of health charges by the UK Labour government in 1951, for example – are not captured by these statistics (Esping-Andersen, 1985; Sked and Cook, 1984, p. 96). Nonetheless, the contrast with the 1940s and the 1960s is quite clear.

A number of reasons have been advanced to explain this comparative decline in social expenditure growth. Some have suggested that need was adequately met by the levels of expenditure established in the late 1940s. Others point to the increased private affluence and low unemployment achieved in the sustained economic growth of the 1950s. For some, the element of mutual risk and austerity which wartime conditions generated had evaporated by the 1950s. Tom Marshall wrote 'that the welfare state reigned unchallenged while linked with the Austerity Society and was attacked from all sides as soon as it became associated with the Affluent Society' (Marshall, 1963, p. 282). Others argued that the succession of defeats of left-wing governments marked a political realignment towards the right and the end of the zeal for reform which had characterized the immediate post-war years.

## 1960–1975: Major Expansion

From about 1960 onwards, we enter a third phase in the post-war development of the welfare state, one that lasts some fifteen years and which is best characterized as an era of major expansion. In terms of the resources devoted to social expenditure, this is perhaps the most remarkable period in the whole evolution of the international welfare states. Thus, the proportion of GDP devoted to social expenditure rose from 12.3 per cent in 1960 to 21.9 per cent in 1975.

**Figure 4.3** The growth of social expenditure in the OECD area, 1960–1981

——— unweighted average for the seven major OECD countries[a]

– – – – unweighted OECD average [a,b]

    a   Prior to 1975 there are no figures for expenditure on education in France. Therefore, only the growth rages for the years after 1975 reflect the growth in expenditure on education in France. The pattern of growth rates over these later years in unaffected by their inclusion.

    b   Average for 17 countries (excluding Denmark and Switzerland except for 1981, where Belgium and Greece are also excluded.

*Source*:   OECD (1985a) p. 19

Both absolute levels and rates of growth varied. By 1975, six countries – France, West Germany, Belgium, Denmark, The Netherlands and Sweden – were devoting in excess of 25 per cent of their GDP to social expenditure. Amongst the seven major OECD economies, only Japan (13.7 per cent), the US (18.7 per cent) and the UK (19.6 per cent) now devoted less than a fifth of GDP to social expenditure. In the 1960–75 period, average annual growth in deflated social expenditure was in excess of 8 per cent in Australia, Denmark, Japan and Norway. It fell below 4 per cent only in the UK and Austria. The overall average for the OECD countries throughout this period was 6.5 per cent per annum (OECD, 1988, p. 11).

As figure 4.3 illustrates, the annual growth rate of deflated social expenditure ranged between 7 and 10 per cent throughout the period 1960–75. It experienced a sharp rise in the period immediately after

1973 but fell sharply after 1975. The average growth rate for the years 1975–81 was little more than half of what it had been in the period prior to 1975.

Again, while there was some international variation, three areas – education, health and pensions – commanded some four-fifths of resources throughout this period. There was some change in the distribution of effort between these three areas as expenditure on education first rose and then declined, while expenditure on health and pensions increased steadily. Of the three, pensions appeared to be least vulnerable to retrenchment following the economic reverses of the mid-1970s. Even with the rapidly rising levels of joblessness in the late 1970s, unemployment compensation remained a minor programme, commanding on average less than 5 per cent of social expenditure (OECD, 1985a).

A number of reasons have been advanced to explain this remarkable growth. In part, these are demographic, reflecting not just the growing numbers of old age pensioners but also the rise in the ratio of elderly (who are also disproportionate users of health services) to the economically active. Some point to the central role of the growth of prosperity in this period as generating the necessary resources for the expansion of social programmes (Alber, 1988b). Others offer more political explanations of the growth of social spending stressing, for example, the mobilization of labour movements, socialist parties and others (including the civil rights movement in the US) in favour of enhanced welfare; the essential role of social spending as a part of the 'capital-labour' accommodation of the post-war consensus; the growing density and capacity of interest groups to mobilize in favour of sectional interests within the welfare state; the increase in urbanization and educational provision leading to greater social and political mobilization.

Many commentators link these explanations of the rapid growth of the welfare state down to 1975 with its problems or 'crisis' thereafter. Indeed, in more or less apocalyptic terms, 1975 is often seen to mark the end-point of nearly 100 years of welfare state growth and to bring the threat or promise of its imminent dismemberment. It is to the distinctive theories and experiences of this period (both on the New Right and the neo-Marxist left) that we turn in chapter 5.

# 5
# Contradiction and Crisis in the Developed Welfare State

Most commentators on the historical evolution of the welfare state have been agreed in identifying a break with a long-standing pattern of growth and development in international social policy from the early or middle years of the 1970s. Some have done no more than draw attention to the slackening pace of welfare state growth in this period (Flora, 1986; Alber, 1988a). Others, particularly those writing from the perspective of the 1970s, drew a much more alarming picture of 'crisis' and 'contradiction' in the welfare state, a condition which challenged either the continuation of the welfare state or even the integrity of the democratic capitalist order itself. It was in this period of the early and mid-1970s that social democratic confidence in the competence of the mixed economy and the welfare state to deliver continuing economic growth allied to greater social equity came under increasing challenge. It was also, as we have seen, the period of the flowering of New Right and neo-Marxist accounts of the welfare state, both of which concentrated on the ubiquity of crisis arising from the inherently unstable and contradictory elements within the post-war welfare capitalist consensus.

Of course, such views were not entirely new. The claim that welfare *rights* were inconsistent with a market economy can be retraced at least to Malthus and Nassau Senior (see p. 9 above). Germany has a history of criticism of the *costs* of the welfare state dating at least from the turn of the century, when social insurance expenditure stood at just 1.4 per cent of GDP (Alber, 1988a, p. 181). Again, Hayek's philosophical case against the welfare state predates the Second World War and was sustained throughout its post-war 'Golden Age'. Turning to the neo-Marxist account, Marx himself had challenged the possibility of reconciling the *real* interests of labour with the dynamics of a capitalist economy, while John Saville's classic article locating the origins of the UK welfare state in turn-of-the-century class struggle dates from 1957–8 (Saville, 1975, pp. 57–69). The more social democratic Asa Briggs argued at the start of the 1960s (and in the middle of the 'Golden Age') that with 'a background of recurring fiscal crises, "paying for services" has replaced "fair shares for all" as a current political slogan' (Briggs, 1967, p. 26). Even as early as 1918, Joseph Schumpeter had written of the fiscal limits of the capitalist state in Austria:

> the state has its definite limits [and these are] limits to its fiscal potential ... [In] bourgeois society ... the state lives as an economic parasite. [It] must not demand from the people so much that they lose financial interest in production. (Schumpeter, 1954, pp. 20–2)[1]

The perspective of contradiction and crisis in the welfare state was not then so much new-found in the writings of the New Right and the neo-Marxists as newly influential. It seemed as if, in an instant, 'complacency about the momentum of the welfare state gave way to doom-mongering by many in the intellectual elite' (Heclo, 1981, p. 399). With astonishing speed, the warnings of a looming crisis (particularly those of the New Right) seemed to replace the benign assumptions of social democracy as a privileged discourse among governing and 'opinion-forming' elites.

Yet precisely what was intended by this discourse of 'crisis' and 'contradiction' is not entirely clear. Alec Pemberton complains that the use of 'contradiction' in Marxist analyses of the welfare state is 'notoriously imprecise'. He identifies two main variants. These were (1) contradiction as *paradox* (as in the claim that 'the working class struggles for welfare rights but this inadvertently strengthens the position of capital'), and (2) contradiction as *opposite effect* (as in the argument that 'the welfare state is introduced to assist the needy and deprived but, in practice, it worsens their position'). The principal difficulty identified in both usages is that it is unclear in what sense the relationships specified are truly 'contradictory'. The outcomes described may be perverse or even establish 'real oppositions', but they do not entail a contradiction which, properly speaking, is a description of the relationship between two logically inconsistent statements (of the kind 'This is the final crisis of capitalism/This is

---

1  It is instructive that Schumpeter here raises the spectre of a 'fiscal crisis of the tax state' only to reject it.

not the final crisis of capitalism') (Pemberton, 1983, pp. 289–308; Benton, 1977; Offe, 1984, pp. 130–46). Although Pemberton's strictures are addressed to the neo-Marxist literature, much the same problem arises in New Right accounts. Indeed, the New Right's use of 'contradiction' is in some sense inherited from a prior Marxist tradition.[2]

Similar difficulties surround the widespread usage, by both right and left, of the idea of a 'crisis' of the welfare state. We may identify three distinct senses in which 'crisis' is employed in contemporary discussions. The first derives from the two associated meanings given to it in its classical origins. These were first a medical usage in which crisis describes 'the turning point in a disease when death or recovery hangs in the balance' and secondly a dramaturgical sense in which crisis describes a 'turning point in a fateful process' when the participants must either succumb to the logic of fate or summon up the moral will or energy to defy it (Rader, 1979, p. 187). This sense of crisis as a decisive phase in which a long-standing or deep-seated struggle must be resolved one way or another has been extended by analogy to describe particularly strategic or decisive episodes in the historical or social process.

'Crisis' is also employed in contemporary discussions in two further senses. First, there is an understanding of 'crisis as a catastrophe caused by an external blow' (Moran, 1988, p. 397). Offe describes this as a *sporadic crisis concept*, in which the crisis is confined to one event or brief series of events. In this sense, 'the crisis event or the defencelessness against it is not seen as a characteristic quality of the system' (Offe, 1984, pp. 36–7). Offe himself prefers a second contemporary notion, that of 'a *processual* concept of crisis'. Here, crises are 'developmental tendencies that can be confronted with "*counteracting tendencies*" ... making it possible to relate the crisis-prone developmental tendencies of a system to the characteristics of the system'. On this reading, crises 'need not be seen as catastrophic events having a contingent origin' (Offe, 1984, pp. 36–7). Rather they relate immediately to Offe's sense of contradiction as 'the tendency inherent within a specific mode of production to destroy those very preconditions on which its survival depends'. These contradictions when seen within the capitalist mode of production may call forth 'counteracting tendencies' (this is, indeed,

---

2  As Brittan acknowledges in an early footnote in his celebrated article on 'The Economic Contradictions of Democracy': 'Strictly speaking only statements can be contradictory, not events or procedures. The title of this paper represents a stretching of the term of the kind in which Marx indulged when speaking of the "contradictions of capitalism"' (Brittan, 1975, p. 129.)

very largely what the welfare state is), but the structural and systemic limitations upon such counteracting tendencies reveal a chronic likelihood 'that contradictions will finally result in a *crisis* of the capitalist mode of production' (Offe, 1984, p. 133). At the same time, all of these more or less technical uses are overlain by the popular and devalued currency of 'crisis' as describing any (and every) large-scale contemporary problem.

For all its advocates, the idea of a 'crisis of the welfare state' may thus have a wide range of meanings. We may isolate the most important of these as:

1   crisis as *turning point*
2   crisis as *external shock*
3   crisis as *long-standing contradiction*

The idea of a crisis or of contradictions surrounding the welfare state is then neither entirely new, nor unproblematically clear. However, we can isolate the early 1970s as the period in which (particularly in the Anglo-American context) the idea of a crisis of the welfare state achieves an unparalleled prominence. The late 1960s had seen the emergence of a growing discontent among both left and right-wing libertarians about the enervating bureaucratic and statist aspects of social welfare (Illich, 1973, 1978; Lasch, 1978, p. 224). It had also been a period of growing political mobilization and renewed industrial action, notably within the public sector trades unions that had themselves been a by-product of welfare state expansion (Jackson, 1987; Hyman, 1989b; Giddens, 1981a). All of these contributed to a climate in which social conflict was of renewed interest. But it was above all the end to uninterrupted post-war economic growth that undermined the incremental confidence of the social democrats and set the stage for 'the new pessimism' (Heclo, 1981, p. 398).

The nature of the 'Golden Age' of post-war capitalism is now itself much debated. There has been some tendency to redraw (and shorten) the parameters of the period of sustained economic growth and comparative social peace – on which both the 'end of ideology' and the perspective of open-ended economic expansion were premised – to cover little more than the fifteen years between 1950 and the mid-1960s.[3] But, wherever one places 'the beginning of the end' of this era, by the early 1970s the signs of economic difficulty were unmistakable and the five-fold increase in oil prices which OPEC

---

3   The earliest version of O'Connor's fiscal crisis theory appeared in 1970. On the post-war period, see Deakin (1987); Kavanagh and Morris (1989).

**Table 5.1** Macroeconomic performance in the OECD, 1960–1981 (%)

| Economic indicator | 1960–73 | 1973–81 |
|---|---|---|
| Unemployment rate | 3.2 | 5.5 |
| Inflation | 3.9 | 10.4 |
| GNP growth | 4.9 | 2.4 |
| Productivity growth | 3.9 | 1.4 |

*Source*: Bruno and Sachs (1985) p. 2

was able to impose in 1973 precipitated (rather than caused) a severe slump throughout the western industrialized world.

A few figures will illustrate the scale of this economic 'crisis'. Between 1965 and 1973, the economies of the OECD countries showed an annual average growth rate of about 5 per cent. In 1974, this annual growth rate fell to 2 per cent and in 1975, nine OECD economies 'shrank', bringing the annual average growth rate below zero. Though there was some recovery from this low point, there was to be a second oil-price 'shock' in 1979, and for the decade 1974 to 1984, annual average growth was little over 2 per cent (Alber, 1988a, p. 187). Nor were these economic difficulties confined to sluggish growth. By 1975, unemployment in the OECD area had risen to an unprecedented 15 million. At the same time, inflation accelerated and there was a growing balance-of-trade deficit throughout the OECD. The 'discomfort/misery index' (the rate of inflation plus the rate of unemployment) which, for the seven major OECD countries, had averaged 5.5 per cent through the 1960s had risen to 17 per cent by 1974–5. At the same time, levels of invest-ment and levels of profitability fell, while the value of disposable incomes stagnated. As table 5.1 shows, governments throughout the developed West were simultaneously failing to achieve the four major economic policy objectives – growth, low inflation, full em-ployment and balance of trade – on which the post-war order had been based (Gough, 1979, p. 132; Goldthorpe, 1984, p. 2).

One of the clearest manifestations of this economic crisis was the growing indebtedness of the public household. As the economic recession deepened, so demands upon public expenditure, and especially social expenditure, grew, in part through the inertia of incrementalism but also through costs that rose directly from econ-omic decline (the costs of enlarged unemployment and social be-nefits claims). At the same time as demand grew, with the slump in tax-generating growth, revenue declined. This manifested itself in a 'yawning gap between expenditure and revenues' and a rapid growth in the public sector borrowing requirement (PSBR). Most acutely in the period 1973–5, as economic growth (and the capacity to fund state expenditure) declined, public expenditure increased (Gough, 1979, p. 132). About half of the 10 per cent growth in the share of GDP devoted to public expenditure in the OECD countries between 1960 and 1975 occurred in 1974 and 1975 (OECD, 1985a, p. 14). In the same period, specifically social spending (on education, health, income maintenance and other welfare services) had taken an increasing share of this enhanced public expenditure, rising from 47.5 per cent in 1960 to 58.5 per cent by 1981 (OECD, 1985a, p. 21). Consequently, concern about state indebtedness and public expenditure was above all concern about the costs of the welfare state.

We shall consider the nature of (differing) governments' (differing) responses to this challenge later in this chapter. In fact, as we shall see, there were important policy differences between the several national governments. Indeed, not only was there the customary discrepancy between what these governments said and what they did but also a divide between what these governments did and what people widely believed them to have done. But we now have sufficient evidence to place in context the 'crisis' theories of the early and mid-1970s, theories which were themselves a response to the economic crisis and the immediate reaction of government agencies.

## OPEC and the 'Contingent Crisis'

Perhaps the earliest response to the economic crisis of the early 1970s was to understand it, in Offe's terms, as a 'sporadic crisis'. Upon this view, the essentially sound and well-ordered international capitalist system had been subjected to an 'external shock' or series of shocks which had temporarily thrown it out of equilibrium. Most prominent among these shocks was the oil price increase of 1973 which had precipitated the deep recession of 1974 and 1975. Other candidates for disruption were the consequences of the long-standing US involvement in Vietnam, the rapid rise of (non-oil) basic commodity costs (notably of basic foods), and the breakdown of international monetary exchange relations. What was crucial about all these 'shocks' was that they were essentially exogenous (from outside the system) and if not non-replicable (after all OPEC could, and did, impose a second oil price hike) then certainly contingent. Paul McKracken's 1977 Report prepared for the OECD, probably the most celebrated statement of this position, concluded that the recession of the early 1970s arose from 'an unusual bunching of unfortunate disturbances unlikely to be repeated on the same scale, the impact of which was compounded by some considerable errors in economic policy' (OECD, 1977). Upon such an account, crisis was external to the welfare state in two senses. First, the source of (temporary) economic problems lay outside the prevailing international market order and second, insofar as there was a knock-on problem of funding for the welfare state, this was one which was wholly attributable to the shortfall in economic product and not to the (damaging) interrelationship between social welfare and economic performance.

However, this essentially optimistic view – of a 'hiccup' in economic growth leading to a temporary pause in welfare state growth – was increasingly overtaken in the welfare state area by studies which stressed the contradictions within the mixed economy (or liberal representative democracy or welfare capitalism) as the real source of crisis. The five-fold increase in crude oil prices was simply the dramatic precipitating event which disclosed the deep-seated structural weaknesses of the post-war political economy which had been in the making for twenty-five years, and manifest to the discerning eye since at least the late 1960s. At the heart of this account is the claim that the end of the period of post-war economic growth was not externally caused but inherent in the social, political and economic order of the post-war consensus and especially in its ameliorating institutions for the management of economically based political conflict.

It will be recalled from chapter 2 that this was precisely the position adopted by both New Right and neo-Marxist commentators in response to the events of the early 1970s. For both schools, this crisis cannot be understood as 'simply' economic. Rather it is a crisis of the social and political order established after 1945 under the rubric of the Keynesian Welfare State. For both, the problems of the early 1970s express the economic and political contradictions inherent in a democratic capitalist society. Such an analysis embraces our two further senses of crisis. First, for all of these commentators the post-war order is threatened by the consequences of deep-seated and 'long-standing contradiction'. Also, typically in its earliest, boldest and most apocalyptic formulations, this perspective raises the spectre of an historical turning point. That is, the contradictions of the post-war order are now so acute that a radical change is no longer simply desirable, it has become unavoidable. Whatever the radical alternatives, the status quo is not an option.

We also saw in chapter 2 that it is extremely difficult to think of the neo-Marxist theory of the welfare state outside of the context of its perceived crisis. For contemporary Marxist thinkers, the welfare state is essentially contradictory, and its crises are but an especially

acute expression of these contradictions. This view was first stated
with some force at the turn of the 1970s in O'Connor's *Fiscal Crisis of
the State*. O'Connor's study centred upon the claim that 'the capita-
listic state must try to fulfil two basic and often mutually contradictory functions – accumulation and legitimization'. On the one hand,
the state must try to maintain or create the conditions under which
profitable capital accumulation is possible; on the other, it must also
try to maintain or create the conditions for 'social harmony'. He
expands the contradiction thus:

> A capitalist state that openly uses its coercive forces to help one
> class accumulate capital at the expense of other classes loses its
> legitimacy and hence undermines the basis of its loyalty and sup-
> port. But a state that ignores the necessity of assisting the process
> of capital accumulation risks drying up the source of its own
> power, the economy's surplus production capacity and the taxes
> drawn from this surplus. (O'Connor, 1973, p. 6)

In essence, these imperatives of accumulation and legitimation are
seen to be contradictory. Expenditure to secure legitimization is
essential, to defray the otherwise potentially explosive social and
political costs of capitalist development, yet these costs must themselves be met via state revenues derived from the profits of capital
accumulation. In this way the costs of legitimization, which are to
secure circumstances for successful capital accumulation, themselves
tend to undermine the very process of profitable accumulation.
Correspondingly,

> The socialization of costs and the private appropriation of profits
> creates a fiscal crisis, or 'structural gap', between state expendi-
> tures and state revenues. The result is a tendency for state ex-
> penditures to increase more rapidly than the means of financing
> them. (O'Connor, 1973, p. 9)

This fiscal crisis is intensified by the pluralistic structure and accessi-
bility of liberal democratic politics, which privileges the servicing of
organized interests, furnishing 'a great deal of waste, duplication
and overlapping of state projects and services'. Thus, 'the accumulation of social capital and social expenses is a highly irrational process
from the standpoint of administrative coherence, fiscal stability
and potentially profitable capital accumulation' (O'Connor, 1973,
p. 9).

By the early 1970s in the US (which was the focus of O'Connor's study), these problems had become intense.[4] Growing tax resistance, intensified hostility to the authority of government, growing mobilization by new social movements among welfare recipients, and heightened politicization among an increasingly unionized state work-force all intensified those pressures upon government which generated fiscal crisis. O'Connor insisted that 'By the late 1960s, the local fiscal crisis was almost completely out of hand' and federal attempts to cope with this simply intensified the difficulties at national level (O'Connor, 1973, p. 212). O'Connor doubted that the crisis could be resolved within the parameters of the existing order. For him, 'the only lasting solution to the crisis is socialism' (p. 221).

## The New Right and the Crisis of Liberal Representative Democracy

Even more influential and dramatic as an account of the crisis of the welfare state in this period were the writings of the New Right. From the turn of the 1970s, the technical arguments of Hayek and the public choice theorists (discussed in chapter 2) were given an enhanced prominence by critics who insisted that the general contradictions underlying social democracy were now beginning to manifest themselves in an immediate and profound crisis of the existing political order. In a 1975 *Report on the Governability of Democracies*, Michael Crozier argued that within Western Europe

> the operations of the democratic process . . . appear to have generated a breakdown of traditional means of social control, a delegitimation of political and other forms of authority, and an overload of demands on government, exceeding its capacity to respond. (Crozier, Huntington and Watanuki 1975, p. 8)

For the neo-conservatives, the core of this 'democratic distemper' lay in the decline in respect for traditional sources of authority and in the break with traditional constraints upon individual aspirations. In the US in the 1960s, so Huntington argued, the 'vitality of democracy . . . produced a substantial increase in governmental activity and a substantial decrease in governmental authority' (Huntington, 1975,

---

4 Although the specific focus of O'Connor's analysis was the post-World War Two US, he did argue that 'many of the ideas presented can be adapted to the experience of other advanced capitalist countries' (O'Connor, 1973, p. 6).

p. 64). Thus at the same time as democratic publics made greatly increased demands of their governments, they were becoming less willing to accept the decisions taken by these public authorities. Indeed, the decline in respect for executive authority and the decline in support for mainstream political parties suggested a general decline in attachment to the traditional forms of representative democratic life. There was a growing mobilization of sectional demands with no recognition of a greater public interest, whether or not represented by the existing government. At the same time, sustained post-war economic growth, the institutionalization of the welfare state and the 'bidding-up' process of adversarial democratic politics had generated a 'revolution of rising expectations' among democratic publics. They were increasingly disposed to claim as non-negotiable 'rights', goods and services to which they had no sound claim. Decline of authority and mutual responsibility within the family meant that social welfare functions traditionally met within the private and family sector generated new claims upon the state – and produced a population increasingly dependent upon state beneficence. Daniel Bell noted as a manifestation of 'the cultural contradictions of capitalism', the fact that capitalism, which required sober, regular and systematically acquisitive individuals for its successful development, tended rather to generate hedonistic and consumption-oriented individuals, resistant to the traditional work ethic (Bell, 1979).

If for the neo-conservatives the major problem was one of declining social control and public authority, for the neo-liberals, following the public choice theorists, the major difficulties lay in the relationship between representative liberal democracy and the market economy. Thus, Samuel Brittan wrote in 1975 of the danger of the (self-) destruction of liberal representative democracy being precipitated by 'two endemic threats': (1) the generation of excessive expectations; and (2) the disruptive effects of the pursuit of group self-interest in the marketplace. He insisted that 'an excessive burden is placed on the "sharing out" function of government', where this function is understood as 'the activities of the public authorities in influencing the allocation of resources, both through taxation and expenditure policies and through direct intervention in the market place'. In essence, the 'growth of expectations imposes demands for different kinds of public spending and intervention which are incompatible both with each other and with the tax burden that people are willing to bear' (Brittan, 1975, pp. 129–31). Marrying Schumpeter's account of democracy as the process of elite competition for votes to the insights of the public choice theorists, Brittan argued that liberal representative democracy is imperilled by two underlying weaknesses.[5] First, the process of political competition generates unrealistic and excessive expectations about the possibilities afforded by government action among a largely (and rationally) uninformed voting public. Parties and politicians are systematically disposed to promise 'more for less'. A party which reminds the electorate of the necessary relationship between income and expenditure is likely to prove unelectable. Secondly, the growth of well-organized sectional interests (most especially trades unions) and especially their willingness to use this power to achieve sectional ends intensifies the difficulties of reconciling liberal and democratic government with national economic solvency. In the short term, this contradiction is likely to manifest itself in rising inflation, but 'in the last analysis the authorities have to choose between accepting an indefinite increase in the rate of inflation and abandoning full employment to the extent necessary to break the collective wage-push power of the unions'. However, such governments may be forced 'to choose between very high rates of unemployment and very high rates of inflation, neither of which can be sustained in a liberal democracy' (Brittan, 1975, p. 143). Consequently, Brittan judged that 'on present indications', liberal representative democracy 'is likely to pass away within the lifetime of people now adult' (Brittan, 1975, p. 129).

There were other elements in these accounts of the early 1970s. Some argued that the growth in resources and personnel directed towards the public sector as a consequence of the rise of the post-war welfare state had 'crowded out' the private sector investment upon which continued economic growth was dependent. Bacon and Eltis argued of the UK experience that there is 'a strong case' for maintaining that 'the great increase in public-sector employment that occurred in Britain in 1961–75 [largely within the welfare state sector] played a significant role in the deterioration of Britain's economic performance' (Bacon and Eltis, 1978, p. 16). Some stressed the growing difficulties of government macro-management in a more open world economy. Others highlighted the particularly entrenched position of public sector trades unions (itself a by-product of expanded (welfare) state employment), whose wages were politically- rather than market-determined (Rose and Peters, 1978, p. 23; Brittan, 1975). Anthony King drew attention to the secular growth in the complexity and interdependency of governmental decisions in all developed societies which would make the governance of even

---

5 On Schumpeter's account of democracy as elite competition, see Schumpeter (1976); Held (1987) pp. 164–85.

the most compliant of democracies more uncertain and problematic (King, 1975).

For many of these commentators, this overload thesis was intimately related to the spectre of growing ungovernability. Rose and Peters, for example, argued that a number of Western governments faced the imminent prospect of 'political bankruptcy' should they fail to show 'the political will to limit growth' of public expenditure in times of declining economic growth and falling take-home pay. While such 'political bankruptcy' would not mean anarchy and fighting in the streets, it would lead to an increase in citizen hostility to the conventional political process, accelerate the process of citizen indifference to the conduct of government and, perhaps most seriously, aggravate the tendency towards tax resistance, with an accompanying growth in the black economy (Rose and Peters, 1978, pp. 31–7). For King, the evidence of ungovernability was already present and, expressing himself 'a little pessimistic about the future', he argued that it was now the duty of political scientists to suggest 'how the number of tasks that government has come to be expected to perform can be reduced' (King, 1975, p. 296). Michael Crozier feared that Western Europe faced the prospect of 'Finlandization', while most apocalyptically, Peter Jay insisted that 'the very survival of democracy hangs by a gossamer thread' and that 'democracy has itself by the tail and is eating itself up fast' (cited in Rose and Peters, 1978, p. 14, n. 17; Jay, 1977: Crozier, Huntington and Watanuki 1975, p. 54).

Not all these commentators were so iconoclastic (nor can they all be identified unproblematically with the New Right). Rose and Peters, for example, insist that any 'attempt to dismantle the policies of the contemporary welfare state would be a response out of all proportion to the cause of the problem' (Rose and Peters, 1978, pp. 38, 232). Yet all were convinced that the continuation of the welfare state status quo was not an option.

## Crisis? What Crisis?

However, by the end of the 1970s, it seemed clear that expectations of a system-threatening crisis – whether a legitimation crisis of welfare capitalism or a crisis of governability of liberal representative democracy – were ungrounded. Nowhere in the advanced capitalist world had the system of representative democracy broken down nor the market system been challenged by mass mobilization in favour of socialism. Certainly, there had been considerable resistance to retrenchment of public expenditure and rising levels of unemployment. There was some (extremely approximate) evidence of growth in the black economy (a 1986 OECD report placed it at between 2 and 8 per cent of total hours worked in the developed economies) and limited evidence of tax resistance, notably in the meteoric rise of the anti-tax Progress Party in Denmark in 1973 and in the passage of Proposition 13 statutorily restricting state taxation in California.[6] Yet none of this represented a real challenge to the prevailing order which had seemingly been endorsed by the electoral success of right-wing parties in the late 1970s and early 1980s. This process was given its definitive expression in the popular election in 1979 and 1980 (and landslide re-election in 1983 and 1984) of self-professedly neo-liberal governments in the UK and the US.

One response to these developments has been to argue that the threat to the system was real enough, but that, just in time, 'the electorate' had recognized 'the incoherence of the providential idea of government in a free society'. Thus, Nevil Johnson argues of the UK that 'there was a shift of opinion and mood just sufficient to yield a modest parliamentary majority at the 1979 general election for a Conservative government committed ... to the reassertion of market principles' (Nevil Johnson, 1987, p. 155). Yet such talk of 'the changing mood of the electorate' really stands in lieu of an explanation and was one of the options seemingly ruled out by the public choice theorists' explanations of 'voting paradox' (see above, pp. 45-7).

Such developments might however be reconciled with a less dramatic view of crisis. Gough raises such a possibility in writing, broadly within the classical Marxist tradition, of crisis as a process of restructuring, in which new circumstances are established for successful capital accumulation. Writing at the end of the 1970s, Gough argued that such a restructuring could only be achieved through a systematic weakening of the power of working-class organizations and a retrenchment of the political and social rights that had been institutionalized in the post-war advanced capitalist world (Gough, 1979, pp. 151-2).

It is this perspective which can be seen to set the agenda for a second and distinctive species of crisis theories that came to dominate discussion in the 1980s (Taylor-Gooby, 1985, p. 14). We may think of these as 'crisis containment theories'. In such accounts, it is argued that the challenge which seemed in the 1970s to be addressed to democratic advanced capitalism itself has, in practice, been

---

6  OECD (1986b): of Proposition 13, it has been observed that it is difficult to sustain a view of California as a state in which the general citizenry faced ruin arising from profligate welfare expenditure.

displaced upon the social and economic policies that constituted the post-war welfare state. In fact, interventions in areas of social and economic policy have been successful in the limited though decisive sense that they have managed to contain and control, if not actually to resolve, those contradictory and crisis tendencies which earlier theorists had thought would imperil the very continuation of liberal democracy. If it is any longer appropriate to speak of a crisis, it is now a crisis within the institutions of welfare state social policy itself.

## Crisis: Containment and Reconstruction

Following Taylor-Gooby, we can isolate three sets of claims as characteristic of this 'crisis containment' theory. First, it is suggested that throughout the advanced capitalist world there has been a break with the political consensus for a managed economy and state welfare that characterized the post-war period. Secondly, this has been made possible by a 'sea-change' in public opinion, which has moved from support for collective solutions to problems of social need to a preference for market provision to satisfy individual welfare demands. Thirdly, and most importantly, these changes have opened the way for cuts in welfare entitlements and a 'restructuring' of public welfare provision. This indicates a move away from the model of a universalist, rights-based welfare state towards a more residualist, needs-governed system of public relief.

### The end of consensus

The argument of 'crisis containment' theorists is that while critics were right to observe a severe challenge to the post-war consensus in the heightened social and political struggles of the early 1970s, they were wrong to identify this with an unmanageable threat to the prevailing democratic capitalist order. The threatening contradictions of welfare capitalism have been, if not definitively resolved, then at least effectively managed. This has been achieved through a radical reconstruction of the social and political order of the advanced capitalist societies, a reconstruction in the interests of capital and parties of the right, achieved through an abandonment of the post-war consensus.

Although this is a process which has taken different forms in different countries, according to specifically local conditions, its definitive and most articulate expression is seen in the rise of 'Thatcherism', both in the UK and, by extension, elsewhere. Despite its self-ascribed single-mindedness and conviction, the precise meaning of 'Thatcherism' remains unclear. (see Jessop et al., 1988, pp. 3–56). For some, perhaps for Mrs Thatcher herself, it signifies, above all else, a rejection of the politics of consensus. According to Gamble, it represents 'a coherent hegemonic project', summarily constructed around the twin themes of 'the free economy and the strong state' (Gamble, 1988, p. 23). It is sometimes given a wider and international resonance, indicating a more generalized policy response to the perceived economic and social problems of the 1970s. Thus, Dennis Kavanagh writes that:

> economic recession and slow economic growth undermined popular support for the welfare consensus in a number of ... states. The Thatcher governments' policies of tax cuts, privatization, 'prudent' finance, squeezing state expenditure and cutting loss-making activities has had echoes in other western states. (Kavanagh, 1987, p. 9)

It is not perhaps surprising that the 'Thatcher agenda' should have an appeal for right-wing governments in the UK, the US and perhaps West Germany. What was seen as still more decisive for the proponents of 'crisis containment' was the extent to which avowedly socialist or social democratic governments were forced to adopt 'austerity' measures which mimicked the policies of right-wing governments. This might be taken to describe the experience of the Labour government in the UK in the late 1970s. To an extent, it even spread into the heartland of the welfare state in Scandinavia (particularly in Denmark). But perhaps most instructive was the experience of the Socialists in France, who, though elected on a radical socialist manifesto in 1981, were abruptly forced to 'U-turn' and embrace the politics of austerity. What seemed to divide this 'Thatcherism with a human face' from the real thing was a lack of enthusiasm for the policies adopted.

## The 'sea change' in popular opinion

This political abandonment of consensus could not have been effected, it is argued, had there not been a wholesale erosion of popular support for existing welfare state arrangements. There are some who argue that the working class never had a strong attachment to the idea of welfare rights and social citizenship, and who trace 'the long hostility of working people to what is perceived as dependency on public provision' (Selbourne, 1985, p. 117). Certainly, most commentators concede that public attitudes to welfare have always been ambivalent and that even where support for the welfare state has appeared to be strong, such strength has often been 'brittle'. Thus, Golding and Middleton identified in the UK of the 1960s 'behind a diffuse and lingering loyalty to the notion of "the welfare state" ... more severe views [that were] readily tapped' by its critics (Golding and Middleton, 1982, p. 229). On this basis, the economic downturn of the early 1970s afforded an opportunity for 'a fullscale assault on the welfare consensus', a consensus which 'has never taken deep root, and [which] was therefore relatively easy to dislodge by the return of an incisive neo-liberal rhetoric in the wake of the significant material shifts in working-class experience in the mid-1970s'. Certainly, '[b]y the 1979 election the thin veneer of the post war welfare consensus had been stripped down to a barely visible remnant' (Golding and Middleton, 1982, pp. 229, 205, 109).

Similarly, John Alt argued that people's support for the welfare state was basically 'altruistic ... supporting a benefit which will largely go to others'. In economic 'good times', when people's earnings are rising, they may be willing to afford such 'altruistic policies'. But times of 'economic stress', such as the 1970s, tend to be associated with 'less generosity' and a preference for 'spending cuts over taxation' (Alt, 1979, p. 258).

Perhaps the single clearest (and most widely challenged) statement of the case for a decline in public support for state welfare has come from the Institute of Economic Affairs. In the most recent of a series of surveys of UK public opinion on welfare, Harris and Seldon claim to have isolated

> a large, latent but suppressed desire for change in British education and medical care among high proportions of people of both sexes, all ages and incomes, whether officially at work or not, and of all political sympathies. (Harris and Seldon, 1987, p. 51; see also Harris and Seldon, 1979, p. 201)

## The decline of the welfare state as a decline of social democracy

Further evidence of this decline in popular support for the welfare state is premised on the growing electoral difficulties of social democratic parties and the renaissance of the political right. Social Democrats have long been identified as 'the party of the welfare state'. Their rise in the 1960s was often associated with the incorporation of the welfare state in advanced capitalist societies. Correspondingly, the decline in their popularity in the 1970s has been seen as evidence of a decline in support for the welfare state itself.

Here again, the most familiar examples are those of the UK, the US and West Germany. But perhaps more important are the examples of a shift to the right in the heartland of the welfare state. Of these, the most important examples are Denmark and, of course, Sweden where the return of a 'bourgeois' coalition in 1976 brought to an end 44 years of continuous social democratic government. But evidence of the decline of socialist parties is Europe-wide. The proportion of votes going to all left-wing parties (Social Democratic, Socialist and Communist) fell from 41.3 per cent in the 1960s to 40.1 per cent in the 1970s. In the same period, support for Conservative parties crept up from 24.6 to 24.9 per cent. In the early 1980s, the proportion of the Conservative vote advanced to 25.3 per cent. A still more dramatic picture emerges if we consider a shorter and more recent period. Thus, between 1977 and 1982, incumbent Socialists were defeated in the UK, West Germany, Belgium, Holland, Norway, Luxembourg and Denmark. In 1975, there were more than twice as many Socialist as Conservative cabinet ministers in European governments (54.1 per cent contrasted with 25.1 per cent). By 1982, the Conservative parties had established a one percentage point lead over the socialists (37.6 per cent Conservative; 36.4 per cent Socialist). Lane and Ersson conclude that the Socialist parties' position 'was reinforced during the 1950s and the 1960s; in the 1970s and early 1980s, however, a decline to a lower level set in'. For the parties of the right, by contrast, the data 'confirm the hypothesis of a conservative revival in the 1970s and early 1980s' (*The Economist*, 1982a, pp. 35–6; Lane and Ersson, 1987, pp. 112–15).

## 'The cuts'

The third, and possibly the most important element in the 'crisis containment' perspective was the spectre of cuts and 'restructuring' in social expenditure. On the basis of a change in popular and electoral opinion and given the successes of parties of the right and the breakdown of the politics of consensus, it seemed that the 1980s must be a decade of welfare retrenchment. For many commentators, both advocates and opponents, it seems as if there was to be a retreat from a universal welfare state based on citizenship towards a more modest policy of the relief of destitution upon the basis of demonstrated need.

The first public expenditure white paper of the newly elected UK Conservative government in 1979 maintained that 'public expenditure is at the heart of Britain's present economic difficulties' and, as we have seen, the single largest (and fastest-growing) aspect of this public spending was social expenditure (H.M. Treasury, 1979). Accordingly, the welfare state looked particularly vulnerable to retrenchment and within a year of Thatcher's election, Ian Gough was arguing that

Britain is experiencing the most far-reaching experiment in 'new right' politics in the Western world. [A number of] policy shifts ... contribute to this aim: legal sanctions against unions, mass unemployment by means of tight monetary controls, the cutting of social benefits for the families of strikers, a reduction in the social wage on several fronts, and a shift to more authoritarian practices in the welfare field. It represents one coherent strategy for managing the British crisis, a strategy aimed at the heart of the post-war Keynesian-welfare state settlement. (Gough, 1983, pp. 162–3)

Much the same process was identified in the US. Here it was said in 1986 that 'the Reagan administration and its big business allies have declared a new class war' against the working class and those reliant on social assistance (Piven and Cloward, 1986, p. 47). Writing in the same year, Michael Katz insists that

In the last several years, city governments have slashed services; state legislatures have attacked general assistance (outdoor relief to persons ineligible for benefits from other programs); and the Reagan administration has launched an offensive against social welfare and used tax policy to widen the income gap between rich and poor. (Katz, 1986, p. 274)

Perhaps even more telling were the prospects for retrenchment in the continental European welfare state. In September 1982, *The Economist* argued that 'during the 1980s, all rich countries' governments ... are likely to make ... big cuts in social spending'. Without such large-scale cuts in the UK, *The Economist* anticipated that public expenditure could reach 60 per cent of GNP by 1990! Within a month, it was reporting 'the withering of Europe's welfare states'. In West Germany, there were to be delays in pension increases, the collection of sickness insurance contributions from pensioners and an end to student grants. Holland faced 'a savage cutback', while the one-time leading welfare state, Denmark, was to seek a 7 per cent cut in public spending by reducing levels of unemployment compensation and introducing new charges for children's daycare. Most saliently, the newly elected Socialist government in France was introducing new charges to meet non-medical hospital costs and increasing social security contributions in a quest to curb spending by $12 billion in a full year. Only the perverse Swedes were 'the exception that proved the rule', re-electing a socialist government on an anti-cuts programme (*The Economist*, 1982b, pp. 67–8).

In contrast to some of the more committed of conservative politicians and the most enthusiastic of their supporters, few academic commentators have ever believed that the future belongs unproblematically to the New Right project. However, the 'crisis containment' perspective did offer a clear account of the breakdown of consensus, a popular political shift to the right and an unpicking of the fabric of the welfare state. It suggested that this change had successfully addressed the threat of systemic crisis that had been identified in the mid-1970s and replaced it with a more modest and piecemeal, if squalid, crisis for those in society who were most reliant upon the support of public services.

## Crisis of the Welfare State: Evaluation

The idea of crisis had a profound impact upon studies of the welfare state in the 1980s. To take just three examples, the Director of Social Affairs for the OECD argued that 'the lower growth of the OECD economies since the early 1970s ... put the Welfare State in crisis' (OECD, 1981). Pat Thane wrote in 1982 of 'a time when the post-war "welfare state" is being actively dismantled', while Ramesh Mishra began his study of *The Welfare State in Crisis* with the claim that 'the welfare state throughout the industrialized West is in disarray' (Mirhra, 1984). Just four years later it seemed as if this perspective had changed. In 1988, Jens Alber insisted 'that the concept of a welfare state crisis is neither necessary nor fruitful', while Michael Moran was still more definitive: 'There is no crisis of the welfare state' (Gass, 1981, p. 5; Thane, 1982, p. viii; Mishra, 1984, p. xiii; Alber, 1988a, p. 200; Moran, 1988, p. 412). It is some twenty years since the discourse of 'crisis' first achieved prominence and we are therefore now in a position to make some substantive judgements about the rise (and fall) of theories of crisis in the welfare state. This assessment is focused upon the three major species of crisis identified above.

### Welfare state crisis as 'external shock'

With the rise of the more dramatic accounts of systemic crisis and given the continuing problems of Western economies, it soon became commonplace to dismiss the idea of crisis arising from an 'external economic shock' as a naïve hankering for the 'good old days' of social peace and economic growth of the 1950s and 1960s. Certainly, it is a view with very real weaknesses. First, its confidence about the early re-establishment of the political and economic status quo ante was misplaced. Secondly, it lacked a sense of the interrelatedness of the political and economic problems of the advanced capitalist societies. Finally, it showed little awareness of the very real changes in the balance of economic and political forces that had been the consequence of twenty-five years of post-war economic growth.

Yet it is an approach which, with the benefit of still more hindsight, can be seen to have had some substantial strengths. Certainly, the crisis presented itself to many contemporaries as a problem of inadequate economic resources (trying to pay for more welfare with a stagnating national product), and there is indeed good reason to think that the crisis of the early 1970s was, in some senses, much more 'purely economic' than later critics were to allow. Thus, much of the perceived 'spiralling' of welfare costs was due not to 'democratic distemper' but to the logic of demographic pressure and statutory entitlement under circumstances of recession. This was simply an expression of the double-bind that the welfare state always faces under circumstances of recession, as national product and taxation revenue *fall*, while demands for welfare compensation *rise*. Further, as the more dire predictions of neo-Marxists and New Right analysts have failed to materialize, so it may seem that the difficulties of the welfare state are indeed more appropriately seen to be based in the shortfall of resources available to fund further growth. Such a belief is buttressed by recent evidence that the best indicator of the capacity of national welfare states to weather the difficulties of the 1970s was not so much a reflection of their *political* complexion (the intensity of their democratic contradictions), as of a given nation's *economic* strength before the 1970s and of its capacity to absorb the oil shock of 1973 (Schmidt, 1983, pp. 1–26).

However, even if we concentrate solely upon economic developments, it is clear that the changes observed in the early 1970s were both more profound and longer lasting than the idea of a one-off 'shock to the system' supposed. This new economic context is not adequately defined by one or two hikes in the price of basic commodities but rather by a whole series of changes in the international political economy which cumulatively shattered the stability of the post-war economic order. Such changes include the decline in stable exchange rates, the loss of the hegemonic role of the US, changing international terms of trade, the rise of newly industrialized countries, changing financial institutions, the impact of new technologies and the continuing de-industrialization/post-industrialization of the advanced capitalist economies. For a number of commentators, changes of this kind add up to a systematic transition from the sorts of *organized capitalism* which had characterized much of the twentieth century towards a new period of *disorganized capitalism*. The changes represent then not so much a crisis for advanced capitalism as the process of establishing what Flora calls 'a changed historical macro-constellation' (Flora, 1985, p. 26). However, the challenge posed to the welfare state may still be severe, since the welfare state was one of the major institutional pillars of that organized form of capitalism which it is suggested is in the process of being transformed (Lash and Urry, 1987; Offe, 1985).

## The welfare state and the crisis of liberal democratic capitalism

The theoretical poverty of the perspective of 'external shock' has often been contrasted with New Right or neo-Marxist critics who are seen to have penetrated the 'depth structure' of contradictions in the welfare state. Certainly, there are considerable strengths in the shared features of these accounts of crisis. They were among the first to develop a modern 'political economy' approach, indicating that while the *symptoms* of the difficulties of the 1970s were economic, their *causes* lay in the interrelation of social, political and economic forces. They were also among the first to indicate that the recession of 1973–4 was not simply a 'blip' in the continuing process of unfettered post-war economic growth, in which 'business as usual' could be restored just so soon as the 'oil shock' had been absorbed. They demonstrated that inflation had not just a political *consequence* but also, in part, a political *cause*. They drew out the political consequences of the growing complexity and complicity of government, of greater bureaucratic and organizational density and of the rise of organized and sectional interests, under circumstances of representative democracy and full employment.

However, the glaring weakness in this analysis is that the substance of its claims about a systemic crisis of advanced capitalism and/or liberal representative democracy remain substantially unfulfilled. In the UK, where the prognoses were often the most gloomy, there has been little real challenge to the political process. There is evidence of growing electoral volatility (masked by the plurality voting system), evidence of declining public deference to government, of the intensified prosecution of sectional interests and of a break with elements of consensus government. There has been an erosion of local government democracy, the circumscription of some civil liberties and the curtailment of trade union rights. All of these have met with more or less fierce resistance. But there has been no real threat of a breakdown of liberal democratic government and limited interest in major constitutional reforms (outside the minor and nationalist parties). In the same period, a right-wing government has been returned to office three times (at least twice with a large plurality of votes), while welfare spending in the major areas (pensions, health and education) has remained largely intact.

Why were analysts on both left and right so mistaken about the consequences of the welfare state structures they helped to reveal? First, there is an element of misunderstanding of the nature of the welfare state. For the New Right, the welfare state was seen largely as an unproductive deadweight on the economy, imposed through the dynamics of irresponsible (social) democracy. In the prevalent Marxist account, the welfare state was the necessary legitimating trade-off for (the unacceptable social costs of) capital accumulation. For both, the inevitable outcome was fiscal crisis. But such a view is difficult to reconcile with the historical development of the welfare state outlined in chapter 4. The welfare state was *not* generally an imposition of organized labour through the pressure of electoral politics. It was as much (if not more) the product of conservative or liberal regimes. It was as frequently (if not more often) status-preserving or market-supporting as it was decommodifying. In fact, evidence that, as both New Right and neo-Marxists seem to assume, the welfare state dampens capitalist economic growth is limited at both 'micro' and 'macro' levels. Similarly, the claims that public spending displaces private investment or that social benefits represent a real disincentive to labour are thinly grounded.[7] Certainly, under some circumstances and as part of a broader constellation of forces, social spending may be complicit in poor economic performance. But this is something different from the claim that social spending *causes* poor economic performance (Pen, 1987, pp. 346–7). Indeed, Nicholas Barr argues that the welfare state has a 'major efficiency role' and that, in a context of market failures, 'we need a welfare state for efficiency reasons, and would continue to do so even if all distributional problems had been solved' (Barr, 1987, p. 421; Blake and Ormerod, 1980; Block, 1987).

The UK case is peculiarly instructive in this context. The UK was often portrayed in the literature of the 1970s as the country with the most pronounced problems of overload, ungovernability and welfare state malaise, so much so that this complex was often identified as 'the English disease' (see, for example, Jay, 1977). Yet, we have seen that the UK was not an especially large welfare spender, nor were the terms of her social benefits either very generous or particularly 'decommodifying'. There were consistently more extensive and generous welfare states with a far better economic record. The size and disposition of the UK public sector and welfare state might

---

7   Nicholas Barr insists that 'the effect of the welfare state on capital accumulation and output growth, despite much research and strident polemics, remains largely *terra incognita*' (Barr, 1987, p. 424).

contribute to its economic difficulties, but only in a context of much longer established problems of economic growth and capital formation (Gamble, 1981). Conversely, as Mishra points out, New Right critics at least tended to neglect those welfare states with a good economic record (Austria, Sweden) or to attribute their success to fortunate and extraneous circumstances (Mishra, 1984, p. 56). In general, this 'Anglocentric' bias (which has long been observed by continental analysts of the welfare state) is also a clue to the weakness of the more apocalyptic theses of contradiction and ungovernability (Flora and Heidenheimer, 1981a, p. 21). Thus Anthony Birch maintains that the New Right thesis is only sustainable for the UK at a very particular historical moment. Seeking to extrapolate from these very particular circumstances, a general theory of the prospects for representative liberal democracy is quite unwarranted (Birch, 1984, pp. 158–9).

Perhaps a clue to these misunderstandings can be found in the problematic use of 'contradiction'. 'Contradiction' as a description of the welfare state can only mean 'perverse outcomes', 'real oppositions' or 'competing objectives'. However, both New Right and neo-Marxist critics have tended to employ it as if its 'proper' sense of irreconcilability (A and not-A) applied to this analogical usage. Correspondingly, they are persuaded to see (irreconcilable) contradictions, where only (deeply problematic but potentially manageable) conflicts exist.

A number of more specific problems can be identified in these accounts. New Right critics in particular have tended to overstate the powers of trades unions. Even at the height of their ascendancy in the early 1970s, unions were essentially the reactive and defensive organizations of labour (Clarke and Clements, 1977; Hyman, 1989a). All governments, and not only those who saw it as potentially therapeutic, have found it difficult to control unemployment. This, in concert with growing international competition and greater capital mobility, has radically curtailed even this limited power of trades unions. Similarly, the last fifteen years have seen no inexorable rise of social democratic parties, irresponsibly promising 'more for less'. (Nor, it should be noted, is the currently fashionable 'ascendancy of the right' likely to prove any more inevitable or permanent.) Despite the ubiquitous talk of governments 'buying' electoral victories through irresponsible manipulation of the economy, such empirical evidence as there is suggests that the impact of the 'political business cycle' has been greatly exaggerated. In Alt and Chrystal's view, 'no one could read the political business cycle literature without being struck by the lack of supporting evidence' (Alt and Chrystal, 1983).

Finally, it is worth drawing attention to the inadequacies of the accounts of legitimacy that underpin many of these accounts of crisis. Both left (notably Habermas and Wolfe) and right suggest that the difficulties surrounding the welfare state are likely finally to express themselves as a crisis of legitimacy of the democratic capitalist order (Habermas, 1976; Wolfe, 1979). But it seems clear that this is to operate with a conception of legitimacy which belongs to constitutional theory rather than to political sociology. The principle of legitimacy as the acknowledged right to rule is not one that has a prominent place in the day-to-day thinking of the democratic citizen. As Rose and Peters indicated, even 'political bankruptcy' does not mean fighting on the streets (Rose and Peters, 1978). Michael Mann has given definitive expression to the view that the 'social cohesion of liberal democracy' rests primarily upon an *absence* of considerations of legitimacy, upon the fact that the average citizen does not have a comprehensive view of the legitimate claims and limitations of governmental authority. It is a mistake to look to a legitimation crisis where legitimacy is not constituted in the way that analysts of its anticipated crisis suppose (Habermas, 1976; Wolfe, 1979; Mann, 1970).

## Crisis Contained?

We have seen that as the prospect of an institutional or constitutional débâcle receded towards the end of the 1970s, a new species of theory, that of 'crisis containment', gained increasing prominence. Upon such an account, any threat posed to the existing social and political order during the 1970s had effectively been displaced into a crisis of the welfare state itself. The end of political consensus (in part premised upon general support for the welfare state), a shift to the right in public opinion and public policy initiatives to cut spending had 'saved' capitalism only by imperilling the post-war welfare state. How convincing is this second school of crisis thinking?

## The End of Consensus?

We saw that it was possible to define consensus as either inter-party or inter-class, but that whichever form it took it could be isolated in policy terms around (1) the maintenance of a comprehensive welfare state, (2) support of the 'mixed economy' and (3) policies of full employment and sustained economic growth. There were always those opposed to consensus, and though we are now inclined to think of the breach with consensus as an intervention from the right, it is worth recalling that some of the earliest mobilization against the social democratic consensus came from the left in the late 1960s and early 1970s. Similarly, while we think of the break being consummated towards the end of the 1970s, 'the beginning of the end of consensus' might be as convincingly retraced to the late 1960s. Even if we identify the demise of consensus with this later date, it is worth recalling that some on the left welcomed this as an opportunity to radicalize politics around the failure of the social democratic 'management of capitalism'.

One of the lessons of empirical research on the welfare state in the 1980s has been to trace the *diversity* of developments in the last twenty years. Faced with similar difficulties, though under national-ly variable circumstances, there has been a variety of responses within the Western welfare states. As the nature of the consensus varied among countries, so too has the process of its 'deconstruc-tion' been far from uniform. Thus the consequences of the election of parties of the right committed to reform in Sweden (1976), the UK (1979) and Germany (1982) are widely different given the variation in national backgrounds.

## The UK: The Definitive End of Consensus?

The most abrupt 'end to consensus' is often ascribed to the UK in which a quarter of a century of Butskellite agreement between Con-servative and Labour parties was seen to yield in 1979 to the rad-ically anti-consensus politics of Thatcherism. Here is potentially the most fruitful ground for the 'end of consensus' theory. Certainly, the polemical hostility to consensus was clear. In 1981, Margaret Thatcher dismissed consensus as

> The process of abandoning all beliefs, principles, values and pol-icies ... avoiding the very issues that have got to be solved merely to get people to come to an agreement on the way ahead. (cited in Kavanagh and Morris, 1989, p. 119)

In the 1979 election campaign, the Conservatives in the UK pre-sented themselves as a party breaking with the exhausted legacy of post-war politics. This break extended to each of the major policy elements of consensus. In terms of the 'mixed economy', there was a commitment to return publicly owned industries to the private sector and to limit government interventions in the day-to-day man-agement of relations between employers and employees. There was a commitment to sustained or enhanced economic growth, but this was to be achieved by an *abandonment* of Keynesian economics and the commitment to full employment in favour of monetarism and supply-side reforms. On the welfare state, there was to be a drive to cut costs by concentrating resources upon those in greatest need, to restrain the bureaucratic interventions of the 'nanny state' in the day-to-day life of citizens, a greater role for voluntary welfare institutions and the encouragement of individuals to make provision for their individual welfare through the private sector (encouraging private pensions, private healthcare and private education).

Certainly, the 1979 general election in the UK may be described as a watershed. Labour had been in office for eleven of the previous fifteen years. This election brought to power a Conservative government that remained in office throughout the 1980s and won three consecutive elections. The 1979 election also saw a major defection of skilled working-class voters from Labour to Conservative. Yet in judging the breach with consensus that it represented, one must be circumspect.

First, the break-up of the consensus pre-dates the election of the Conservatives in 1979. As early as 1970, Richard Crossman heard 'the sound of the consensus breaking up' (Crossman, 1970). The first two years of the Heath government (1970–2) had been committed to the sort of neo-liberalism that the 1979 Thatcher government promised. It was the Labour government of 1974–9 that presided over the earliest retrenchment in welfare spending and a (then) unprecedented rise in post-war unemployment. The ill-fated 'Social Contract' may be seen less as the culmination of post-war collaboration of capital, labour and the state than as a desperate attempt to hold together forms of corporatist bargaining which had already been undermined and were destined to issue in the sort of débâcle that was seen in 'the Winter of Discontent' of 1978/9 (Deakin, 1987, pp. 2–3).

Turning to the record of the post-1979 Thatcher government, political practice did not always match party rhetoric. Certainly, unemployment was allowed to reach unheard-of levels (officially in excess of three million) and a string of major public corporations and utilities were returned to the private sector (notably British Telecom, British Gas, British Airways and water supply and sewerage services). There was a major (and popular) drive to sell off public housing and there were limited cuts in expenditure on education. Yet in the period of the first Thatcher administration total social expenditure showed a significant growth of about 10 per cent, rising as a proportion of GDP from 21.7 per cent to 23.6 per cent. Much of this increase was the consequence of extremely high levels of unemployment and low economic growth (Taylor-Gooby, 1985, p. 72).

In 1985, the government Green Paper on *The Reform of Social Security* ('The Fowler Reviews') promised 'the most fundamental examination of our social security system since the Second World War' (DHSS, 1985). The proposals – and especially the abolition of State Earnings Related Pensions (SERPS) which had been introduced as a bipartisan policy as recently as 1975 – were condemned by the government's critics as a break with the welfare state consensus (Kavanagh, 1987, p. 27). But when government legislation was brought forward, it contained substantial concessions and, most importantly, a scaling-down rather than abolition of SERPS. There were limited inducements for private welfare provision and a deterioration in the terms of welfare services for the least privileged. But the major and mainstream pillars of the welfare state (public pensions and the National Health Service) were largely unscathed and there was no effective cut in social expenditure. In 1985/6, this stood at £36 billion, a third higher than its 1979 level (Kavanagh, 1987, p. 217). More recently, the government has made efforts to address the issue of reforms within the NHS. However, these proposals focus upon 'internal market' reforms rather than a wholesale commitment to the privatization of healthcare and retain the commitment to a service 'available to all, regardless of income, and to be financed mainly out of general taxation' (Thatcher, 1989). Even so, the government has run into acute public and professional resistance and the political outcome remains unclear.

The Thatcher governments were significantly different from those that preceded them. In the area of the welfare state, there have been important changes – the sale of council houses, the 'contracting out' of ancillary services in hospitals, the 'opting out' of schools from local government control, the depreciation of child benefit, the promotion of private healthcare. But these changes have not necessarily meant a saving to the public purse. Greater home ownership, for all its promise of greater self-reliance, imposes a financial burden in tax expenditures on mortgage interest relief. This increased by almost five times between 1963/4 and 1983/4 rising in the period from 1979 to 1983 alone by 44 per cent. In 1985/6, the cost of mortgage interest relief was officially estimated to have been about £4.5 billion (rising to £5.5 billion in 1988/9), exemption from capital gains tax approximately £2.5 billion and council house sales discounts a further £1 billion (Taylor-Gooby, 1985, p. 84; Forrest and Murie, 1988; Forrest, 1988; CSO, 1990, p. 93). The 'heartlands' of the welfare state – pensions and healthcare – have proven extremely difficult to restrain. On healthcare, the government has increased real spending, while facing charges from all quarters of systematic underfunding.[8] This looks like a very traditional problem of post-war governments. Finally, Mrs Thatcher's successor, John Major, in distancing himself from the New Right's more radical proposals for reform, has insisted that 'the welfare state is an integral part of the British instinct. It will remain an integral part of the British instinct' (cited in The *Guardian*, 1990).

Indeed, the problem of funding pensions and health is one which the Thatcher administration has shared with governments throughout the advanced industrialized world (OECD, 1984; OECD, 1986a). It is to this international context that we turn in the remaining pages of this chapter. Earlier we identified three areas as the definitive testing ground for an 'end to welfare state consensus'. These were (1) changing public opinion, (2) the decline of 'welfare state parties' and (3) changes in public policy. We shall consider each of these in its international context.

## Changes in Public Opinion

One of the principal claims of 'crisis containment' was that, in contrast to the period in which the post-war consensus was constructed and sustained, popular opinion has shifted away from support for equity and citizenship through the welfare state. Crudely put, public welfare was something which people would support in economic 'good times', when both public and private consumption could rise, but to which they were much less sympathetic in times of economic stagnation. A strictly temporary and provisional support for the welfare state had been dissipated through an appeal to traditional and much more deep-seated hostility to the poor and indolent.

Perhaps the fullest review of international public opinion on the welfare state is Coughlin's *Ideology, Public Opinion and Welfare Policy*. Across a sample of eight rich nations he found that

> public attitudes toward the principles of social policy have developed along similar lines both of acceptance and rejection. The

---

8   This seeming paradox of increasing expenditure and a worsening record of meeting demand is often explained in terms of (1) the demographic pressure of an ageing population, (2) the 'technological push' of new medical technologies making more treatments possible, (3) the 'relative price effect' that follows from the labour-intensive nature of healthcare and (4) supplier control over the level of production (Cullis and West, 1979; Ashmore, Mulkay and Pinch, 1989).

idea of collective responsibility for assuring minimum standards of employment, health care, income, and other conditions of social and economic well-being has everywhere gained a foothold in popular values and beliefs. And yet the survey evidence suggests a simultaneous tendency supporting individual achievement, mobility, and responsibility for one's own lot, and rejecting the elimination of aspects of economic life associated with capitalism. (Coughlin, 1980, p. 31)

Levels of support varied between 'big spenders', such as Sweden and France, and 'low spenders', such as the US and Australia. Generally, 'a country's mix of economic collectivism and economic individualism will match its social spending and taxing and the actual amount of government intervention' (Wilensky, 1980, p. xii). But broadly the same patterns of support were revealed. The same areas – pensions, public health insurance, family/child allowances – were most popular (and expensive) and the same sort of provision – unemployment compensation and public assistance – the least popular. Not only between nations, but between social classes and across political sympathies, it seemed that everyone liked pensions and no-one liked 'scroungers' (Coughlin, 1980, p. 52).

More recently, Tom Smith has drawn together international survey material that reveals a similar pattern. Collating evidence for the US, Austria, West Germany, Italy and the UK, Smith records very strong endorsements of government responsibility for health care (94.5 per cent) and for ensuring 'a decent standard of living for the old' (95.2 per cent). His more recent evidence shows majority support everywhere for increased government spending on healthcare and an average of 57 per cent in favour of increased retirement benefits. In both these areas, questions controlled clearly for 'tax blindness', and again in both areas the UK showed the highest disposition for increased spending (at 87.8 and 74.6 per cent, respectively). In the more stigmatized area of unemployment benefit, the proportion favouring increased spending was much lower (at 33.3 per cent) but this was still greater than those who favoured a reduction in such support (at 21.9 per cent). The endorsement by an average of 70.2 per cent of respondents of the view that it was 'the government's responsibility to ... provide a job for everyone who wants one' suggests that the question of unemployment elicits responses to perceived indolence rather than to state intervention in the economy. Again, given the choice, respondents everywhere saw the government's responsibility to keep unemployment down as more important than its responsibility to control inflation (Smith, 1987).

Taylor-Gooby's recent review of the international evidence, looking at the same five countries plus Australia, reveals lower absolute *levels* of popular support, but a similar *ranking* of both countries and programmes (Taylor-Gooby, 1989). The survey material recorded majorities everywhere for increased state spending on healthcare (88 per cent in the UK and 81 per cent in Italy), and a clear (unweighted) majority for increases in old age pensions (with support highest again in the UK and Italy, which had positive responses of 75 and 76 per cent, respectively). As in Smith's survey, the endorsement of increased state spending on the unemployed was much lower, with only the Italians mustering majority support (Taylor-Gooby, 1989, p. 41). Yet Smith has continued to record substantial majorities everywhere supporting increased state spending on benefits for the poor (Smith, 1989, p. 62). Overall, Taylor-Gooby has concluded that

> the attitudes of the citizens of the six nations correspond more closely to the traditional post-war settlement than they reveal any enthusiasm for change, although within this framework there are substantial national variations ... Social welfare that provides for mass needs is warmly endorsed, but provision for minorities, whose interests challenge the work ethic, receives meagre approval. Direct social engineering to advance equality of outcomes is not endorsed. (Taylor-Gooby, 1989, p. 49)

Taylor-Gooby's more detailed if parochial survey of public opinion in the UK reveals a similar pattern. His evidence suggests that

> a general climate of opinion exists among the public that strongly supports services for the elderly, the sick and disabled, education and the NHS, and is antipathetic to benefits for the unemployed, low paid, lone parents and children ... (Taylor-Gooby, 1985, p. 29)

In the favoured areas there is support for increased spending even when the tax consequences are made explicit. Least favoured are those areas of provision to minorities – one-parent benefits, unemployment benefits – from which most taxpayers do not foresee themselves benefiting. Taylor-Gooby reports an ambivalent attitude to public/private provision. Generally, the public is concerned with the nature of the benefits received and their cost. Delivery through the public or private sector is not a pressing concern. Many persist in endorsing both public and private provision, persuading Taylor-Gooby to conclude that the 'sentiments that support privatisation are real. They coexist with countervailing sentiments of collectivism' (Taylor-Gooby, 1986, p. 244). Furthermore, Coughlin's analysis 're-vealed that in all the nations for which we have data, anti-tax/welfare sentiments are nowhere expressed by clear majorities of national populations, and that continued popular support for im-proved programs is broadly based' (Coughlin, 1980, p. 151).

Overall, the pattern of popular attitudes to state welfare is com-plex but stable. There is public hostility to certain areas of state provision, probably some repressed demand masked by state com-pulsion, hostility to certain categories of beneficiary and some sup-port for private/market provision of welfare services. However, these views are not new and they coexist with widespread popular endorsement of the most expensive and extensive elements of state provision. There is little evidence here of large-scale popular back-lash against the welfare state.

## The Demise of 'the Welfare State Party'

We have seen that, however doubtful is the *historical* basis of such a claim, the welfare state has come to be strongly identified with socialist and particularly social democratic parties. Another source of evidence of decline in popular support for the welfare state is thus to be found in the decline of these parties of the welfare state. Evidence of such a decline was considered above. It included (1) a series of defeats of social democratic governments in Europe and North America between 1977 and 1982, (2) a long-term decline in left-wing voting after 1960 and (3) a fall of more than a third in socialist participation in government between 1975 and 1982. It is clear that there was a movement (perhaps more properly a counter-movement) against the left in this period. However, obituaries for 'the strange death of social democracy' are surely premature (Kava-nagh, 1987, pp. 4–5). Thus, the combined electoral strength of the left in Western Europe, which had stood at 40.1 per cent through the 1970s, advanced to 42.5 per cent in the period 1980–3. In the 1980s, while the right has taken or retained power in the UK, the US and West Germany, the left has retained or been restored to office in Sweden, France, Spain, Portugal and Greece (*Keesing's World Events*, 1989). Following the 1989 European Parliament elections, the Social-ists formed the single largest group (with 180 members), while the Conservatives were reduced to 34 members, with the Christian Democrats forming the second-largest grouping of 121 MEPs (*Keesing's World Events*, 1989, p. 36818). Throughout this period it has tended to be the socialist/social democratic parties which have

**Table 5.2**   Changing patterns of electoral support for left-wing parties

|  | Most recent election (up to 1987) % | Average of previous three elections % | Change % |
|---|---|---|---|
| Greece | 57.5 | 40.3 | +17.2 |
| New Zealand | 42.6 | 39.7 | +2.9 |
| Spain | 47.9 | 46.1 | +1.8 |
| West Germany | 45.3 | 43.6 | +1.7 |
| Norway | 46.9 | 45.5 | +1.4 |
| Sweden | 50.1 | 48.8 | +1.3 |
| Belgium | 29.4 | 28.5 | +0.9 |
| Netherlands | 35.1 | 35.2 | −0.1 |
| Australia | 46.3 | 47.4 | −1.1 |
| Denmark | 46.6 | 48.5 | −1.9 |
| Switzerland | 23.7 | 26.8 | −3.1 |
| UK | 31.3 | 35.5 | −4.2 |
| Finland | 37.7 | 42.1 | −4.4 |
| France | 42.9 | 49.5 | −6.6 |
| Austria | 43.8 | 50.7 | −6.9 |
| Portugal | 39.4 | 52.0 | −12.0 |

*Source*:   Pulzer (1987) p. 387

gained ground *within* the left everywhere (including the stronghold of the former Communist Party in Italy).[9]

In fact, the experience of the left in the 1980s was a mixed one, as table 5.2 illustrates. On the basis of this evidence, Peter Pulzer insists that there is no reason to presume that we are witnessing 'a long-term and unstoppable decline of parties of the democratic Left' (Pulzer, 1987, p. 388).

Writing of the ascendancy of the Reagan presidency in the US, Kelley insists that there is 'almost no support for the view that the Reagan administration came to power as the result of an increasingly insistent popular demand for the economic and welfare policies Reagan had proposed'. He concludes that 'opposition to New Deal-like policies won some support for Reagan, but it had won support

---

9   In Italy, the PCI (communists) outvoted the PSI (socialists) by a proportion of less than 2:1 in the 1989 European parliamentary elections, compared with a proportion of 3:1 in the previous European elections of 1984 (*Keesing's World Events*, 1989, p. 36876). Indeed, after much soul searching, the PCI decided to reconstitute itself as the Democratic Party of the Left (PDS).

in roughly equal measure for all Republican candidates since 1952'
(Kelley, 1988, p. 7). Of course, a revival of the social democratic left
might be much less important if these were no longer 'the parties of
the welfare state', that is, if the period of right-wing ascendancy had
so transformed the political agenda that a *new consensus* had been
formed in which the welfare state now had a much reduced place.
There is some evidence that certain traditional goals of the left, such
as public ownership, may have been downgraded, though as much
in response to changes in the international political economy as
to the ascendant ideology of the New Right. To assess claims that
the welfare state may be similarly displaced, we need to consider
the way that the welfare state has itself fared over the past ten to
fifteen years.

## 'The Cuts'

We have already reviewed the general evidence of cuts in welfare
state provision since the early 1970s. However, a fuller survey of the
evidence reveals that while most states enacted some programme
cutbacks, most also introduced new forms of entitlement and in
most countries social spending has continued to grow faster than
GDP. Alber notes that in 'all countries except Germany ... the
social transfer expenditure ratio [was] higher in 1984 than in 1975'
(Alber, 1988a, p. 187). Certainly, there has been a major restraint in
the levels of *growth* of social expenditure. Between 1960 and 1975,
real growth in social expenditure stood at about 8 per cent a year.
Between 1975 and 1981, this rate of real growth was halved to just
over 4 per cent (OECD, 1984). But only four countries (the US,
Canada, the Netherlands and West Germany) saw reduced social
expenditure ratios (of a maximum of 1.1 per cent in West Germany),
while these ratios continued to increase substantially in seven countries (Sweden, France, Belgium, Austria, Japan, Italy and Finland).
While in some countries (West Germany, Switzerland, Norway,
Finland, the US) welfare state expansion largely came to a halt after
1985, in others (Sweden, Denmark, Belgium, France, Ireland and, to
a lesser extent, Austria and Italy) it continued to expand. Reviewing
this evidence, Jens Alber concludes:

> the welfare state has continued to grow in most Western European
> countries even throughout the most recent period of austerity.
> Only in four countries have the expansionary trends come to a
> visible halt. Nowhere, however, did the expenditure ratios fall
> below the record levels reached in the early 1970s. This suggests
> an interpretation of the recent period as a phase of consolidation
> rather than of welfare state dismantling. (Alber, 1988b, p. 463)

Table 5.3 offers a useful summary of recent Western European evidence on welfare retrenchment and backlash.

**Table 5.3** Welfare state curtailments and popular reactions in Western European countries

| Country | Curtailments | Backlash symptoms | Mass attitudes (survey results) |
|---|---|---|---|
| Sweden | Starting in 1981–2 (bourgeois government); cuts in health, housing, various transfers including pensions; extensions in child allowances and unemployment benefits | 1976 electoral victory of bourgeois parties, 1982 Social Democrats re-elected; polarization between employers' associations and trade unions weakening corporatist consensus on social policy | Declining welfare state support during late 1970s; trend turned in favour of welfare state in 1980s; majority in favour of welfare state schemes |
| Denmark | Starting in 1980 (social democratic government), continued with more severe cuts under bourgeois government; cuts in health, social assistance, unemployment benefits; pensions relatively safeguarded; extensions in various programmes | 1973 rupture of established party system with rise of anti-tax party whose share of the votes halved in subsequent years; 1982 election victory of bourgeois parties, re-elected in subsequent years; declining social policy consensus among major parties | Declining welfare state support in 1973; rising support in subsequent years; in 1984 highest welfare state support since 1969 |
| Finland | Starting in 1977 (social democratic government); cuts in health and various transfers; extensions in some fields mixed with cutbacks in others | Basic pro-welfare state consensus among all major parties | Declining welfare state support between 1975 and 1980, rising support after 1980; majority across all social groups in favour of welfare state |

| | | | |
|---|---|---|---|
| Norway | Starting in 1980–1 (social democratic government); continued under conservative government; cuts in health and various transfer schemes; extensions especially for low-income groups | Foundation of anti-tax party in 1970s; 1981 government turnover in favour of bourgeois parties, later re-elected | Sudden decline in welfare state support in 1973 which later disappeared; large, but slightly declining pro-welfare state majorities; percentage in favour of cutbacks in 1980 same as in 1965 |
| UK | Starting in 1980 under conservative government; cuts in housing, education, unemployment benefits and various transfers; segmentation into protected schemes (pensions) and marginal sectors susceptible to curtailments | Government turnover to Conservatives in 1979, later re-elected; increasing ideology in social policy since 1970s | Move in favour of social programmes after 1979; percentage in favour of tax cuts halved between 1979 and 1983 |
| West Germany | Starting in 1975 (social democratic government), continued more severely under conservative governments; cuts in social assistance, unemployment compensation, health and various transfers; pensions relatively safeguarded; minor re-extensions since 1985 | 1982 government turnover to bourgeois parties, later re-elected; no symptoms of an organized backlash | Declining welfare state support from 1978 to 1983; turning of trend in 1984 with growing resistance against further cutbacks; large pro-welfare state majorities across all social groups |

**Table 5.3** *(Cont.)*

| Country | Curtailments | Backlash symptoms | Mass attitudes *(survey results)* |
|---------|--------------|-------------------|-----------------------------------|
| Italy | Starting in 1978 under national solidarity government with communist support; more severe cuts from 1981 to 1983; cutbacks targeted on health and pensions; several extensions counteracting restrictive measures | Politicization of welfare state issues with group formation against or in favour of social programmes; growing white-collar mobilization against selectively targeted benefits | Slightly declining welfare state support between 1978 and 1982, but still large majorities in favour of existing social programmes |
| Ireland | Starting in 1980; cutbacks targeted on health, unemployment compensation and various services; pensions safeguarded; some minor extensions | Growing resistance after 1979, dying out in 1983; growing party consensus on welfare state issues | (no longitudinal data) |

*Source:* Alber (1988a) p. 194

# Conclusion

Evidence of crisis in any of the principal senses in which it has been addressed in this chapter is extremely thin. Claims about the de-stabilization of liberal democracy, the decimation of social expenditure and the withdrawal of public support for major welfare programmes have been poorly vindicated. Certainly, since 1975, 'the growth party is over' and growth in the welfare state has been severely (though varyingly) restrained. However, in contrast to the rather grand generalizations of both New Right and neo-Marxists, Manfred Schmidt may be right to identify 'muddling through' as the generic form of government policy throughout this period (Schmidt, 1983, pp. 14ff). Taylor-Gooby concludes rather bleakly that, far from being transformed, 'The forces that mould the status quo are still alive' (Taylor-Gooby, 1985, p. 142).

However, this does not mean that all is well with the welfare state. First, the reconstruction of the international political economy has definitively altered the circumstances in which welfare states have to operate. Exposing national economies and national corporatist arrangements to an unregulated world economy has transformed the circumstances under which any government might seek, for example, to pursue a policy of full employment. The long-term consequences for the welfare state of this change in the world economy are likely to be profound. Secondly, changes in the economy nationally and internationally may transform the configuration of individuals' interests and the political articulation of those interests. The character of a welfare state cannot be adequately measured by levels of aggregate spending. Long-term high levels of unemployment amidst societies of generally rising affluence, increasingly segmented labour markets and new patterns of consumption may change the disposition of social expenditure. Rising levels of social spending and continuing public endorsement of the popular elements of the welfare state may well be consistent with an internal transformation from a solidary, universalistic, citizenship-based welfare state towards a system based on the more generous provision of insurance-style entitlement and a further deterioration in the position of the poor and stigmatized (Alber, 1988a, pp. 187–9; see also Parry, 1986, pp. 155–240).

Finally, what may remain in the face of all our evidence is an *intellectual* crisis of the welfare state. That is, the social democratic vision of the welfare state as the mechanism for taming capitalism through redistributive social policy may be losing its authority. Its core elements, the commitment to economic growth, the enabling capacity of the state bureaucracy and the attempt to exercise indirect control over capital are increasingly under challenge. The 'welfare state malaise' of which Therborn writes, is identified not only by the New Right or neo-Marxist left but also by 'supply-side socialists' and ecologists (Therborn, 1986). On both left and right, the claims of mutualism, voluntarism and self-help are being reassessed. It is to these prognoses for the future of the welfare state that we turn in the final chapter.

# 6
# Beyond the Welfare State?

In this final chapter, I return explicitly to the issue of whether and in what sense we are moving towards social and political arrangements that are 'beyond the welfare state', and particularly to the challenge that such changes pose for traditional social democracy. Some of the most important grounds for anticipating such a transformation in welfare arrangements were contained in propositional form towards the end of the Introduction. Summarily, these suggested that existing welfare state arrangements were unlikely to survive because of (1) the long-term incompatibility of the welfare state with a market economy, (2) changes in the international political economy leading to an erosion of class compromise between organized labour and organized capital, (3) changes in class structure and patterns of consumption leading to an erosion of the alliance for public welfare between middle and working classes, (4) changes in class structure and patterns of consumption leading to an erosion of class solidary action within the 'broad' working class itself and (5) the incompatibility of a growth-based welfare state with the securing of genuine individual and social well-being. This final chapter is given over to an assessment of these claims in the light of the evidence considered in earlier chapters. We shall see that at least some of the problems raised in the Introduction, and more fully elaborated in the following theoretical chapters, arise from a serious misunderstanding of the nature and history of the international welfare states, but also that a very serious challenge remains, particularly for social democrats.

## Markets v. the Welfare State

This element of misunderstanding is particularly clear in some of the more apocalyptic claims made about the incompatibility of the welfare state and the market economy. In chapter 5, we saw that claims of crisis and contradiction in the welfare state were largely misplaced, and the more dramatic forebodings of the mid-1970s much exaggerated. In part, this misunderstanding arose from imprecision in the use of the core terms 'crisis' and 'contradiction'; in part, it built upon misreadings of the political forces behind the rise of the welfare state, of the nature of its interaction with the economy and indeed of the extent to which welfare states have always been (varyingly) subordinate to the logic of the market. It was also informed by some improbable claims about the ways in which varying interests within the welfare state could find effective political expression and mobilize real political power.

Of course, this does not mean that there are not very real structural problems thrown up by non-market distribution in a market-based economy, nor that the structure of costs and benefits which this implies may not have a very substantial impact upon economic performance (however this is measured). In fact, the salience of these concerns is heightened by the very different international economic order in which the welfare states of the 1990s operate, compared with those of the 1950s and 1960s. But the claim that we have now to choose to have *either* a market economy *or* a welfare state, or indeed the belief that we can choose to have a market economy *without* some form of state provision of welfare, is no more compelling now than it was twenty or even a hundred years ago.

However, it might be argued that, while historically we have avoided this choice between state and market, such an accommodation will no longer be available to us in the twenty-first century. Students of the welfare states' 'growth to limits' have argued that the failure to constrain future growth in the welfare budget (at least as a proportion of national wealth) will tend in the long run to undermine popular support for welfare state institutions (as public expenditure increasingly squeezes out the choices of private consumers). Could it be that the pressures arising from *demographic change* in the twenty-first century will so overburden the public welfare system as rather belatedly to trigger an institutional crisis of the welfare state?

## A Demographic Crisis of the Welfare State?

Clearly the demographic challenge of an ageing population is a real one and has been a pressing concern of social policy makers for

more than a decade (Atkinson and Altmann, 1989; Thane, 1987).
The UK government in 1985 proposed the wholesale abolition of the
earnings-related element of state pensions precisely as a response to
the overburdening of the productive economy and the tax base
which it anticipated this would bring in the twenty-first century
(DHSS, 1985, pp. 15–17, 21–5). Similar concerns have been expressed by the OECD. One recent report notes that 'with the proportion
of retired people rising, welfare systems may undergo a financial
crisis', while another insists that 'restructuring retirement provision
has become an arithmetic necessity in all countries' (Blot, 1990,
p. 21; Holzmann, 1986, p. 10; Hagemann, 1989).

In practice, the demographic impact of an ageing population is
likely to vary quite substantially between different countries. Within
the OECD, 'between 1986 and 2040, increases in the number of
elderly people over 75 are likely to vary between 30 per cent
(Sweden, Denmark) to nearly 400 per cent (Australia, Canada, Turkey)' (OECD, 1988, p. 10). Overall, it has been estimated that 'the
effect of demographic changes could be to raise pension expenditure
by about 5 per cent of national income by the year 2020', (OECD,
1987, p. 170). Clearly, there is a fear that as dependency ratios rise,
so the rising demands placed upon current workers to fund services
for the growing numbers of pensioners may lead to a breakdown of
the 'intergenerational contract' upon which pension provision in a
Pay-As-You-Go system depends. Inasmuch as the welfare state is a
system of provision for the elderly, which substantially it is, it
clearly faces a formidable challenge in the early to middle years of
the next century.

However, this will not necessarily precipitate a crisis for the welfare state. While predictions of the numbers of elderly in this period
are fairly reliable, most of the other variables upon which dependency projections are premised are very provisional. Such long-range
predictions are extremely sensitive to even quite minor changes in
rates of economic growth, labour force participation rates, patterns
of labour migration, fertility rates and changes in retirement age.
The interaction of these several variables makes forecasting for the
middle years of the twenty-first century extremely hazardous. Nor is
it clear that the population over 65 years old in forty or fifty years'
time will necessarily be uniformly 'dependent' and a 'burden' on the
productive economy.[1] Consequently, Pat Thane and Peter Taylor-
Gooby, for example, have both cautioned against making precipitate
policy changes now, on the basis of extremely tentative predictions
and questionable assumptions about the elderly population in 2040

---

1  Nor is it clear that we can so describe the *current* elderly population.

(Thane, 1987; Taylor-Gooby, 1988). It is also worth noting that even quite sluggish economic growth may have a significant cumulative effect upon the capacity of the developed economies to support a growing dependent population. In one of the few assessments of its kind, made amidst the doom-mongering of the mid-1980s, Davies and Piachaud indicated that in the UK, at least in the brief period between 1984 and 1989, very modest economic growth (of 1–2 per cent) would allow some upgrading of benefits without a growth in the proportional 'take' of welfare from the national economy. The major constraint upon such modest upgrading, as they saw it, was the government's greater commitment to tax cuts for the population in work (Davies and Piachaud, 1985). This suggests that the real limits of the welfare state may be set not so much by the faltering capacity of the economy as by (changing) patterns of political will and political support. We shall return to this issue, and particularly its consequences for social democracy, below.

Finally, it is worth noting that insofar as there is a 'demographic problem' of an ageing population in the twenty-first century, this is a challenge not just for the welfare state but for the developed societies and their economies much more generally. In whatever way, the costs of supporting an ageing dependent population will have to be met from current economic output. Some alternative mix of public and private provision *may* ease the burden on the public sector and this *may* be economically more efficient. But no juggling of the labels 'private' and 'public' can dissolve the core requirement to support a growing dependent population out of current economic production.

## Welfare State Regimes

There are then rather limited grounds for supposing that either now or in the envisageable future the welfare state will collapse because of its incompatibility with a market-based economy or because of the unsustainable burden of an ageing population. In fact, amidst the seemingly ubiquitous talk of widespread cuts and a generalized crisis over the last ten to fifteen years, even those governments most powerfully committed to a reduction of the welfare state have found it to be stubbornly evasive of financial constraint. In the UK, the Conservative government enjoyed uninterrupted tenure of office through the 1980s and evinced a strong ideological commitment to lessening the role of the state in welfare and reducing the 'burden' of public expenditure. Yet, even here, welfare state expenditure rose consistently throughout the decade (Taylor-Gooby, 1988). In the US,

David Stockman, the disgruntled ex-Director of the Budget in the Reagan Administration, asked why the Republicans had failed to 'tame' the welfare state.

> In the answer lies the modern dirty little secret of the Republican Party: the conservative opposition helped build the American welfare state brick by brick during the three decades prior to 1980. The Reagan Revolution failed because the Republican Party decided to stick with its own historic handiwork. (Stockman, 1986, p. 437)

That these most committed and entrenched New Right governments failed to transform existing welfare state expenditures does *not* mean that nothing has changed. Of statutory provision for the unemployed in the UK, for example, Atkinson and Micklewright argue that changes in the 1980s 'made the system less generous and have weakened the role of unemployment *insurance* as opposed to unemployment *assistance*', (Atkinson and Micklewright, 1989, p. 125). In the US, Katz argues that the first Reagan administration had considerable success in cutting income maintenance and social service programmes (such as AFDC, food stamps and child nutrition) (Katz, 1986, pp. 286–9). But, as we saw in chapter 5, while 'unpopular' areas of welfare state expenditure have been subject to considerable constraint, the most popular (and expensive) areas have proven much more difficult to control. In the US, for example, Katz argues that while the Reagan administration enjoyed successes in its 'offensive against social welfare . . . social insurance . . . has proved nearly impregnable' (Katz, 1986, p. 274). In the UK, the budget of the NHS rose throughout the 1980s, while repeatedly popular complaints were of *under-* rather than of *over-*spending (Bosanquet, 1988).

For some commentators, this resilience of mass-consumption areas of the welfare state is evidence of the irreversibility of what Therborn calls 'the universal welfare state'. For them, the most basic and crucial fact about the modern welfare state is its deep and massive presence in the day-to-day lives of millions of citizens. Therborn argues that the welfare state is 'alongside liberal democracy . . . the most pervasive feature of the everyday politics and policy of western countries', while Alber insists that 'because extended welfare states develop self-perpetuating features as the numerical importance of welfare state clients in the electorate grows, . . . the basis for a large-scale anti-welfare state backlash in the future appears rather weak'. Therborn concludes that 'a radical anti-welfare state party or coalition will find it virtually impossible to succeed under democratic rules of universal sufffrage and rights to industrial action' (Therborn, 1989, pp. 62, 91; Alber, 1988a, p. 196).

It is difficult to be quite so sanguine about the future of the welfare state as are Alber and Therborn. Nonetheless, it is highly improbable that the welfare state in any advanced industrial society will simply 'disappear'. What seems much more likely is that welfare states will be varyingly 'reconstructed' so as to reflect a new pattern of rights and interests. In chapter 5, we saw that such a process of 'reconstruction' is already underway and in the future we might expect not only that this process will continue, but also that under its impact what are already considerable differences between national welfare states will become still more pronounced. This 'reconstruction' cannot be adequately measured by simply plotting changes in aggregate social expenditures. 'The crucial issue' as Esping-Andersen observes, is 'not aggregate expenditures, but welfare state structuration' (Esping-Andersen, 1990, p. 118). Thus, what may be most important in assessing likely futures for the welfare state is not so much sheer survival nor even the level of expenditure but the *type of welfare state regime*. It is this last feature that may be changing most rapidly and profoundly.

## A Typology of Welfare State Regimes

We can begin to think about these differing types of welfare state regime by considering some of the criteria in table 6.1. In fact, in themselves these criteria are insufficient to define even a simple 'left-right' division in welfare state regimes. While it is hard to imagine a 'left' welfare state being (intentionally) regressive in its redistribution, the support of earnings-related benefits may have a place in both a 'right' welfare state (preserving existing status/ income differentiation) and a 'left' welfare state (ensuring broad support for the welfare state beyond the poorest and militating against 'residualism'). Similarly, means-testing is often seen as a policy favoured by the right as a way of minimizing welfare costs. However, it is sometimes seen, when combined with funding from progressive general tax revenue, as, for example, at the inauguration of the Australian welfare state, as a strategy for effective redistribution of resources towards the poor (see Shaver, 1988). Finally, a number of commentators have remarked upon the seeming similarity between the calls from both left and right for reforms to integrate the taxation and benefit systems and between the left's schemes for a basic guaranteed income and the New Right's call for a negative income tax (Hill, 1990, pp. 157–67).[2]

---

2  Even the call for vouchers, long seen as an exclusively right-wing proposal, has recently been taken up on the left (Le Grand and Estrin, 1989, pp. 198–204).

**Table 6.1**  Criteria defining welfare states

| | |
|---|---|
| Scope | Universal/Selective |
| Range | Expansive/Delimited |
| Quality | Optimal/Minimal |
| Instruments | Public consumption/Social transfers |
| Financing | Tax-based/Contributory |
| Benefit type | Earnings-related/Flat-rate |
| Redistribution | Progressive/Regressive |

*Source*:   Alber (1988b) p. 452

Thus, these general criteria must themselves be placed in some overall *strategic* context. One of the most influential attempts to offer such a further classification is to be found in Titmuss' three models of social policy. Titmuss isolated:[3]

1  The *residual welfare model*, which is 'based on the premise that there are two "natural" (or socially given) channels through which an individual's needs are properly met; the private market and the family. Only when these break down should social welfare institutions come into play and then only temporarily'.

2  The *industrial achievement-performance model*, which 'incorporates a significant role for social welfare institutions as adjuncts of the economy. It holds that social needs should be met on the basis of merit, work performance and productivity'.

3  The *institutional redistributive model*, which 'sees social welfare as a major integrated institution in society, providing universalist services outside the market on the principle of need'.

Titmuss's classification remains a useful one but as a typology for welfare states, it has been criticized both because most actual welfare states embrace elements of all three models and because in practice it has been used to underpin *evolutionary* accounts of the development of the welfare state from a residual through an industrial achievement–performance towards an institutional basis.

Finally, we can consider two contemporary typologies which seek to address these weaknesses. Goran Therborn's recent work on the welfare state was considered in chapter 1. There we saw that he was anxious to stress the ubiquity of the modern welfare state, but he also insists that there are important differences within the welfare states that the configuration of the Keynesian Welfare State and the general prosperity of the 1960s have concealed. Therborn orders his classification of welfare states along two dimensions: (1) level of

---

3   Titmuss (1974), pp. 30–1.

**Table 6.2**　Classification of welfare states

|  | | Social entitlements | |
| --- | --- | --- | --- |
|  | | High | Low |
| Commitment to full employment | High | Strong interventionist welfare states | Full employment-oriented small welfare states |
| | Low | Soft, compensatory welfare states | Market-oriented small welfare states |

*Source*:　Therborn (1987)

social entitlements and (2) orientations to the labour market and full employment. This determines a four-fold classification, shown in table 6.2. This, in turn, yields the following four categories:[4]

**Strong interventionist welfare states**:   Sweden, Norway, Austria
  (extensive social policy, strong   (Finland)
  commitment to full employment)

**Soft compensatory welfare states**:   Belgium, Denmark,
  (generous social entitlements, low   Netherlands (France, West
  commitment to full employment)   Germany, Ireland, Italy)

**Full employment-oriented, small**   Switzerland, Japan
**welfare states**:
  (low social entitlements, but
  institutional commitment to full
  employment)

**Market-oriented welfare states**:   Australia, Canada, US, UK,
  (limited social rights, low   New Zealand
  commitment to full employment)

We can contrast this with the classification developed by Gosta Esping-Andersen and organized around the idea of welfare state 'regime clusters'. If it is appropriate to think of all the states of developed capitalism as welfare states, these are clearly welfare states of rather differing kinds. Such differences are not however linearly distributed between low spenders and high spenders or between residual and institutional models. Indeed *level* of social expenditure may not be a reliable indicator of the character of any given welfare state. Rather do the differing welfare states cluster around three ideal typical regime types.[5]

---

4　Therborn (1987).
5　Esping-Andersen (1990) pp. 26–33; see also Rein, Esping-Andersen and Rainwater (1987).

1   The *liberal welfare state* is dominated by the logic of the market. Benefits are modest, often means-tested and stigmatizing. The principle of 'less eligibility' requires that welfare should not undermine the propensity to work. The state encourages the private provision of market forms of welfare (private insurance/occupational welfare).
    *Typical examples*: US, Canada, Australia

2   In the *conservative/'corporatist' welfare state*, 'the liberal obsession with market efficiency and commodification was never pre-eminent' and correspondingly the granting of social rights was never so contested. Private insurance and occupational welfare are 'minimal'. However, the emphasis of social rights is upon upholding existing class and status differentials and its redistributive effects are 'negligible'. Such welfare states often have their origins in pre-democratic or authoritarian regimes which sought to use social policy as a means of defusing the threat of working class mobilization (Bismarck in Germany, Taafe in Austria). In many cases, corporatist regimes are shaped by the Church, and this tends to determine their conservative attitude to the family (gender differential benefits to support the traditional form of the male-dominated family) and their support of the principle of *subsidiarity* (in which the state should support and deliver only those forms of welfare which other intermediary institutions, and notably the church, are unable to provide).
    *Typical examples*: Austria, France, Germany, Italy

3   The *social democratic welfare state* is characterized by universalism and the usurpation of the market. It is envisaged as 'a welfare state that would promote an equality of the highest standards, rather than an equality of minimal needs'. Benefits are graduated in accordance with earnings, but this is a way of securing universal support for, and participation in, a universal insurance system. Unlike the other regimes, the state is not seen as a second or last resort, but as the principal means of realizing the social rights of all its citizens. It is, of necessity, committed to the principle of full employment, since 'the enormous costs of maintaining a solidaristic, universalistic and de-commodifying welfare state' can be best and perhaps only achieved 'with most people working, and the fewest possible living off social transfers'.
    *Typical examples*: Sweden and Norway

## Welfare State Regimes in Flux?

The 'real' agenda for the future of the welfare state may then be much less concerned with its disappearance than with its prospective 'restructuring' or a shift in its dominant regime types. At the start of this chapter, we rehearsed a number of 'restructuring imperatives' which, while not generally leading to the disappearance of the welfare state, would nonetheless tend to force it ever closer to a 'residual', 'market-oriented' or 'liberal' welfare state regime (in the respective terminologies of Titmuss, Therborn and Esping-Andersen). We can now assess these claims in the light of the historical and comparative material reviewed in this study.

First, changes in the global economy do seem to have curtailed opportunities for the further development of national welfare states. The deregulation of international markets and of financial institutions, in particular, have tended to weaken the capacities of the interventionist state, to render all economies more 'open' and to make national capital and more especially national labour movements much more subject to the terms and conditions of international competition.[6] Inasmuch as the post-war welfare state truly was a *Keynesian* welfare state, those changes in the international economy which have precipitated a decline of Keynesianism may be seen to have had a very material effect on the welfare state. The prospects for sustaining long-term, corporatist arrangements within particular nation states (including the institutionalization of a 'social wage') seem even less promising in a deregulated international economy.[7]

Yet we need to be cautious in drawing firm predictions about the future of the welfare state from this evidence. Many commentators insist that under the new international economic order, the state will still be interventionist. Indeed, the state may actually increase its interventions in, for example, training and re-training and in the transition from school to work (Offe, 1987). Also, insofar as welfare state interventions have an *efficiency* effect, we might expect such interventions to *increase* under more internationally competitive circumstances (see Therborn, 1989; Barr, above, p. 162). At the same time, the rise of supranational institutions in the new economic order may enhance welfare state interventions. Thus, for example, the harmonization of social policy throughout the European Community, the adjudications of the European Court and the enactment of the European Social Charter will force certain member states to *increase* their welfare provision (*Social Europe*, 1990). And while

---

6  Though it is worth noting that, historically, it was often those (small) countries with 'open' economies that had the most developed welfare states.

7  On the much-contested relationship between corporatism, organized capitalism and the welfare state, see Middlemas (1979); Cawson (1986); Panitch (1986); Pierson (1991).

Lash, Urry and others have isolated some important tendencies of the contemporary political economy in their thesis of 'disorganizing capitalism', the unravelling of the welfare state which they antici- pate is as yet largely unproven (Lash and Urry, 1987, pp. 228–31). Several of their critics have argued that their thesis exaggerates the tendency towards disorganization by highlighting selected features of particular occidental economies, and amongst these, neither the most successful nor those at the 'leading edge' of social and econo- mic change (see Clegg, 1989). We must also anticipate that the process of 'disorganization' is likely to proceed quite differently in countries which developed differently under organized capitalism (Pierson, 1990; see Lash and Bagguley, 1988).

A second tendency identified above was the move away from a welfare state based upon an 'historic compromise' of the interests of capital and labour, a change most frequently associated with the rise of 'Thatcherism' in the UK (and elsewhere). Here, the exclusion of organized labour from social policy-making, the reorientation of welfare provision towards the private sector and the advocacy of targeted rather than universal provision have been quite explicit. At the same time, containing social expenditure – one of the clearest ambitions of the Thatcher administration – has proven extremely difficult. Despite the talk of targeting, the reconstruction of the UK welfare state has tended to see a squeeze upon the standard of provision for those poorest and most dependent on the state and at least a partial protection of the mainstream and popular areas of the mass welfare state (education, health and pensions), as well as a transfer of public spending effort from public to private sector hous- ing (Taylor-Gooby, 1985; Taylor-Gooby, 1988).

Certainly, amongst both organized capital and organized labour, it is possible to identify a decline in support for the 'historic comprom- ise' welfare state. For capital, this may be because the changing balance of power in the new economic order makes the compliance of organized labour a much less essential condition of long-term profitability. For organized labour, it may reflect a strategic weaken- ing of its position, a changing division of labour (leading to a diminution of the communality of interest among all wage workers) and the emergence of a disadvantaged core of unemployed and underemployed in a largely non-unionized secondary labour market.

However, in a properly historical perspective, such changes are not particularly startling nor shockingly new. As we have seen repeatedly, the welfare state has never been a simple 'engine of equality' and the tangle of measures and practices of which it con- sists has always tended to reflect both the balance of social forces and the (variable) authority of the market. We have seen that historically both organized labour and organized capital have taken quite different views of the desirability of welfare state provision at different times. While the present period may mark a conjunctural rather than simply a cyclical change in the balance of forces between capital and labour, this does not mean that there may not be future circumstances in which either or both might see their interests lying in a restoration of state authority over welfare. We should also remember that evidence of a decline in support for the welfare state within public opinion is extremely limited (see pp. 168–71 above) and that despite the widespread concern within political parties and amongst political commentators about the unpopularly oppressive nature of state provision of welfare, it is not clear that this coincides with public dissatisfaction with state provision. *British Social Attitudes* surveys from 1983 onwards show that in the (perhaps uniquely popular) National Health Service, growing *dissatisfaction* with the quality of the service provided is coupled with a growing *endorsement* of the principle of universal state provision of healthcare, free at the point of delivery (Bosanquet, 1988, p. 93). Walzer's comment in *Spheres of Justice* seems apposite:

> what is most common in the history of popular struggles is the demand not for deliverance [from the state] but for performance; that the state actually serve the purposes it claims to serve, and that is does so for all its members. (Walzer, 1983, p. 74)

A third premiss of structural change was the suggestion that, in the long run, it is the previous *successes* of the welfare state which undermine the circumstances for its continued well-being. This claim takes a number of forms. First, it is argued that a changing division of labour and changing taxation regimes under the welfare state generate a new social and electoral division between those primarily dependent upon the welfare state (for income and/or employment) and those whose welfare is more immediately dependent upon the private sector. This is seen to undermine that alliance between working and middle classes or that commonality of interest within the broad working class upon which the post-war welfare state was constructed. Sectoral differences (of public v. private) override more traditionally defined class differences (of manual v. non-manual workers). In electoral terms, the welfare state now attracts a broad but minority coalition of interests (within both middle and working classes). But this is characteristically outweighed by a majority which favours the nurturing of the private sector, a majority which now embraces a significant section of the skilled, regularly employed and often home-owning working class (see, *inter alia*, Dunleavy, 1980; Dunleavy and Husbands, 1985; Heath and Evans, 1988).

Secondly, it is argued that the very security and affluence which the welfare state has guaranteed (above all to the securely employed middle classes within the welfare state sector), generates a growing incentive for these same social actors to *defect* from reliance upon state-provided welfare. The defection of sections of the middle class (and increasingly of the more affluent and securely employed sections of the working class) from support of public provision encourages a transformation from a mass-based universal welfare state towards a system of much more residual provision for the poor and dependent. This process is encouraged by a general rise in affluence and 'consumer sovereignty' in the developed industrial countries. As the population becomes increasingly used to exercising its enhanced purchasing power to acquire non-standardized goods and services within an increasingly diverse marketplace, so, it is argued, do consumers wish to exercise increasing choice and discretion over such vital commodities as health care and educational provision. All these changes will not lead to the disappearance of the welfare state, it is suggested, but they will move it ever more clearly from a 'universal' towards a 'residual' regime (OECD, 1988; Offe, 1987).

The UK, in which the process of change is seen to have been most pronounced, is a useful testing ground for these claims. Evidence of a change in patterns of electoral support is keenly contested and other cleavages (for example, those based upon geographical or functional region) are sometimes given greater weight than the public sector/private sector divide (Johnson, Pattie and Allsopp, 1988). Nonetheless, considerable evidence has been marshalled to suggest that the public/private divide is an important component of the remarkable electoral successes of the Conservative governments of the 1980s, particularly in explaining the limited shift of middle-class votes towards the Labour Party and of skilled working-class votes towards the Conservatives (Dunleavy, 1980; Dunleavy and Husbands, 1985; Heath and Evans, 1988). Changes in government spending and tax allowances have encouraged a continuation of the long-term post-war trend of growth in owner-occupation of housing and in private pension schemes. Private health insurance has increased rapidly (from a very low base) and there has been some expansion of private education. While there is continuing popular support for mainstream areas of the welfare state, there is also some evidence that this support may be becoming increasingly fragile and that it 'coexists with concern at standards in the state sector' (Taylor-Gooby, 1988, p. 14).

However, these changes do not straightforwardly evidence a transfer of support from public to private welfare premised on the self-defeating successes of the welfare state. First, as we have seen, the welfare state has never been straightforwardly a barometer of popular sympathy for collective provision. Just as there were sources other than public opinion at the origins and in the development of the welfare state, so we should anticipate that other policy sources and objectives will influence its 'restructuring'. Secondly, the privatization of welfare builds upon already well-established forms of the non-state allocation of goods. Thus, for example, the growth of owner occupation and of occupational pensions was as much a feature of the 'Golden Age' of the welfare state as it has been of the years of retrenchment and 'restructuring'. Thirdly, 'private' welfare does not always correspond to individual consumers making welfare choices within an unregulated welfare market. For many of the beneficiaries of private health insurance, these benefits are provided by their employers and are properly a part of the system of occupational welfare. Similarly, it is state interventions, especially in the form of tax expenditures, that make particular forms of private welfare – be it schooling or housing or pensions – sufficiently attractive to trigger 'defections' or 'opting out' of the state system. As Taylor-Gooby notes, the choice of private rather than public provision is influenced by 'the capacity to pay, the structure of subsidies and the availability and quality of alternatives' (Taylor-Gooby, 1988, p. 9; see also, Taylor-Gooby and Papadakis, 1987). While there is a long-standing belief that for workers 'affluence = privatism', at least in the field of welfare, the picture is more complex (see, *inter alia*, Sombart, 1976; Goldthorpe et al., 1968). Greater affluence (the capacity to pay) may make private provision a possibility. However, the take-up of this opportunity is likely to be further influenced by (1) the ways in which state or employers *subsidize* particular types of welfare choices, (2) the extent to which the state offers an attractive alternative and (3) the extent to which 'anti-defection' incentives are built into the public system.

To accept that greater affluence and the expression of greater consumer choice must *necessarily* lead to a defection from welfare state provision is to concede too much to the New Right position, before their claims have been properly tested. However, at the same time, it should be recognized that there is no unshiftable alliance in favour of a citizenship, mass-based and universal welfare state. Whatever sort of welfare state we have is likely to be shaped by political choices and state structures. Under present circumstances, that political alliance which will support mass welfare state provision must be seen to be potentially fragile and the welfare state correspondingly vulnerable to a process of deep-seated 'restructuring'.

## Growth to Limits or Limits to Growth?

One final proposition about the transformation of the welfare state raised in the Introduction needs to be considered here. It is of a rather distinct character from the other claims. In essence, it is the view that further development of the welfare state should be resisted not because historically it has been anti-progressive, but because the welfare state is irrevocably tied to a strategy of economic growth and the imperatives of this economic growth are no longer consonant with the meeting of real human needs and the sustainable securing of human welfare. We have seen that this is the core claim of the green critique of the welfare state.

It is certainly true that, while the welfare state has frequently been held responsible for depressing economic growth, the expansion of the welfare state has itself been premised upon the remarkable growth of the Western industrialized economies after 1945. Most advocates of the welfare state's growth have seen the generation of a greater economic product as the necessary basis for enhanced (re-) distribution. Recent years have seen the rising popularity of a series of arguments which insist that present patterns of economic growth – and particularly the exhaustion of finite resources and the generation of waste which it is beyond the capacity of the ecosystem to absorb – are inconsistent with the long-term sustainability of the human species. In this most fundamental sense, the growth-based welfare state is inconsistent with the securing of general human welfare. It is also argued that the human and social costs of economic growth – stress-related illness, the diseases of affluence, unsatisfying labour and the direct economic costs of these social ills – make the 'economy of the welfare state' self-defeating. Inasmuch as the welfare state is irretrievably tied into an unsustainable pattern of economic development, it is antithetical to the realization of real long-term welfare.

These are powerful arguments. While the precise parameters of sustainability remain contested, and estimations of the required changes in our economic practice fluctuate wildly, there is little doubt that existing patterns of economic exploitation and economic growth cannot be supported indefinitely (Pearce, Markandya and

Barbier, 1989; Dobson, 1990). As is now widely recognized, however, the issue is not necessarily one of arresting economic growth. The problem is rather one of ecological equilibrium, or sustainability, and a sustainable economy may permit of economic growth. It is *unsustainable* growth – growth which overloads the capacity of the ecosystem to process natural waste or which exhausts finite resources without offering substitutes – that is inimical to long-term welfare. There is lively disagreement about precisely how sustainability should be defined and how it can be achieved, whether through a more regulated market and tax incentives, through a more interventionist state or through the decentralization of economic and decision-making to the most local level (Jacobs, 1989; Pearce, Markandya and Barbier, 1989; Dobson, 1990).

Whatever the economic parameters of this problem, it is clear that it presents a very specific and intractable social and political challenge. Amidst the many general difficulties, we can identify at least three specific challenges which immediately confront the welfare state. First, it seems impossible any longer to proceed as if the welfare state could be solely concerned with the *redistribution* of an exogenous economic product. Some sort of positive-sum welfare state economy *may* still be possible, but the belief that economic growth can be allowed to proceed untrammelled and its dysfunctions compensated for by the welfare state is no longer tenable when the character of growth and its consequences for social welfare is so problematic. Secondly, if we take the global nature of the problem of economic growth and its welfare consequences seriously, we cannot continue to understand the securing of welfare as a purely national issue, as an issue for conventional national welfare states. It is now widely recognized that the neighbourhood effects and external costs of economic growth fall upon an international or even upon a global community. Thirdly, changing parameters of economic growth and a global economy mean raising not only the issue of intergenerational welfare, but also the more immediate question of intra-national or interregional equity. Sustainable development may allow of some economic growth, but given the sorts of constraints which sustainability may require us to impose, is it possible for the Western welfare state economies to continue to command even their present proportions of economic resources? In this sense, the problem for the future of the welfare state is not primarily an economic one (sustainable growth might make available a modestly growing social product). The real and more daunting challenge is to discover political institutions which are consistent with the dictates of sustainability and the securing of general human welfare, and then to realize them.

# Beyond the Welfare State: The Challenge to Social Democracy

Overall, evidence that we are moving towards circumstances that are 'beyond the welfare state' is then rather mixed. Certainly, there is limited reason to believe that we face a crisis brought on by the economic, political or demographic contradictions of the welfare state. Some system of public provision of welfare looks set to stay with us into the indefinite future. But the types of welfare state which we will inhabit (and these are already quite different throughout the Western industrialized world) seem liable to change under the impact of a range of economic, social, political and ecological pressures. These pressures, and the changes that may follow from them, present varying problems for many of the accounts of welfare state development which we have reviewed in this book. But for none of these is the challenge as acute as it is for social democracy, both as a political practice and as a political ideology. We have seen that it is mistaken to describe the welfare state as 'the institutional embodiment of social democracy' and while the welfare state has had an important place in social democrats' strategic thinking, it is probably also mistaken to think that they have characteristically seen the welfare state as an 'engine of equality' (see Hindess, 1987). Yet the challenge facing the welfare state is peculiarly severe for social democrats. Changes in the global economy have done much to discredit the traditional political economy and the generally reformist strategy of social democracy. Changes in the class basis of the welfare state and the imperilling of the sorts of social and electoral alliances upon which this was built are above all threats to the social base of social democratic forces. Finally, the critique of a policy based on the extraction of a social levy upon a growing market economy seems above all to confront the rationale of post-war social democracy and the 'costless' social change which the Keynesian welfare state seemed to promise.

The challenge of a 'restructured' welfare state is above all then a challenge for social democracy, and in the closing pages of this chapter I turn to two alternative responses to this impasse. Broadly described, these respond to the difficulties of the social democratic welfare state by advocating (1) a checking of the powers of the state through an enhanced principle of citizenship or through the regeneration of the sphere of civil society and (2) some form of socialization of the investment function. In assessing these alternatives, I draw some general conclusions about the nature of the state and of democratization under any revised form of social democracy.

## Welfare and the Enhancement of Citizenship

One of the most widely acknowledged sources of the New Right's political success over the last decade has been its ability to capture the discourse of freedom and choice and to characterize social democracy as the embodiment of statism, bureaucratization, conformity and insensitivity to individuals' needs and desires. The *locus classicus* of this 'nanny statism' has often been found in the institutions and practices of the welfare state.

One increasingly influential response to this challenge has been to take up and seek to augment the classical idea of *citizenship*. Seeking to distance the entitlement to welfare from the unpopular statism associated with public corporations and producer-controlled welfare bureaucracies, social citizenship is advanced as a mechanism for empowering ordinary individuals in the face of the dominance of both the state and the principal market actors (including both capital *and*, at times, organized labour). Citizenship is, in fact, one of the oldest terms in political discourse, probably as old as the idea of the political community itself, and in the more general call for constitutional reform, the idea of citizenship is often given an appropriately broad background.[8] However, in its application to welfare and the social rights of citizenship, the terms of reference are much narrower. Here there is a very clear indebtedness to Tom Marshall and his occasionally acknowledged forerunners (such as Hobhouse and T. H. Green) in the tradition of New Liberalism (on Marshall, see above, pp. 22–4). Particular weight is given to their conception of 'positive' freedom. For all these earlier thinkers, while social rights might underpin some general sense of national community (and Green and his contemporaries clearly held that the state could in some sense be the representative of society's 'common good'), they were not principally a means of securing some form of *collective* provision. They were not a means of articulating, but rather of avoiding, the politics of class interest (see, for example, Hobhouse quoted in Richter, 1964). Their intention was, through the guarantee of some social minimum, to ensure that all individuals enjoyed the autonomy with which to pursue their various and self-defined 'life plans'. Autonomy was a prerequisite of citizenship and where necessary the enabling state could legitimately intervene so as to create the circumstances for autonomy. For the New Liberals,

---

8   See, for example, the advocacy of Charter 88 (*New Statesman and Society*, 1988).

there could be no true liberty if a man was confined and oppressed by poverty, by excessive hours of labour, by insecurity of liveli-hood ... To be truly free he must be liberated from these things ... In many cases, it was only the power of law that could effect this. More law might often mean more liberty. (Herbert Samuel, cited in Vincent and Plant, 1984, p. 73)

Echoes of these earlier arguments about autonomy can be found in contemporary advocacy of a revived and enhanced social citizenship. Thus, Albert Weale argues that a normative basis for the mandatory provision of a welfare minimum resides in the 'overrid-ing imperative [of] *the principle of autonomy'*. This stipulates 'that all persons are entitled to respect as deliberate and purposive agents capable of formulating their own projects, and that as part of this respect there is a governmental obligation to bring into being or preserve the conditions in which this autonomy can be realized' (Weale, 1983, p. 42). Similarly, King and Waldron argue 'for public provision of a minimum level of welfare as a universal entitlement, defining a threshold below which people will not be allowed to fall without diminishing their sense and capacities of citizenship' (King and Waldron, 1988, p. 436). In *Rethinking Welfare*, Bill Jordan calls for a guaranteed basic income as part of 'a redefinition of the terms of citizenship' which would guarantee the capacity of individuals to pursue their self-ascribed life plans (Jordan, 1987, pp. 149–64; for similar arguments, see also Campbell, 1983; Vincent and Plant, 1984). The principal intention appears to be that the hostility of both the New Right and an increasingly disenchanted public towards the bureaucratic and domineering welfare state might be met by reallo-cating power from the state to the rights-exercising individual.

A second major source for the defence of welfare citizenship is found in the contractarian principles of John Rawls' *A Theory of Justice* (1973). In brief, Rawls' ambition is to establish those social, economic and political principles which would define a just society. In King and Waldron's paraphrase, 'a society is just ... if we can show that its institutions satisfy certain principles that people would have agreed to as basic terms of co-operation, had they been given the opportunity to decide' (King and Waldron, 1988, p. 440).

Individuals under the special circumstances of the imaginary 'original position' (stripped of their specific social indentities and positions), would, according to Rawls, choose two principles as the contractual basis of a just social order. These are, in order of priority:[9]

---

9 Rawls (1973) p. 302

1   Each person is to have an equal right to the most extensive total system of equal basic liberties compatible with a similar system of liberty for all.
2   Social and economic inequalities are to be arranged so that they are both:
    (a)   to the greatest benefit of the least advantaged [the 'Difference Principle'] ... and
    (b)   attached to offices and positions open to all under conditions of fair equality of opportunity.

Two consequences follow for a conception of welfare citizenship:

1   No-one in the 'original position' could 'enter into agreements that may have consequences they cannot accept'. Since no 'normal' human being could be expected to accept social circumstances in which she was denied the basic necessities of life, those placed in the 'original position would opt for social arrangements in which 'the government guarantees a *social minimum*' to meet the most basic human needs of all citizens (Rawls, 1973, pp. 176, 275).

But Rawls, in fact, argues that the circumstances of the 'original position' would generate more than this commitment to a 'basic' social minimum.

2   The Difference Principle [the requirement that social and economic inequalities are to be arranged so that they are to the greatest benefit of the least advantaged] may, in fact, require the very substantial redistribution of resources. The Difference Principle is not a principle of economic equality (since wealth differentials may always be justified by their capacity to sponsor improvements in the social well-being of society's least advantaged). However, once 'the difference principle is accepted ... it follows that the minimum is to be set at that point which ... maximizes the expectations of the least advantaged group' (Rawls, 1973, p. 285).

For its welfarist advocates, the great strength of the Rawlsian account of justice lies in its principled defence of an extensive and redistributive welfare state based on the entitlements of citizens. Such a theory may then be used to countermand those accounts of justice and freedom with which the New Right seeks to undermine the claims to any but the most minimal state provision of welfare.

A second initiative which has been even more immediately concerned with the overweening presence of the state is to be found in that strategy which calls for the renewal of a reconstituted civil society to countermand the excessive powers of the interventionist state. This view, most effectively popularized during the 1980s by John Keane, holds that the origins of 'the dwindling popularity of the Keynesian welfare state or [as Keane calls it] "state administered socialism" [lie in the failure] to recognize the desirable form and limits of state action in relation to civil society' (Keane, 1988a, p. 3; see also Keane, 1984; Keane and Owens, 1986; Keane, 1988b).[10] In Keane's view, the problems of social democracy in Western European countries arise primarily from its over-reliance upon the state as an instrument of social change. For whatever historical reasons, social democracy, in adopting the programme of the Keynesian welfare state, abandons the *mobilization* of its supporters for radical social change, in favour of the *management* of ever more areas of social life, in the belief that 'state power could become the caretaker and modernizer of social existence' (Keane, 1988a, p. 4). In this process, the state replaces the self-activity of citizens with the promise that its many-faceted interventions in social life can ensure commodious living, social peace and real 'social security'. To try to redeem this promise, the state is required to intervene ever more intrusively and bureaucratically in the day-to-day social life of its citizens, 'to encourage the passive consumption of state provision and seriously to undermine citizens' confidence in their ability to direct their own lives' (Keane, 1988a, p. 4). This mixture of state intrusion and citizen passivity might just have been tolerable so long as the welfare state seemed able to 'deliver the goods' (in which task, over the last twenty years, it has been repeatedly seen to have failed). However, as Habermas has argued, it is not just that the welfare state was *economically* ineffective. There was also an inherent contradiction between its goal – 'the establishment of forms of life that are structured in an egalitarian way and that at the same time open up arenas for individual self-realization and spontaneity' – and its methods – those of legal and administrative intervention (Habermas, 1989a, p. 59; see above, pp. 65–7). Correspondingly, the success of the neo-conservatives was built not only upon the inadequacy of welfare state outcomes, but also upon 'the actual experience of many citizens in daily contact with welfare state institutions ... that socialism means bureaucracy, surveillance, red tape and state control' (Keane, 1988a, p. 4).

---

10  This was not perhaps *the* dominant theme in the revival of interest in civil society in the 1980s, especially in the first half of what Piccone styled 'the decade of Gramscism' (Piccone, 1976, p. 485). On the Gramscian usage of civil society, see, *inter alia*, Anderson (1977); Bobbio (1988); Bellamy (1987).

The lesson for those hostile to the neo-conservatives is that a return to the Keynesian welfare state is neither possible nor desirable. The only appropriate form for rekindling the traditional socialist aspiration for both liberty and equality is through redefining the relationship between the state and a reconstituted civil society. Keane defines civil society as

> an aggregate of institutions whose members are engaged primarily in a complex of non-state activities – economic and cultural production, household life and voluntary associations – and who in this way preserve and transform their identity by exercising all sorts of pressures or controls upon state institutions. (Keane, 1988a, p. 14)

'Actually-existing civil societies' – dominated by white heterosexual males and private corporations – are inadequate to the task of reform without themselves undergoing substantial change. But it is only through returning many of the functions of welfare previously annexed by the state to the competence of individual and social actors in a 'legally guaranteed and democratically organized' civil society that the impasse of social democracy and the unhelpful opposition of 'the state or the market' can be overcome.

The same theme is taken up by Pierre Rosanvallon. The Keynesian welfare state is too bureaucratized, centralized and impersonal. It is also 'bursting at the seams' (Rosanvallon, 1988, p. 213). Social welfare can now only be realized through 'a three-pronged approach of reducing the requirement for state intervention, reinstating mutual support as a function of society, and creating greater visibility for the social' (Rosanvallon, 1988, p. 202). Overcoming the fruitless dichotomy of state or market requires us 'to bring into being a civil society of greater density and to develop its scope for exchange and mutual support, instead of "externalizing" these needs and abandoning their satisfaction to the twin poles of market or state' (Rosanvallon, 1988, p. 204).

A third initiative, closely related to both the advocacy of revived citizenship and the renewal of civil society, is the call for an enhanced role for voluntary welfare provision in a context of greater welfare pluralism. Welfare pluralists argue that current over-reliance upon state provision of welfare can be relieved through a reallocation of responsibilities into the informal, commercial and voluntary sectors. Amongst these, the voluntary sector is seen to have a particular attraction as the repository of social and altruistic impulses, without many of the vices such as compulsion, centralization and inflexibility which undermine the state as a vehicle for society's well-being (Hadley and Hatch, 1981; Kramer, 1981; Norman Johnson, 1987).

Regeneration of the voluntary sector has an appeal across a range of political positions. Thus, for some neo-conservatives, the move away from state responsibility for welfare towards a voluntary response has the advantage of reviving the moral economy of charity, with the uplifting largesse of the donor and the humble gratitude of the recipient replacing the forcible transfer of resources from the wealthy (and the not-so-wealthy) to an ungrateful population of dependants. For others, withdrawal of the state leaves room for 'active citizenship', for the performance of 'good works' and the rendering of 'help to the community' which had been squeezed out by the 'monopoly' of state welfare (Gilder, 1982; Murray, 1984; Raison, 1990; Knight, 1990).

For those more sympathetically critical of social democracy, the strengths of enhanced voluntarism are rather different. First, the voluntary sector is seen to have a much greater sensitivity than the state to the needs of its welfare community, to be more responsive to change and better able to initiate new programmes and services. Secondly, voluntary organizations, being typically small, specialized and organized 'from the bottom up', are seen to be less vulnerable to formalization or to capture by (self-interested) groups of professional workers. Thirdly, the independence of the voluntary sector makes it more effective in representing welfare needs to government, compared with the always unequal intra-governmental battle between welfare ministries and finance ministries. Finally, and most importantly, 'self-help' and 'self-organization' empowers those citizens who were the passive clients of state welfare. Thus empowered, such individuals, groups and communities are able to sense their (collective) strength and identity and lobby more effectively for what they really want and need, and not for those needs which welfare professionals have attributed to them.

## Welfare Citizenship: An Assessment

In their several ways, the claims made for a revival of citizenship, civil society and voluntarism have much to commend them. It is hardly to be doubted that the welfare state does, *in certain contexts*, disempower its citizens, weaken the fabric of mutual and communal support and entrench the directive powers of the state and its professionals. (It has also, of course, brought to these same citizens rights which they did not previously enjoy.) Enhanced and robust principles of citizenship, a reformed and empowered civil society clearly separated from the state, and a greater emphasis upon welfare voluntarism represent a powerful response to the statism which seems to be inherent in the welfare state 'project'. And yet it is unclear that any of these responses will resolve the strategic dilemmas of social democracy in its thinking about the welfare state.

First, the advocacy of enhanced social citizenship is generally too reliant upon Tom Marshall and his New Liberal precursors. For all the strengths and subtleties of Marshall's work (which are often lost in secondary accounts), it reflects a very partial and particular understanding of the nature of citizenship. It is not just that Marshall's work may be, as his critics have variously argued, Anglocentric, evolutionary and historicist (see Turner, 1986, 1990; Mann, 1987; Giddens, 1981b, 1985; Roche, 1987; Held, 1989; and p. 36 above). It is also that Marshall offers what is, in many ways, too benign an account of the relationship between citizenship, rights, welfare and the state. First, Marshall often writes as if the welfare state were itself simply an expression of the extension of social rights of citizenship. Yet we have seen that, especially outside the UK context, the welfare state is only very partially a fulfilment of the struggle for citizenship rights, and that all sorts of other interests and practices are inscribed in its institutions. Secondly, Marshall shows a limited sense of the 'dark' side of the expansion of state powers which came with the extension of citizenship. At the same time as the New Liberals were advocating the freedom-enhancing expansion of state powers, Dicey was warning against the 'new despotism' of greater state authority and Weber lamenting society's ensnarement by the 'iron cage' of bureaucracy (Dicey, 1962; Weber, 1968). Thirdly, while both Marshall and more particularly Green and the social liberals had a keen sense that citizenship entailed not only rights but also duties, this is understated and is certainly substantially lost from sight in contemporary discussions. Other strands of citizenship thinking – for example, French republicanism or Soviet constitutional theory – show a much stronger sense that citizenship entails sometimes onerous duties (including compulsory military service), as well as rights (Kelsen, 1955; Brownlie, 1971, pp. 25–8). Such assessments often show a much keener sense of the costs of citizenship and of the requirements of membership of a political community which citizenship implies. Fourthly, the ways in which we exercise our citizenship rights are seen to be relatively unproblematic. But, in fact, inasmuch as our social rights rest solely upon the fact that the state or the community recognizes and is willing to uphold them, we may well find that they are most difficult to exercise precisely when they are most desperately needed. At the same time, citizenship rights are something which we can be said to hold over against the state, indeed the state is generally the only agency that can redeem them, and this must entail some *strengthening* of the powers of the state. Ironically, if the scope and effectiveness of citizenship rights are to be enhanced, it is likely that this can only be achieved through a strengthening of the power and authority of the state.[11]

Turning to the Rawlsian defence of welfare citizenship, a number of further difficulties can be identified. First, there is an extensive literature which challenges the philosophical bases of Rawls' understanding and especially the claim to reason from contractarian premises (see, for example, Daniels, 1975; Weale, 1983). Secondly, several critics have insisted that those placed in the 'original position' would not choose those principles which Rawls identifies or that the provision beyond a 'basic' minimum which he derives from the 'original position' is not justified (Waldron, 1986). Thirdly, as a philosophical work, *A Theory of Justice* is seen to be silent on those most pressing issues that surround the welfare state – what economic system will best serve the principles of citizenship, how is a just society to be achieved, how can government redistribution avoid the vices of bureaucratization, how can justice between generations be imposed?

Clearly, these reservations do not invalidate the approaches of either Marshall or Rawls, nor do they undermine their adoption by latter-day advocates of social citizenship. They do however suggest that such a policy will be keenly resisted and that the belief that 'costless' growth of citizenship could somehow replace 'costless' economic growth as the touchstone of social democratic welfare state development is misplaced. They also require us to refocus our attention upon a slightly different issue. There may be good grounds for seeking enhancements of citizenship and citizenship rights and these may represent advances in freedom and autonomy (in Herbert Samuel's sense, that more law may make for more freedom). But such enhancements of the power of the citizen cannot effectively be made by reducing the powers of the state. This suggests that, for social democracy, the key issue in reforming the

---

11 Des King, for example, calls for a strengthening of citizenship through the addition of 'the right to full employment through an active labour market policy; and women's rights, which requires a significant change in existing values in society as well as in the way social citizenship rights have been conceptualised' (King, 1987, p. 177). It is difficult to see how such an enhancement of social citizenship rights could be achieved without giving greatly increased powers to the state to intervene in both the economy and civil society.

welfare state is the finding of ways in which the relationship between state and citizen can be redefined so as to ensure that the
legal and administrative powers of the state are at the service of the
citizens, rather than the citizens at the service of the state.
Citizenship implies a state which is both strengthened *and* more
circumscribed – a constitutionally self-limiting state. In this context,
the real difficulty is to establish how citizens are to exercise effective
control over a state from which their capacities as citizens derive.
Here Marshall and his New Liberal forerunners offer little guidance.

Similar difficulties are to be found in the attempt to use a revital-
ized civil society as the mechanism for resolving the problems facing
social democracy and the contemporary welfare state. Here again it
should be stressed that the initiative for returning forms of social
provision to a reconstituted civil society, and redefining the relationship between civil society and the state, is a valuable and innovative one. But, as it stands, there are real difficulties with this
position. In part, these arise from the mistaken attempt to identify
the post-war welfare state with a social democratic form of socialism.
While some social democrats some of the time have understood the
welfare state in this sense, it is difficult to accept that the Keynesian
welfare state, as we have described it in this study, can be properly
redescribed as 'state administered socialism'. This may be a suitable
label for the regimes of Eastern Europe after 1945, but it seems more
appropriate to describe the Western welfare state as a form of 'state-
administered capitalism'. This is not to raise a purely 'theological'
issue about what constitutes 'real socialism'. Describing the post-war
welfare state as a form of state socialism has real analytic consequences. One minor drawback lies in the possible elision of the
experiences of the Soviet Empire under Stalin and Western Europe
since 1945 as twin forms of 'authoritarian statism' (Poulantzas,
1978, p. 256). This is polemically attractive (especially to neo-
conservatives) but analytically unhelpful. However, a more important
consequence of this usage is that it allows of the dichotomy 'state-
administered socialism' versus 'neo-conservative capitalism', or
more simply of 'state versus market', which dichotomy can be overcome by embracing the alternative strategy of a reconstruction of
state and civil society. In claiming, by contrast, that both the welfare
state and neo-conservatism are better understood as differing forms
of *capitalist* regime, I do not want to dust down and rehabilitate the
time-worn (and misleading) rubric that all forms of capitalism are
basically the same, and all ought correspondingly to be confronted
with the same spectre of (traditionally defined) socialism. I do
however want to suggest that Keane's reformulation contains both a

misappraisal of the nature of the welfare state and, more importantly, a comparative neglect of the bases of economic power.

The relationship between 'civil society' and 'the economy' has always been somewhat ambivalent. For some commentators (for example, John Urry), the economy is a third sphere alongside the state and civil society (Urry, 1981). For others, perhaps above all for Marx, civil society was reduced to little more than the economy or 'the realm of needs' (Pierson, 1986, pp. 9–14). For Keane, economic relationships belong within civil society, and he is certainly mindful that 'taming the power of private capital' within civil society is one of the prerequisites of effective reform. He also recognizes that there are profound inequalities within civil society based upon gender and ethnicity, and that simply to return social functions to civil society without the (reformed) state as guarantor and adjudicator risks turning civil society into 'a battlefield, in which the stronger . . . enjoy the freedom to twist the arms of the weaker' (Keane, 1988a, p. 22). Thus the system of pluralism and complex equality which he recommends requires an arbitrating and adjudicating state.

Yet there is little indication of the ways in which the vast disparities of power which characterize existing civil society are to be addressed, let alone overcome. 'Taming the power of private capital' is to be effected 'through social struggles and public policy initiatives', but it is unclear which social movements or social actors will be able to control the economically stronger and prevent civil society continuing to be the realm of their 'freedom to twist the arms of the weaker' (Keane, 1988a, p. 14). There is similarly little indication of the ways in which existing powers within and upon the interventionist state are to be refashioned so as to secure a greater realm of freedom and autonomy for ordinary citizens.

As a part of his strategy, Keane makes out a strong case for institutions that secure complex equality and liberty. But as Walzer makes clear in his own defence of a similar idea, the existence of complex equality is dependent upon society having no dominant good which is both monopolized by some groups of men and women and 'convertible' from one social sphere to another. As Walzer recognizes, capital, however imperfectly, does enjoy these dual qualities in a capitalist society and correspondingly any strategy for a society of complex equality and liberty must address this question of the power of private capital (Walzer, 1983, pp. 10–17). It is the absence of such a discussion which gives Keane's recommendations for a reformed and empowered civil society its slightly unreal sound. The characteristic institutions that would inhabit a reformed civil society range from 'self-governed trade unions and enterprises or housing co-operatives to refuges for battered women, independent communications media, and neighbourhood police monitoring associations' (Keane, 1988a, p. 15). The autonomy and effectiveness of such organizations would surely be imperilled as much by the power of capital as by the powers of an overweening state. We might also anticipate that they would face an unequal struggle with the several sorts of powers that already inhabit their respective spheres of civil society. Such a consideration may also point up a misunderstanding of traditional socialist attitudes to the state. For, while some elements of the labour movement have certainly grown to be too sanguine about the beneficence of the state, a significant element in its appeal has been (and continues to be) its status as the one agency capable of exercising some sort of constraint over the powers of private capital.[12]

Socialism has been so variously described, that one cannot properly speak of some essential 'core' which any definition must include. However, virtually all classical definitions of socialism have seen it as involving, in whatever varying ways, collective or social control of economic decision-making. This element is missing from Keane's redefinition of socialism as 'the vitalization of civil society and the democratic reform of state power' (Keane, 1988a, p. 25). The limitation of Keane's strategy as a resolution of the problems of social democracy is its partial confrontation of the powers of private capital. It is only this neglect that allows for an over-simple resolution of the dilemmas involved in social democracy's commitment to state action.

These several reservations about citizenship and civil society strategies as a way of overcoming the problems of social democracy and its welfare state are reinforced when we turn to the third initiative raised above – that is the call for an enhanced role for welfare voluntarism. Here comment can be confined to three points. First, it is far from clear that, in practice, the voluntary sector displays the sorts of qualities which its advocates argue make it so much better a provider than the state. In what remains the fullest empirical assessment of the voluntary sector, Kramer argues that 'while one can acknowledge the importance of sustaining altruism and citizen participation in a welfare state, there may be a tendency to exaggerate the virtues of both volunteerism and voluntary agencies' (Kramer, 1981, p. 211). He found (1) that there is little evidence

---

12 In this it has not always been conspicuously successful, and it is the case that globalization of the capitalist economy may be making the state a (still) less effective tool for the control of private capital.

to suggest that voluntary agencies are more sensitive or innovative than their public sector counterparts, (2) that voluntary agencies soon succumb to classical processes of bureaucratization, (3) that voluntary agencies are substantially dependent upon state financing (through payment for services) and (4) that (at least in the US, 'where voluntary effort remains a larger part of total welfare effort than in other advanced societies'), individual giving as a proportion of personal income has been falling since the early 1960s (Kramer, 1981). While sympathetic to the importance of the voluntary sector, he concludes that

> Voluntarism is no substitute for services than can best be delivered by government, particularly if coverage, equity, and entitlements are valued ... there is a danger that those who have jumped on the bandwagon of the era of limits, signaling the end of the welfare state by advocating more volunteerism, are being coopted by others who have less concern with social justice than with tax reduction. (Kramer, 1981, p. 283)

The second point to stress is that even those who are most enthusiastic for an enhancement of the voluntary sector, and most convinced of 'the failure of the state', acknowledge that the state will have to continue to be the dominant welfare agency (Hadley and Hatch, 1981). For example, Hadley and Hatch, in calling for 'a pluralist strategy which ... seeks to develop roles for each of the [welfare] sectors and, in particular, to maximize the voluntary and informal contributions', recognize that 'the instrument for formulating a strategy must necessarily be the state' (Hadley and Hatch, 1981, p. 101).

Thirdly, while some areas of existing state provision probably could be replaced by (compulsory) social insurance, it is quite unrealistic to suppose that the social needs of the least advantaged could be adequately met by their own (or anyone else's) voluntary effort (Ware, 1989; *Charity Trends*, 1990; De Swaan, 1988).

## Welfare States and the Socialization of Investment

A second major response to social democracy's present difficulties with the welfare state focuses upon renewal of the traditional socialist commitment to social ownership of the economy or, more specifically, to 'social control of the investment function'. In chapter 1, we saw how the discovery of Keynesianism seemingly 'resolved' what had become a profound dilemma for democratic socialists – how to complete the hazardous and costly transition to socialism through the institutions of liberal parliamentary democracy. Keynesianism offered a solution because it seemed to render formal ownership of the economy, and correspondingly the traditional strategy of socialization of ownership, irrelevant. Economic *control* could be exercised by the government's manipulation of key macroeconomic variables and the owners of capital could be *induced* to act in the long-term interests of social democracy. In this way, social demo- crats could pursue a socialist strategy without venturing the hazar- dous expropriation of private capital. The 'decline of Keynesianism' represents a severe challenge to this social democratic strategy of 'indirect' socialization and contemporary social democrats are again faced with that dilemma for which Keynesianism proved to be only a temporary solution – how to achieve socialization of the economy under the circumstances of liberal parliamentary democracy.

This perspective is well represented in the recent work of Gosta Esping-Andersen. While endorsing the historical development of the welfare state as progressive, he insists that existing welfare state strategies are no longer consonant with development towards social- ism. Changes in the structure of advanced capitalism, themselves in part the product of welfare state development, mean that the con- tinuing prosecution of traditional welfare state policies is, in fact, likely to *undermine* the preconditions for socialism. He argues that 'the leading social democratic movements are at a crossroads where, for an array of reasons, the leap from a politics of social citizenship [the welfare state] to one of economic citizenship must be attempted' (Esping-Andersen, 1985, p. xiv). In the absence of this 'leap for- ward', the social democratic parties (and with them the existing coalition of support for the welfare state) face not just stagnation but accelerating decline.

Esping-Andersen follows the power resources model (pp. 29–31 above) in arguing that social democracy can form the basis for the prosecution of a transformative socialist strategy. Where he departs from this perspective is in arguing that this social democratic politics cannot be based exclusively upon the interests of the working class. Since social democratic strategy is of necessity majoritarian, and yet the traditional working class has never and will never form a major- ity of the population, it must be premised upon support beyond the working class. Within the definite limits set by class structure (given by the prevailing social division of labour), it has always been the business of social democratic parties to seek to mobilize class forma- tion and to sponsor class alliances that will serve the interests of its natural core constituency, the broad working class. Effective class mobilization is above all else dependent upon the use the social democrats make of state power. To unify and mobilize its class base, it is first and foremost important that social democracy should be able to implement strategies that *de-commodify* labour — through full employment and welfare provision. Protecting workers from the imperatives of the market is seen to be the indispensable basis for effective collective action and the central principle of the welfare state.

Under these circumstances, it is social democracy's capacity for political mobilization *beyond the working class* that has always underlain its success and above all its promotion of the welfare state. But, Esping-Andersen insists, it is 'in the long run a potentially incompatible strategy for mobilization. If not corrected and supplemented with other policies, it is likely to boomerang and provoke the decomposition of social democracy.' Thus,

> unless the social democratic movement manages to relieve the state of its sole responsibility for welfare distribution, decommod-ification, and solidarity and to reallocate that responsibility in the economy, the movement risks a backlash against the welfare state. (Esping-Andersen, 1985, p. 35)

This exhaustion of the existing welfare state settlement has two components. First, its class basis has been eroded. This may reflect either the decline of traditional intermediary classes (particularly in the agricultural sector) or else the shrinking of the traditional working class itself. Secondly, Keynesian strategies of indirect government intervention to control the capitalist business cycle have proven to be increasingly unsuccessful — generating the now familiar pattern of high taxation, inflation, growing unemployment and so on. Both problems call for radical remedies. First, if the integrity of social democracy is to be protected, it must seek to transfer to a strategy based upon an alliance with what under contemporary capitalism is an expanding white-collar middle stratum. But it is precisely and disproportionately upon this white-collar group that the growing costs of an increasingly inefficient traditional welfare state fall. Thus, if social democracy is to promote and sustain this new alliance, it must move from indirect Keynesian forms of intervention in the capitalist business cycle to direct socialization of the investment function (the very commitment that social democracy abandoned in entering its earlier historic compromise with capital and the agrarian classes). The new class alliance will depend upon expansion of the economy and the preservation of full employment. Since private capital cannot be relied upon to be 'induced' to secure such conditions, the social democratic state must itself intervene *directly* to ensure adequate investment. Engaging the issue of control of the economy is the necessary basis for forging a new class alliance without which the incipient process of social democratic party decline and the erosion of welfare state gains will necessarily accelerate.

However, if socialization is to be restored as a strategic priority for the social democrats, this must also mean reviving the dilemma that they faced down to the 1930s – how to reconcile the short-term costs of transition to socialism with the institutions of liberal democracy. Social democracy has therefore to seek out a strategy which avoids the unacceptable costs of transition, is consistent with the constitutional demands of liberal parliamentary democracy, and yet which is able to address the question of the *direct* socialization of major economic decision-taking. Esping-Andersen finds a solution in the form of *wage-earners' funds*.

## Wage-earners' Funds and the Social Democratic Dilemma

Modern proposals for a system of wage-earners' funds were first presented by a working party of the Swedish Trades Union Congress (LO), under its principal economist Rudolf Meidner, in 1975. Originally, they were canvassed as a solution to certain anomalies which had been generated by Sweden's unusually lengthy experience of welfare capitalism. First and foremost, the trades unions' solidaristic wage policy – which had sought to standardize pay rates throughout the national economy – had generated a problem of 'excess profits' in highly efficient firms. While some of this excess was offset against local wage drift, the unions wanted to resolve this problem in a way that would not prejudice their commitment to equalize incomes. At the same time, they wished to confront and overcome other problems generated by the long period of 'historic compromise' with organized capital. Among the most important of these, Meidner listed the need 'for the community and the trades unions to acquire a greater say in the allocation of profits for investment purposes', 'to check the concentration of wealth among traditional groups of owners' and 'to increase employee influence'. However, in meeting these ambitions, the trades unions wanted a policy which would maintain a high level of capital formation, promote economic growth and be 'neutral with respect to costs, wages and prices' (Meidner, 1978, pp. 14, 17). While the details of the wage-earners' funds are complex, the principle of the Meidner proposal, which was to reconcile these several constraints and ambitions, was quite straightforward:

The ownership of a part of the profits which are ploughed into an enterprise is simply transferred from the previous owners to the employees as a collective. A proportion of the profit is set aside for the employees. This money does not however leave the business. Instead, a company issues shares to that amount, and these are transmitted to the employee fund. (Meidner, 1978, p. 47)

For Esping-Andersen, the Meidner proposal, at least in principle, defines a social democratic strategy for implementing *direct* communal or workers' control over economic decision-making, but in a gradualist form which avoids the threat of capital flight and the trough of economic underproduction and civil unrest which more conventional strategies for transition have always implied. The wage-earners' funds initiative is thus seen to offer a strategy through which the social democratic movement can press beyond the welfare state and welfare capitalism towards social control of the investment function and thus towards gradual socialization of the economy. According to John Stephens, it represents 'a brilliant solution to the political and tactical problems of social democracy in its attempt to go beyond the welfare state towards socialism' (Stephens, 1979, p. 190).

## Wage-earners' Funds as Social Democratic Strategy

How effectively does the strategy proposed by Esping-Andersen address the dilemmas facing the social democratic welfare state? We should begin by acknowledging the strengths of the wage-earners' funds proposals. Whatever have been the difficulties in implementing Meidner's plans, they represent an imaginative and elegant solution which far outstrips the kind of parochial and unimaginative thinking which usually passes for social democratic 'strategy'. It is also a great strength of Esping-Andersen's work that he recognizes at least some of the profound historical changes, beyond a simple crisis of public indebtedness, which threaten the long-term coherence of social democracy, particularly changes in the class structure of contemporary welfare capitalism. Yet significant difficulties remain.

First, even given the unique strengths of the Swedish labour movement, such a strategy probably underplays the increase in the powers of capital over against collective labour which the process of internationalization and globalization of the world economy brings. While there has been some faltering internationalization of the labour movement and of citizenship rights in recent years, it remains the case that labour movements and social citizenship rights are essentially *national* institutions. Both are significantly weakened by the increasing mobility of international capital. Capital can be transmitted around the globe in seconds, while citizenship rights remain essentially claims upon national governments, conditional and often painfully slow to be processed. 'National capital' and 'capital flight' seem increasingly archaic terms, when capital is in a constant flurry of movement around the world economy. This must clearly present difficulties for a strategy which is premised upon 'taming private capital' *within national boundaries*. Again, Esping-Andersen seems to canvass the gradual expropriation of capital as a political power without any serious interruption in the process of capital formation and accumulation, as a process to which resistance will be severely limited. In this, he is perhaps too sanguine about the quiescence of capital. After all, one of the developments which inspired the call for wage-earners' funds in Sweden was precisely the concentration of the private ownership of capital that the social democrats' own labour market policy had unintentionally promoted. Even the sustained electoral success of social democratic parties may have a limited impact, given that the power of capital does not principally rest upon the size of its electoral support. In addition, the optimistic expectation that stockholders might acquiesce in the gradual expropriation of capital because wage-earners' funds do not undermine the immediate value of their assets has hardly been vindicated by the bitter and polemical response of the Swedish conservatives.

A second set of difficulties surround changes in the class structure of the welfare state. It is to Esping-Andersen's considerable credit that he was one of the first to recognize that welfare state policies would not necessarily continue to consolidate the class basis of social democracy's support, and to draw the conclusions that followed for traditional welfare state strategies. Thus, he does not argue that the capacity for economic democracy rests upon a majoritarian working class (indeed, he denies just such a possibility). Nor does he argue that the outcome of political struggles over class is predestined to favour labour. However, there remain problems with his account of the class politics of the welfare state. For example, it is not at all certain that the white-collar new middle strata are available for the sort of wage-earners' alliance that Esping-Andersen envisages. We have seen that Dunleavy and Husband's studies of class and voting patterns in the UK suggest that the division between public and private sector employment may be becoming a stronger indicator of social democratic voting intention than the traditional blue-collar/white-collar divide or 'wage-earner' status. (Dunleavy and Husbands, 1985). It is not clear that public sector white-collar employees – many of whose jobs have emerged from the expansion of the welfare state – will necessarily share a community of interests with other white-collar workers or blue-collar workers in the private sector, whose experience of high levels of taxation will not be offset by an immediate interest in the continued sponsorship of public employment (Lash and Urry, 1987). Easing the state's responsibility for welfare may not have the effect of solidifying a class alliance between working and middle strata. Secondly, Esping-Andersen's recommendations convey very little sense of an active and contested political struggle. Insofar as it is recognized at all, political class struggle is seen to be mediated either through parties or through the formal organizations of labour and capital. Correspondingly, the model of transition – built around wage-earners' funds – itself tends to be technocratic, premised upon the (however brilliant) resolution of a set of *technical* problems of accumulation through changes in formal ownership rather than upon the overcoming of the *political* contradictions established by capitalist development. Indeed, for its advocates, one of the great strengths of the wage-earners' funds policy is that it promotes a process of more or less painless and costless expropriation of capital. Thus, there appears once again the possibility of continuing to enjoy, uninterrupted, the benefits of capitalist economic growth while gradually stripping capital of its effectiveness as a form of ownership. In this way, the problem of declining productivity occasioned by economic disruption and capital flight/resistance, which is one of the most widely cited problems of mobilizing mass support for the transition to socialism, can be avoided. Seen from a rather different angle, as Offe suggests, what seems to be offered is a technical (and *dirigiste*) strategy for changes in formal ownership without any indication of how this is to articulate with a mass movement for social change (Emmanuel, 1979; Gustaffson, Giddens and Offe, 1982).

Thirdly, however broad may be the alliance of working-class and middle-class workers, it is uncertain that *any* wage-earners' alliance will be sufficiently broadly representative of society's interests as to carry forward the political project which Esping-Andersen advocates. As Adam Przeworski has argued, while the trend *within* the working population may be towards growing 'proletarianization', the more general social trend is for growing numbers – among them those in higher education and particularly old age pensioners – to be located *outside* the categories of wage labour and capital, and correspondingly to be open to 'politicization' around quite differing issues (Przeworski, 1985, p. 82; see also Przeworski and Sprague, 1986). Left-wing social democrats in Scandinavia might well have been

sensitized to such political issues defined *outside* the sphere of production by the historic electoral defeat of the Social Democrats in
1976, which Korpi attributed not so much to the unpopularity of the
novel wage-earners' funds proposals as to the government's commitment to nuclear power (Korpi, 1979, 1983). The attitude to civil
and military nuclear power is widely perceived to be among the
most pressing, contentious and class-crossing of contemporary political issues, especially 'after Chernobyl'. The salience of post-
materialist issues and electoral ambivalence on the welfare state are
the common experience of social democratic movements throughout
Western Europe. In the face of this, it would appear that any effective socialist or – more appropriately – 'emancipatory' politics is
likely to be defined around an alliance that goes beyond the preponderance of wage-earners and beyond the issues of growth,
security and state welfare (Offe, 1985/6).

This brings us to a third issue – that of wage-earners' funds and
the attitude to economic growth. It is increasingly unlikely that the
circumstances in which wage-earners' funds might be used as a
means of transition to socialism would involve simply a reallocation
of the fruits of unproblematic economic growth. While wage-
earners' funds promise intervention in the direction of the processes
of production, they still constitute a strategy tied to continued economic growth. But, as we have seen, this problematic of continued
economic growth and its attendant disutilities is now *itself* politically
contentious ground, not least amongst those white-collar elements
whose support social democracy requires. In addition, wage-
earners' funds can do little to address point-of-production and
labour-process politics, nor those other issues, such as women's
rights or the quality of natural environments, which are of increasing salience particularly to that growing number of citizens located
outside the world of work. Indeed, in concentrating upon a politics
of producers, the wage-earners' funds not only neglect what are
widely conceived to be major contemporary political problems –
such as civil and military nuclear policy, environmental and sexual
politics – they also neglect that growing number of citizens who lie
outside the active working population (Lash and Urry, 1987).

But perhaps the sternest and most instructive challenge to the
Esping-Andersen model has come from the recent experience of the
Swedish Social Democrats themselves. While the drop in the Swedish Social Democrats share of the vote in the 1988 election was small
(and about half that of their conservative opponents), there was a
major upsurge of support for the Greens (*Electoral Studies*, 1989).
Meanwhile, unemployment has crept up to the historically high
figure of 4 per cent, and there has been further erosion of wage

solidarity, growing evidence of division of interests between differing sectors of the trades union movement and a virtual moratorium on new wage-earners' funds (Lash and Urry, 1987). That the success of the wage-earners' funds initiative should have been so limited upon what appears to be the most favourable terrain suggests the profound difficulties which must confront it as a strategy for social democracy elsewhere.

Despite the great strengths of Esping-Andersen's work, which recognizes the importance of non-determined political struggles, the open-endedness of social democratic development, and even the necessity of unseating the welfare state settlement, there remains the axiomatic social democratic commitment to economic growth, to traditional 'full employment' and to mobilization around the uniformity of wage-earners' interests. But it is precisely these expectations that the economic crisis of the 1980s and the politics of the new social movements have in their differing ways challenged. What is offered is certainly a radical attempt to address the problems of traditional social democracy. But it may be that the challenge of fostering a transition to socialism within the framework of liberal democracy has itself been overtaken by further social development.

# Conclusion: Defending the Welfare State

At the end of the twentieth century, no-one can write innocently of the benevolent power of the state. If the experience of Stalinism and Fascism, to name but two of the most infamous tyrannies of the twentieth century, were not enough, there is also a tradition, perhaps best represented by Foucault, which charts the chronic and petty incursions of the state in the day-to-day life of the modern citizen. If we add to this the rather more mundane 'failures' of social democracy, there can be little surprise that the state in general, and the welfare state in particular, should have become so uniformly unfashionable. Yet, in these concluding pages I wish to mount a partial defence of the state's role in welfare, based on the comparative and historical evidence collated in this study.

The most important premise of this defence is the seeming ubiquity of the welfare state. We have seen that welfare states come in a variety of forms and sizes, supported by disparate political and economic forces, seeking to realize differing social outcomes. Certainly, the state may not be needed in all those areas in which it presently intervenes and it may be that such interventions as it does make need not take their present form. Nonetheless, the prospects of any developed society moving towards a 'minimal state' are extremely remote and the idea of marginalizing the welfare state is likely to prove to be both Utopian and socially regressive. As we saw in chapter 6, within the envisageable future, the 'real' issue is not going to be whether we have a welfare state (nor even how much it will cost), but what sort of a welfare state *regime* it will be. The state's allocation of welfare may be changing (perhaps to become more fiscally regressive), but nowhere is it disappearing or yielding to a minimal state uninterested in the welfare status of its population.

One popular response to this universality of the welfare state is to insist that, if it has to be maintained as a 'regrettable necessity', we should at least be seeking to minimize its social interventions. This aspiration to move welfare allocation away from the state takes two especially influential forms. First, there is an initiative, popular in a range of new social movements, to bypass the state by returning welfare to more localized, non-hierarchical and non-bureaucratized forms of communal self-administration. Secondly, there is the neo-conservative strategy of limiting the state's intervention by returning the allocation of welfare to markets. Whatever the practical limitations of these initiatives (and I have attempted to show earlier in the book that these are considerable), they also suffer from a number of weaknesses in principle.

On the first initiative, critics are surely right to point to the difficulties of securing personalized and sensitive social provision through the massified institutions of a legal–administrative state apparatus. But while the development of new forms of welfare self-administration which they recommend is extremely healthy (and ought where appropriate to be supported by the state itself), this is not best understood as an *alternative* to the welfare state. For example, there are circumstances in which anonymity, non-discretionary provision and a professional relationship (which are often seen as characteristic *weaknesses* of the state sector) may be preferable to a less formal and community-based response. It is also difficult to see how the compulsory revenue-raising power of the state, or many of the services that it funds, could be replaced by some other agency and we may feel, as Titmuss argued, that there is a special moral quality in meeting the 'needs of strangers' which may be best effected through the anonymity of the state (Titmuss, 1970). It is also clear that the strengthening of social citizenship and civil society, and indeed the guaranteeing of the integrity of the sorts of alternative welfare institutions which the new social movements commend, may also require a selective strengthening of the powers of the interventionist state.

In turning to the neo-conservative response, it is necessary to confront directly the claim that returning welfare functions from the state to the market can be properly considered a process of empowering ordinary citizens. It may certainly enhance the power of certain actors (and sometimes quite 'ordinary' ones) in certain contexts, but consumer sovereignty is not a surrogate for citizen sovereignty. Returning the allocation of (still more) welfare opportunities to the market is likely to make welfare outcomes still less equitable than under existing welfare state regimes. Furthermore, it is not clear that the intensified individuation of welfare choices is a viable long-term option. In many ways our current global position requires us to make more not fewer collective choices and necessitates, alongside a possible enhancement of the market in some areas, its stricter regulation in others.

Some of these points can be illustrated by turning to the green agenda for social and political reform. Green activists are amongst those who call for a decentralization of welfare provision and for more local, informal and discursive forms of decision-taking ('thinking globally and acting locally'). Yet the problems which the greens have helped to isolate – of unsustainable growth and maldistribution of global resources – clearly require enhanced decision-making and powers of enforcement at a national and especially a supra-national level. Certain green welfare initiatives (for example, a guaranteed minimum income or a guaranteed right to sabbatical leave in all forms of employment) seem to imply a much larger role for the state (Dobson, 1990, pp. 112–15). Inasmuch as green politics is something more than an act of faith, the question of institutional and constitutional reform in large-scale contexts is unavoidable. The market, with its seeming decentralization of decision-making, is not a solution. If we think of a position that is sympathetic to both the green agenda and to markets (as, for example, in the Pearce report *Blueprint for a Green Economy*), we see that markets can give environmentally 'efficient' allocations only within a previously given and *politically chosen* framework. Pearce argues that markets can maximize efficiency and effectiveness at a given level of resource exhaustion or environmental spoliation, but these framework-setting levels (and crucially decisions about intergenerational distribution) must be the outcome of political processes and can only be reached through the agency of the state (Pearce, Markandya and Barbier, 1989). Thus, if we accept even a very *weak* and market-sympathetic form of the green argument that unsustainable economic growth cannot be allowed to continue, then we have a very *strong* case for the increased politicization of economic decision-making. Esping-Andersen is right to argue that the welfare state cannot carry all the burden of society's responsibility for social welfare and collective provision, while leaving the economy 'to look after itself' (Esping-Andersen, 1985). However difficult it may prove to be, socialists and social democrats have to confront the question of how to politicize economic decision-making without repeating the mistakes of 'actually existing socialism' and 'actually existing social democracy' (see Miller, 1989; Le Grand and Estrin, 1989).

At the heart of all these difficulties in the welfare state lies something like a collective loss of political nerve. More than twenty years ago, Habermas identified the coming of 'social welfare state mass democracy' with the process of 'depoliticization':

> the depoliticization of the mass of the population and the decline of the public realm as a political institution are components of a system of domination that tends to exclude practical questions from public discussion. The bureaucratized exercise of power has its counterpart in *a public realm confined to spectacles and acclamation*. (Habermas, 1971, p. 75; see also Habermas, 1989b)

Inasmuch as social democratic practice ever reflected a line of strategic thinking, we have seen that depoliticization or demobilization of its political support was a key feature of the advocacy of the Keynesian welfare state in the 1930s and 1940s.[1]

In their differing ways, the neo-conservatives and the new social movements seek to avoid the traditional terrain and institutions of massified democracy. Yet I have suggested that any attempt to circumvent the politics of welfare is a diminishing option, as the prospects of open-ended, positive-sum economic growth recede. If there is a crisis of the welfare state (paralleling the impasse of social democracy), it may be this, that the very circumstances which make for a *depoliticization* of welfare provision themselves require a willingness to *repoliticize* issues of welfare.

The call for a simultaneous democratization and sectoral strengthening of the powers of the state is not a fashionable one. The coinage of 'democracy' is little less debased in the popular estimation than is 'the state's promotion of the common good' and strengthening the powers of the democratic state has long been recognized as a double-edged process (at least since the French and American Revolutions). Post-modernism is heir to a long and well-documented account of the dangers of strengthening the state so as better to secure democracy and the rights of its citizens. This criticism is also able to draw upon a deep-seated and well-grounded public and academic scepticism about the democratic credentials of the state and its capacity for reform. Yet this profound pessimism is only partially justified.

Few commentators would now want to defend democracy as a transparent and benign mechanism for expressing society's collective will and still fewer argue for a strengthening of the coercive

---

1   See Schmidt, (p. 177 above), who concludes that the most characteristic governing strategy on the welfare state over the past twenty years has been one of 'muddling through'.

powers of existing state institutions on the basis of this popular legitimacy. Democracy is now widely recognized to embrace not only majority rule, but also the protection of the rights of individual citizens and statutory limitations upon government. An enhancement of some capacities of the state (in, for example, the allocation of welfare opportunities) may need to be complemented by a much stricter delimitation of the ways in which the state may act in other spheres. One of the most important initiatives to have arisen from the recent experience of Eastern Europe has been the call for the sovereignty of the state to be curtailed by its submission to lawful and constitutional mechanisms. Reform in Western Europe might well require that both the state and its claims to sovereignty should be less absolutist. What is required is not so much more or less state power, as the reformation of a constitutionally self-limiting state. Such reform need not increase the intrusive involvement of the state bureaucracy in the day-to-day life of its citizens. Specifically in the welfare area a whole series of self-limitations by the state – the 'lease-back' of welfare institutions, the statutory prioritization of citizen's interpretations in cases of dispute, state funding rather than state delivery of services and so on – may enhance its role as guarantor rather than provider. The prospects for such reform may not be very promising and it certainly sounds wiser to say that 'nothing can be changed' than to insist that 'anything is possible'. But neither of these claims is wholly convincing. However one understands the changes in the state in Eastern Europe at the turn of the 1990s, it is surely a trivialization to say that nothing has changed. Similarly, the state in the West may not be wholly beyond reform.

Of course, the spectre of 'repoliticizing' society is not an especially attractive one. Few people (and then possibly the 'wrong' ones) will want to spend seven nights a week in political meetings. Historically, societies of 'total political mobilization' have often been extremely unattractive and dangerous places in which to live and have themselves encouraged the withdrawal towards the private sphere as a haven of security. The constitutional challenge is to find political arrangements that allow ordinary citizens in a variety of local, national and supra-national contexts to make effective and informed decisions about at least the broad outlines of economic, social and political policy, without becoming 'new men and women' in a society of total mobilization. Such reform is neither easy nor readily avoidable.

This need for both institutional reform and a continuing presence of the state in a context of the 'politicization' of welfare can be illustrated by returning briefly to the feminist perspective on welfare. First, it is quite clear that the institutional structure of actual welfare states has significantly disadvantaged women. It has under-pinned existing patriarchal structures, it has reinforced traditional definitions of 'women's natural role', it has formalized material dif-ferences in benefit and pension rights and it has exploited women in a range of low status and poorly paid work. At the same time, it has represented some advances for women in, for example, the limited provision of healthcare and nursery facilities and as an avenue of job mobility for professional women less restricted than that of the private sector. Overall, we may well judge that welfare states have done more to disadvantage women than to assist them. However, this does not mean that feminists should or can abandon the welfare state. For, under any envisageable social formation, womens' social advancement will depend upon the state's provision of welfare. As Linda Gordon argues:

> the core notions of socialism imply that welfare as we know it . . . need not exist. In fact, the implication of recent feminist thinking suggests that, short of a purely communist set of arrangements, such a hope may be futile, because reproductive responsibilities towards children, the aged, and the disabled may always leave some citizens less able to contribute to production than others. (Gordon, 1990, pp. 171–2)

In chapter 3, we concluded that women had not been well served by the welfare state. But the kinds of claims that women in particular need to make outside the market – in terms of childcare, health provision, protection against male violence and so on – while they may require a very different state and a very different relationship with that state, cannot realistically be built upon its wholesale aban-donment.

## Conclusion

The welfare state is certainly paradoxical. On the one hand, it is extraordinarily mundane, concerned with the minutiae of the pen-sion and benefit rights of millions of citizens. On the other, the sheer scale of its growth is one of the most remarkable features of the post-war capitalist world and it remains one of the dominant, if sometimes unnoticed, institutions of the modern world. In recent years, it has become a major political concern of both the political left and, more especially, the political right. But this new or revived interest is, as we have seen, often based upon a quite mistaken reading of its historical evolution and its political consequences.

Recommendations from most political quarters are substantially weakened by these misunderstandings.

In particular, we have seen that the notorious spectre of a 'crisis of the welfare state' is itself a part of this wider misunderstanding. For many, the crisis was real enough, but is now passing. In fact, many of the most difficult and the most 'political' decisions about welfare lie in the future. Questions about the relationship between economic and social policy, between employment and income, between political decision-making and economic decision-making, between state and market, between this and subsequent generations, will have to be addressed anew. When they are, the consensus presently forming around the competence of the market may look no stronger than the consensus which once seemed to cocoon the welfare state.

# Bibliography

Acker, J. 1988: Class, Gender and the Relations of Distribution. *Signs*, 13 (3) 473–97.

Addison, P. 1977: *The Road to 1945*. London: Quartet.

Alber, J. 1982: *Von Armenhaus zum Wohlfahrtsstaat*. Frankfurt: Campus.

Alber, J. 1986: Germany. In P. Flora (ed.), *Growth to Limits*, vol. 2, pp. 1–154. Berlin: De Gruyter.

Alber, J. 1988a: Is there a Crisis of the Welfare State? Cross-national Evidence from Europe, North America, and Japan. *European Sociological Review*, 4 (3) 181–207.

Alber, J. 1988b: Continuities and Changes in the Idea of the Welfare State. *Politics and Society*, 16 (4) 451–68.

Alestalo, M. and Uusitalo, M. 1986: Finland. In P. Flora (ed.), *Growth to Limits*, vol. 1, pp. 197–292. Berlin: De Gruyter.

Alston, L. J. and Ferrie, J. P. 1985: Labour Costs, Paternalism and Loyalty in Southern Agriculture: A Constraint on the Growth of the Welfare State. *Journal of Economic History*, 45 (March), 95–117.

Alt, J. 1979: *The Politics of Economic Decline*. Cambridge: Cambridge University Press.

Alt, J. and Chrystal, K. A. 1983: Political Business Cycles. In J. Alt and K. A. Chrystal (eds), *Political Economics*, pp. 103–25. Brighton: Wheatsheaf.

Amenta, E. and Carruthers, B. G. 1988: The Formative Years of U.S. Social Spending Policies: Theories of the Welfare State and the American States During the Great Depression. *American Sociological Review*, 53, 661–78.

Amenta, E. and Skocpol, T. 1989: Taking Exception: Explaining the Distinctiveness of American Public Policies in the Last Century. In F. G. Castles (ed.), *The Comparative History of Public Policy*. Cambridge: Polity.

Anderson, P. 1977: The Antinomies of Antonio Gramsci. *New Left Review*, 100, 5–78.

Arber, S. and Gilbert, N. 1989:   Men: The Forgotten Carers. *Sociology*, 23 (1) 111–18.

Ashford, D. E. 1982:   *British Dogmatism and French Pragmatism: Central–Local Policymaking in the Welfare State*. London: Allen and Unwin.

Ashford, D. E. 1986a:   *The Emergence of the Welfare States*. Oxford: Blackwell.

Ashford, D. E. 1986b:   The British and French Social Security Systems: Welfare States by Intent and Default. In D. E. Ashford and E. W. Kelley (eds), *Nationalizing Social Security in Europe and America*, pp. 245–71. London: Jai Press.

Ashford, D. E. and Kelley, E. W. (eds) 1986:   *Nationalizing Social Security in Europe and America*. London: Jai Press.

Ashmore, M., Mulkay, M. and Pinch, T. 1989:   *Health and Efficiency: A Sociology of Health Economics*. Milton Keynes: Open University Press.

Atkinson, A. B. and Altmann, R. M. 1989:   State pensions, taxation and retirement income, 1981–2031. In Atkinson, A. B. (ed.), *Poverty and Social Security*. London: Harvester Wheatsheaf.

Atkinson, A. B. and Micklewright, J. 1989:   Turning the Screw: benefits for the unemployed, 1979–1988. In Atkinson, A. B. (ed.), *Poverty and Social Security*. London: Harvester Wheatsheaf.

Axinn, J. and Levin, H. 1975:   *Social Welfare: A History of the American Response to Need*. New York: Dodd, Mead and Co.

Bacon, R. and Eltis, W. 1978:   *Britain's Economic Problem: Too Few Producers*. London: Macmillan.

Balbo, L. 1987:   Family, Women and the State: Notes towards a Typology of Family Roles and Public Intervention. In C. S. Maier (ed.), *Changing Boundaries of the Political*. Cambridge: Cambridge University Press.

Bane, M. J. 1988:   Politics and Policies of the Feminization of Poverty. In M. Weir, A. S. Orloff and T. Skocpol (eds), *The Politics of Social Policy in the United States*, pp. 381–396. Princeton, NJ: Princeton University Press.

Barbalet, J. M. 1988:   *Citizenship: Rights, Struggle and Class Inequality*. Milton Keynes: Open University Press.

Barnett, C. 1986:   *The Audit of War*. London: Macmillan.

Barr, N. 1987:   *The Economics of the Welfare State*. London: Weidenfeld and Nicolson.

Barrett, M. 1980:   *Women's Oppression Today: Problems in Marxist Feminist Analysis*. London: Verso.

Beechey, V. and Perkins, T. 1987:   *A Matter of Hours: Women, Part-time Work and the Labour Movement*. Cambridge: Polity.

Bell, D. 1979:   *The Cultural Contradictions of Capitalism*. London: Heinemann.

Bellamy, D. F. and Irving, A. 1989:   Canada. In J. Dixon and R. P. Scheurell (eds), *Social Welfare in Developed Market Countries*, pp. 47–88. London: Routledge.

Bellamy, R. 1987:   *Modern Italian Social Theory*. Cambridge: Polity.

Bendix, R. 1970:   *Embattled Reason: Essays on Social Knowledge*. New York: Oxford University Press.

Benton, T. 1977:   *Philosophical Foundation of the Three Sociologies*. London: Routledge and Kegan Paul.

Berkowitz, E. and McQuaid, K. 1980: *Creating the Welfare State: The Political Economy of Twentieth-Century Reform*. New York: Praeger.

Bernstein, E. 1909: *Evolutionary Socialism*. London: Independent Labour Party.

Beveridge, W. H. 1942: *Social Insurance and Allied Services*. London: HMSO.

Birch, A. 1984: Overload, Ungovernability and Delegitimation. *British Journal of Political Science*, 14 (2) 135–160.

Blake, D. and Ormerod, P. 1980: *The Economics of Prosperity: Social Priorities in the Eighties*. London: Grant Macintyre.

Blitz, R. C. 1977: A Benefit–Cost Analysis of Foreign Workers in West Germany. *Kyklos*, 30, 479–502.

Block, F. 1987: Social Policy and Accumulation: A Critique of the New Consensus. In M. Rein, G. Esping-Andersen and M. Rainwater, *Stagnation and Renewal in Social Policy: The Rise and Fall of Policy Regimes*. New York: Sharpe.

Block, F., Cloward, R. A., Ehrenreich, B. and Piven F. F. 1987: *The Mean Season: The Attack on the Welfare State*. New York: Pantheon Books.

Blot, D. 1990: The Demographics of Migration. *OECD Observer*, 163, 21–5.

Bobbio, N. 1988: Gramsci and the Concept of Civil Society. In J. Keane (ed.), *Civil Society and the State*. London: Verso.

Bosanquet, N. 1983: *After the New Right*. London: Heinemann Education.

Bosanquet, N. 1988: An Ailing State of National Health. In R. Jowell, S. Witherspoon and L. Brook (eds), *British Social Attitudes*, 5th edn, pp. 93–108. Aldershot: Gower.

Bottomore, T. and Goode, P. (eds) 1978: *Austro-Marxism*. Oxford: Oxford University Press.

Bowles, S. and Gintis, H. 1982: The Crisis of Liberal Democratic Capitalism: The Case of the US. *Politics and Society*, 11 (1) 51–93.

Bowley, M. 1967: *Nassau Senior and Classical Economics*. New York: Octagon.

Brenner, J. and Ramas, M. 1984: Rethinking Women's Oppression. *New Left Review*, 144, 33–71.

Briggs, A. 1967: The Welfare State in Historical Perspective (1961). Reprinted in C. Schottland (ed.), *The Welfare State*, pp. 25–45. London: Harper.

Brittan, S. 1975: The Economic Contradictions of Democracy. *British Journal of Political Science*, 5 (2) 129–59.

Brody, D. 1980: The Rise and Decline of Welfare Capitalism. In D. Brody (ed.), *Workers in Industrial America: Essays on the Twentieth-Century Struggle*, pp. 48–81. New York: Oxford University Press.

Brown, C. 1984: *Black and White Britain: The Third PSI Survey*. London: Heinemann.

Brown, M. and Madge, N. 1982: *Despite the Welfare State: A Report on the SSRC/DHSS Programme of Research into Transmitted Deprivation*. London: Heinemann Educational.

Brownlie, I. (ed.) 1971: *Basic Documents on Human Rights*. London: Oxford University Press.

Brubaker, W. R. (ed.) 1989:   *Immigration and the Politics of Citizenship in Europe and North America*. London: University Press of America.

Bruce, M. 1968:   *The Coming of the Welfare State*, 4th edn. London: Batsford.

Bruno, M. and Sachs, J. D. 1985:   *Economics of Worldwide Stagflation*. Oxford: Blackwell.

Cameron, D. R. 1978:   The Expansion of the Public Economy: A Comparative Analysis. *American Political Science Review*, 72 (4) 1243–61.

Campbell, T. C. 1983:   *The Left and Rights: A Conceptual Analysis of the Idea of Socialist Rights*. London: Routledge and Kegan Paul.

Carby, H. V. 1982:   White Woman Listen! Black Feminism and the Boundaries of Sisterhood. In Centre for Contemporary Cultural Studies, *The Empire Strikes Back*, pp. 212–35. London: Hutchinson.

Carens, J. H. 1988:   Immigration and the Welfare State. In A. Gutmann (ed.), *Democracy and the Welfare State*, pp. 207–30. Princeton, NJ: Princeton University Press.

Cashmore, E. E. and Troyna, B. 1983:   *Introduction to Race Relations*. London: Routledge and Kegan Paul.

Castles, F. G. 1978:   *The Social Democratic Image of Society: A Study in the Achievements and Origins of Scandinavian Social Democracy in Comparative Perspective*. London: Routledge and Kegan Paul.

Castles, F. G. 1982:   The Impact of Parties on Public Expenditure. In Castles, F. G. (ed.), *The Impact of Parties: Politics and Policies in Democratic Capitalist States*, pp. 21–96. London: Sage.

Castles, F. G. 1985:   *The Working Class and Welfare*. Wellington, New Zealand: Allen and Unwin.

Castles, F. G. (ed.) 1989:   *The Comparative History of Public Policy*. Cambridge: Polity.

Cawson, A. 1986:   *Corporatism and Political Theory*, Oxford: Blackwell.

*Charity Trends* 1990:   *Charity Trends*, 13th edn. Tonbridge, Kent: Charities Aid Foundation.

Childs, M. 1961:   *Sweden: The Middle Way*. New Haven, Conn.: Yale University Press.

Clarke, T. and Clements, L. (eds) 1977:   *Trades Unions under Capitalism*. London: Fontana.

Clegg, S. 1989:   Review of Lash and Urry, *The End of Organized Capitalism. Contemporary Sociology*, 18 (1) 48–9.

Collier, D. and Messick, R. E. 1975:   Prerequisites versus Diffusion: Testing Alternative Explanations of Social Security Adoption. *American Political Science Review*, 69 (4) 1299–315.

Commonwealth Bureau of Census and Statistics (Australia) 1910– : *Official Year Book of the Commonwealth of Australia*. Canberra.

Cook, J. and Watt, S. 1987:   Racism, Women and Poverty. In C. Glendinning and J. Millar, *Women and Poverty in Britain*, pp. 53–70. Brighton: Wheatsheaf.

Coughlin, R. 1980:   *Ideology, Public Opinion, and Welfare Policy*. Berkeley, Calif.: University of California Press.

Crosland, A. 1964:   *The Future of Socialism*. London: Cape.

Crossman, R. 1970: Introduction to W. Bagehot, *The English Constitution*, pp. 1–57. London: Fontana.

Crozier, M., Huntington, S. P. and Watanuki, J. (eds) 1975: *The Crisis of Democracy*. New York: New York University Press.

CSO (Central Statistical Office) 1989: *Social Trends 19*. London: HMSO.

CSO 1990: *Social Trends 20*. London: HMSO.

Cullis, J. G. and West, P. 1979: *The Economics of Health*. Oxford: Martin Robertson.

Cutright, P. 1965: Political Structure, Economic Development, and National Social Security Programs. *American Journal of Sociology*, 70, 537–50.

Dale, J. and Foster, P. 1986: *Feminists and State Welfare*. London: Routledge and Kegan Paul.

Daniels, N., (ed.) 1975: *Reading Rawls*. New York: Basic Books.

Davies, G. and Piachaud, D. 1985: Public Expenditure on the Social Services: The Economic and Political Constraints. In R. Klein and M. O'Higgins (eds), *The Future of Welfare*, pp. 92–110. Oxford: Blackwell.

De Swaan, A. 1988: *In Care of the State: Health Care, Education and Welfare in Europe and the USA in the Modern Era*. Cambridge: Polity.

Deakin, N. 1987: *In Search of the Postwar Consensus*. London: Suntory International Centre for Economics and Related Disciplines, LSE.

Delphy, C. 1984: *Close to Home*. London: Hutchinson.

Department of Health (UK) 1989: *Working For Patients*. London: HMSO.

DHSS (Department of Health and Social Security, UK) 1985: *The Reform of Social Security*, Cmnd. 9517, vol. 1. London: HMSO.

Dicey, A. V. 1962: *Law and Opinion in England in the Nineteenth Century*. London: Macmillan.

Dixon, J. and Scheurell, R. P. (eds.) 1989: *Social Welfare in Developed Market Countries*. London: Routledge and Kegan Paul.

Dobson, A. 1990: *Green Political Thought*. London: Unwin Hyman.

Donnison, D. 1979: Social Policy since Titmuss. *Journal of Social Policy*, 8 (2) 145–56.

Downs, A. 1957: *An Economic Theory of Democracy*. New York: Harper and Row.

Doyal, L., Hunt, G. and Mellor, J. 1981: Your Life in Their Hands: Migrant Workers in the NHS. *Critical Social Policy*, 1 (2) 54–71.

Dryzek, J. and Goodin R. E. 1986: Risk-sharing and Social Justice: The Motivational Foundations of the Post-War Welfare State. *British Journal of Political Science*, 16 (1) 1–34.

Dunleavy, P. 1980: The Political Implications of Sectoral Cleavages and the Growth of State Employment. *Political Studies*, 28, 364–84 and 527–49.

Dunleavy, P. and Husbands, C. 1985: *British Democracy at the Crossroads: Voting and Party Competition in the 1980s*. London: Allen and Unwin.

Dyer, C. 1978: *Population and Society in Twentieth-Century France*. New York: Holmes and Meier.

*The Economist* 1982a: Europe's Socialists are Losing their Taste for Power. *The Economist*, 284 (7249).

*The Economist* 1982b:   The Withering of Europe's Welfare States. *The Economist*, 285 (7259).

*Electoral Studies* 1989:   *Electoral Studies*, 8 (1) 102.

Emmanuel, A. 1979:   The State in the Transitional Period. *New Left Review*, 113/4, 111–31.

Ensor, R. C. K. 1936:   *The Oxford History of England 1870–1914*. Oxford: Clarendon Press.

EOC (Equal Opportunities Commission) 1987:   *Women and Men in Britain: A Statistical Profile*. London: HMSO.

Ermisch, J. 1985:   Work, Jobs and Social Policy. In R. Klein and M. O'Higgins (eds), *The Future of Welfare*, pp. 59–71. Oxford: Blackwell.

Esping-Andersen, G. 1985:   *Politics Against Markets*. Princeton, NJ: Princeton University Press.

Esping-Andersen, G. 1990:   *The Three Worlds of Welfare Capitalism*. Cambridge: Polity.

Esping-Andersen, G. and Korpi, W. 1984:   Social Policy and Class Politics in Post-War Capitalism: Scandinavia, Austria and Germany. In J. Goldthorpe (ed.), *Order and Conflict in Contemporary Capitalism*, pp. 179–208. Oxford: Oxford University Press.

Esping-Andersen, G. and Korpi, W. 1987:   From Poor Relief to Institutional Welfare States: The Development of Scandinavian Social Policy. In R. Erikson et al. (eds), *The Scandinavian Model: Welfare States and Welfare Research*. Armonk, NY: Sharpe.

Evans, E. J. 1978:   *Social Policy 1830–1914: Individualism, Collectivism and the Origins of the Welfare State*. London: Routledge and Kegan Paul.

Ferrera, M. 1986:   Italy. In P. Flora (ed.), *Growth to Limits*, vol. 2, pp. 385–482. Berlin: De Gruyter.

Ferrera, M. 1989:   Italy. In J. Dixon and R. P. Scheurell (eds), *Social Welfare in Developed Market Countries*, pp. 122–46. London: Routledge.

Finch, J. and Groves, D. 1983:   *A Labour Of Love: Women, Work and Caring*. London: Routledge and Kegan Paul.

Firestone, S. 1979:   *The Dialectic of Sex*. London: The Women's Press.

Flora, P. 1985:   History and Current Problems of the Welfare State. In S. N. Eisenstadt and O. Ahimer (eds), *The Welfare State and its Aftermath*. London: Croom Helm.

Flora, P. (ed.) 1986:   *Growth to Limits*, vols 1 and 2. Berlin: De Gruyter.

Flora, P. (ed.) 1987a:   *Growth to Limits*, vol. 4. Berlin: De Gruyter.

Flora, P. (ed.) 1987b:   *State, Economy and Society*, 2 vols. London: Macmillan.

Flora, P. and Alber, J. 1981:   Modernization, Democratization and the Development of Welfare States in Western Europe. In P. Flora and A. J. Heidenheimer (eds), *The Development of Welfare States in Europe and America*, pp. 37–80. London: Transaction.

Flora, P. and Heidenheimer, A. J. (eds) 1981a:   *The Development of Welfare States in Europe and America*. London: Transaction Books.

Flora, P. and Heidenheimer, A. J. 1981b:   The Historical Core and Changing Boundaries of the Welfare State. In P. Flora and A. Heidenheimer (eds), *The Development of the Welfare States*, pp. 17–34. London: Transaction.

Foot, M. 1975: *Aneurin Bevan*, vol. 2. London: Paladin.

Forrest, R. 1988: *The Political Economy of Owner Occupation*. London: Hutchinson.

Forrest, R. and Murie, A. 1988: *Selling the Welfare State: The Privatisation of Public Housing*. London: Routledge.

Foucault, M. 1975: *Discipline and Punish*. Harmondsworth: Penguin.

Fowle, T. W. 1890: *The Poor Law*. London: Macmillan.

Fraser, D. 1973: *The Evolution of the Welfare State*. London: Macmillan.

Fraser, D. 1981: The English Poor Law and the Origins of the British Welfare State. In W. Mommsen (ed.), *The Emergence of the Welfare State in Britain and Germany 1850–1950*, pp. 9–31. London: Croom Helm.

Fraser, N. 1989: Women, Welfare and the Politics of Need Interpretation. In P. Lassman (ed.), *Politics and Social Theory*. London: Routledge.

Freeman, G. P. 1986: Migration and the Political Economy of the Welfare State. *Annals of the American Academy of Political and Social Science*, 485, pp. 51–63.

Friedman, M. 1962: *Capitalism and Freedom*. Chicago: University of Chicago Press.

Freidman, M. and Friedman, R. 1980: *Free to Choose*. London: Secker and Warburg.

Furniss, N. and Tilton, T. 1979: *The Case for the Welfare State*. London: University of Indiana Press.

Gale Research Company 1985: *Encyclopedia of Associations*. Detroit: Gale Research Co.

Gamble, A. 1981: *Britain in Decline*. London: Macmillan.

Gamble, A. 1988: *The Free Economy and the Strong State: The Politics of Thatcherism*. London: Macmillan.

Gass, J. R. 1981: Preface. In OECD, *The Welfare State in Crisis*, pp. 5–6. OECD: Paris.

*General Household Survey* 1987: London: HMSO.

Giddens, A. 1981a: *The Class Structure of the Advanced Societies*. London: Hutchinson.

Giddens, A. 1981b: Class Division, Class Conflict and Citizenship Rights. In A. Giddens (ed.), *Profiles and Critiques in Social Theory*. London: Macmillan.

Giddens, A. 1985: *The Nation-State and Violence*. Cambridge: Polity.

Gilbert, B. B. 1966: *The Evolution of National Insurance in Great Britain*. London: Michael Joseph.

Gilbert, B. B. 1970: *British Social Policy 1914–1939*. London: Batsford.

Gilder, G. 1982: *Wealth and Poverty*. London: Buchan and Enright.

Ginsburg, N. 1979: *Class, Capital and Social Policy*. London: Macmillan.

Glass, D. 1940: *Population: Policies and Movements in Europe*. Oxford: Clarendon Press.

Glendinning, C. and Millar, J. 1987: Invisible Women, Invisible Poverty. In C. Glendinning and J. Millar (eds), *Women and Poverty in Britain*, pp. 3–27. Brighton: Wheatsheaf.

Godfrey, M. 1986: *Global Unemployment: The New Challenge of Economic Theory*. Brighton: Wheatsheaf.

Golding, P. and Middleton, S. 1982: *Images of Welfare*. Oxford: Blackwell.

Goldthorpe, J. H. 1984: *Order and Conflict in Contemporary Capitalism*. Oxford: Oxford University Press.

Goldthorpe, J. H., Lockwood, D., Bechofer, F. and Platt, J. 1968: *The Affluent Worker*. Cambridge: Cambridge University Press.

Goodin, R. 1988: *Reasons for Welfare*. Princeton, NJ: University of Princeton Press.

Goodin, R. E. and Le Grand, J. 1987: *Not Only the Poor: The Middle Classes and the Welfare State*. London: Allen and Unwin.

Gordon, L. 1990: The Welfare State. Towards a Socialist-Feminist Perspective. In R. Miliband, L. Panitch and J. Saville (eds), *The Socialist Register*, pp. 171–200. London: Merlin.

Gorz, A. 1985: *Paths to Paradise*. London: Pluto.

Gough, I. 1979: *The Political Economy of the Welfare State*. London: Macmillan.

Gough, I. 1983: Thatcherism and the Welfare State. In S. Hall and M. Jacques (eds), *The Politics of Thatcherism*, pp. 148–68. London: Lawrence and Wishart.

Graham, H. 1987: Women's Poverty and Caring. In C. Glendinning and J. Millar (eds), *Women and Poverty in Britain*, pp. 221–40. Brighton: Wheatsheaf.

Grammenos, S. 1982: *Migrant Labour in Western Europe*. Maastricht: European Centre for Work and Society.

Gramsci, A. 1971: *The Prison Notebooks*. London: Lawrence and Wishart.

The *Guardian* 1990: *Guardian* 26 November 90, p. 2.

Gustaffson, B., Giddens, A. and Offe, C. 1982: Beyond Welfare Capitalism: Review Symposium. *Acta Sociologica*, 25 (3) 301–18.

Habermas, J. 1971: *Toward a Rational Society: Student Protest, Science and Politics*. London: Heinemann.

Habermas, J. 1976: *Legitimation Crisis*. London: Heinemann Educational.

Habermas, J. 1989a: The New Obscurity: The Crisis of the Welfare State and the Exhaustion of Utopian Energies. In *The New Conservatism*, pp. 48–70. Cambridge, Mass.: MIT.

Habermas, J. 1989b: *The Structural Transformation of the Public Sphere: An Inquiry into a Category of Bourgeois Society*. Cambridge: Polity.

Hadley, R. and Hatch, S. 1981: *Social Welfare and the Failure of the State: Centralised Social Services and Participatory Alternatives*. London: Allen and Unwin.

Hage, J., Hanneman, R. and Gargan, E. T. 1989: *State Responsiveness and State Activism*. London: Unwin Hyman.

Hagemann, R. 1989: Aging Population and the Pressure on Pensions. *OECD Observer*, 160, 12–15.

Hall, P. 1952: *The Social Services of Modern England*. London: Routledge and Kegan Paul.

Hammar, T. 1990: *Democracy and the Nation State: Aliens, Denizens and Citizens in a World of International Migration*. Aldershot: Avebury.

Hammar, T. and Lithman, Y. G. 1987: The Integration of Migrants: Experiences, Concepts and Policies. In OECD, *The Future of Migration*, pp. 234–56. Paris: OECD.

Harris, J. 1977: *William Beveridge: A Biography.* Oxford: Clarendon Press.

Harris, R. and Seldon, A. 1979: *Over-ruled on Welfare.* London: Institute of Economic Affairs.

Harris, R. and Seldon, A. 1987: *Welfare Without the State: A Quarter-Century of Suppressed Public Choice.* London: Institute of Economic Affairs.

Hartmann, H. 1981: The Family as the Locus of Gender, Class, and Political Struggle: The Example of Housework. *Signs*, 6 (3) 366–94.

Hay, J. 1975: *Origins of the Liberal Welfare Reforms of 1908–14.* London: Macmillan.

Hay, J. 1978a: *The Development of the British Welfare State, 1880–1975.* London: Edward Arnold.

Hay, J. 1978b: Employer's Attitudes to Social Policy and the Concept of Social Control, 1900–1920. In P. Thane (ed.), *The Origins of British Social Policy*, pp. 107–25. London: Croom Helm.

Hay, R. 1977: Employers and Social Policy: The Evolution of Welfare Legislation 1905–14. *Social History*, 4, 435–55.

Hayek, F. 1960: *The Constitution of Liberty.* London: Routledge and Kegan Paul.

Hayek, F. 1982: *Law, Legislation and Liberty*, 3 vols. London: Routledge and Kegan Paul.

Heath, A. and Evans, G. 1988: Working-class Conservatives and Middle-class Socialists. In R. Jowell, S. Witherspoon and L. Brook (eds), *British Social Attitudes*, 5th edn, pp. 53–69. Aldershot: Gower.

Heclo, H. 1974: *Modern Social Politics in Britain and Sweden: From Relief to Income Maintenance.* London: Yale University Press.

Heclo, H. 1981: Towards a New Welfare State? In P. Flora and A. Heidenheimer, *The Development of Welfare States in Europe and North America*, pp. 383–406. London: Transaction.

Heikkinen, E. 1984: Implications of Demographic Change for the Elderly Population. In A. D. Lopez and R. L. Cliquet (eds), *Demographic Trends in the European Region*, pp. 161–75. Copenhagen: World Health Organization.

Held, D. 1987: *Models of Democracy.* Cambridge: Polity.

Held, D. 1989: Citizenship and Autonomy. In D. Held (ed.), *Political Theory and The Modern State.* Cambridge: Polity.

Hennock, E. P. 1987: *British Social Reform and German Precedents: The Case of Social Insurance 1880–1914.* Oxford: Clarendon Press.

Henriques, U. R. O. 1979: *Before the Welfare State.* London: Longman.

Hewitt, C. 1977: The Effect of Political Democracy and Social Democracy on Equality in Industrial Societies: A Cross-National Comparison. *American Sociological Review*, 42, 450–64.

Hicks, A. 1988: Social Democratic Corporatism and Economic Growth. *The Journal of Politics*, 50, 677–704.

Hicks, A. and Swank, D. 1984: On the Political Economy of Welfare Expansion: A Comparative Analysis of 18 Advanced Capitalist Democracies, 1960–1971. *Comparative Political Studies*, 17 (1) 81–119.

Higgins, J. 1981: *States of Welfare: Comparative Analysis in Social Policy.* Oxford: Blackwell/Martin Robertson.

Hill, M. 1990: *Social Security Policy in Britain.* Aldershot: Edward Elgar.

Himmelstrand, U., Ahrne, G., Lundberg, Leif and Lundberg, Lars 1981: *Beyond Welfare Capitalism.* London: Heinemann.

Hindess, B. 1987: *Freedom, Equality, and the Market: Arguments on Social Policy.* London: Tavistock.

H. M. Treasury, U. K. 1979: *The Government's Expenditure Plans 1980–1,* Cmnd. 7746. London: HMSO.

Holzmann, R. 1986: Pension Reform: Sharing the Burden. *OECD Observer,* 138, 3–10.

Huntington, S. 1975: The US. In M. Crozier et al. (eds), *The Crisis of Democracy,* pp. 59–118. New York: New York University Press.

Hyman, R. 1989a: Class Struggle and the Trades Union Movement. In R. Hyman (ed.), *The Political Economy of Industrial Relations.* London: Macmillan.

Hyman, R. 1989b: *Strikes.* London: Macmillan.

Illich, I. 1973: *Deschooling Society.* Harmondsworth: Penguin.

Illich, I. 1977: *Disabling Professions.* London: Boyars.

Illich, I. 1978: *The Right to Useful Employment.* London: Boyars.

Jackson, B. and Jackson, S. 1979: *Childminder: A Study in Action Research.* London: Routledge and Kegan Paul.

Jackson, M. P. 1987: *Strikes.* Brighton: Wheatsheaf.

Jacobs, M. 1989: What is Sustainability? Paper presented to the Green Politics Seminar, Nottingham, May, 1989.

Jay, P. 1977: Englanditis. In R. E. Tyrrell (ed.), *The Future That Doesn't Work,* pp. 167–85. New York: Doubleday.

Jennings, E. T. 1979: Competition, Constituencies, and Welfare Policies in American States. *American Political Science Review,* 73 (2) 414–29.

Jessop, B. 1988: *Conservative Regimes and the Transition to Post-Fordism.* Colchester: University of Essex Papers.

Jessop, B., Bonnett, K., Bromley, S. and Ling, T. 1988: *Thatcherism: A Tale of Two Nations.* Cambridge: Polity.

Johansen, L. N. 1986: Denmark. In P. Flora (ed.), *Growth to Limits,* vol. 1, pp. 293–381. Berlin: De Gruyter.

Johnson, Nevil 1987: The Break-up of Consensus: Competitive Politics in a Declining Economy. In M. Loney (ed.), *The State or the Market,* pp. 144–60. London: Sage.

Johnson, Norman 1987: *The Welfare State in Transition: The Theory and Practice of Welfare Pluralism.* Brighton: Wheatsheaf.

Johnson, R. J., Pattie, C. J. and Allsopp, J. G. 1988: *A Nation Dividing? The Electoral Map of Great Britain 1979–1987.* London: Longman.

Jones, C. 1985: *Patterns of Social Policy.* London: Tavistock.

Jones, M. A. 1980: *The Australian Welfare State.* London: Allen and Unwin.

Jordan, B. 1987: *Rethinking Welfare.* Oxford: Blackwell.

Joshi, H. 1987: The Cost of Caring. In C. Glendinning and J. Millar (eds), *Women and Poverty in Britain,* pp. 112–33. Brighton: Wheatsheaf.

Joshi, S. and Carter, B. 1984: The Role of Labour in the Creation of a Racist Britain. *Race and Class,* 25 (3) 53–70.

Kaim-Caudle, P. 1973: *Comparative Social Policy and Social Security.* Oxford: Martin Robertson.

Katz, M. 1986:  *In the Shadow of the Poorhouse.* New York: Basic Books.

Kautsky, K. 1909:  *The Road to Power.* Chicago: Bloch.

Kautsky, K. 1910:  *The Class Struggle.* New York: Kerr.

Kautsky, K. 1983:  *Selected Political Writings.* London: Macmillan.

Kavanagh, D. 1987:  *Thatcherism and British Politics: The End of Consensus?* Oxford: Oxford University Press.

Kavanagh, D. and Morris, P. 1989:  *Consensus Politics from Attlee to Thatcher.* Oxford: Blackwell.

Keane, J. 1984:  *Public Life and Late Capitalism: Toward a Socialist Theory of Democracy.* Cambridge: Cambridge University Press.

Keane, J. 1988a:  *Democracy and Civil Society.* London: Verso.

Keane, J. (ed.) 1988b:  *Civil Society and the State.* London: Verso.

Keane, J. and Owens, J. 1986:  *After Full Employment.* London: Hutchinson.

*Keesing's World Events* 1989: Harrow: Longman.

Kelley, S. 1988:  Democracy and the New Deal Party System. In A. Gutmann (ed.) *Democracy and the Welfare State*, pp. 185–205. Princeton, NJ: Princeton University Press.

Kelsen, H. 1955:  *The Communist Theory of Law.* London: Stevens.

Kennedy, F. 1975:  *Public Social Expenditure in Ireland.* Dublin: The Economic and Social Research Institute.

Keohane, R. O. 1984:  The World Political Economy and the Crisis of Embedded Liberalism. In J. Goldthorpe (ed.), *Order and Conflict in Contemporary Capitalism*, pp. 15–38. Oxford: Oxford University Press.

Keynes, M. 1973:  *The General Theory of Employment, Interest and Money.* London: Macmillan.

King, A. 1975:  Overload: Problems of Governing in the 1970s. *Political Studies*, 23 (2/3) 284–96.

King, D. S. 1987:  *The New Right: Politics, Markets and Citizenship.* London: Macmillan.

King, D. and Waldron, J. 1988:  Citizenship, Social Citizenship and the Defence of Welfare Provision. *British Journal of Political Science*, 18, 415–43.

Klein, R. 1983:  *The Politics of the NHS.* London: Longman.

Knight, K. 1990:  State of Activity. *New Socialist*, Oct/Nov, 1990, 7–9.

Korpi, W. 1979:  *The Working Class in Welfare Capitalism.* London: Routledge and Kegan Paul.

Korpi, W. 1983:  *The Democratic Class Struggle.* London: Routledge and Kegan Paul.

Korpi, W. 1989:  Power, Politics, and State Autonomy in the Development of Social Citizenship: Social Rights during Sickness in Eighteen OECD Countries since 1930. *American Sociological Review*, 54 (3) 309–28.

Kramer, R. M. 1981:  *Voluntary Agencies in the Welfare State.* Berkeley, Calif.: University of California Press.

Kristol, I. 1978:  *Two Cheers for Capitalism.* New York: Basic Books

Kudrle, R. T. and Marmor, T. R. 1981:  The Development of Welfare States in North America. In P. Flora and A. J. Heidenheimer (eds), *The Development of Welfare States in Europe and America*, pp. 81–121. London: Transaction.

Kuhnle, S. 1981:  The Growth of Social Insurance Programs in Scandinavia

Outside Influences and Internal Forces. In P. Flora and A. J. Heiden-heimer, (eds), *The Development of Welfare States*, pp. 125–50. London: Transaction.

Lane, J.-E. and Ersson, S. O. 1987: *Politics and Society in Western Europe*. London: Sage.

Langan, M. and Lee, P. (eds) 1989: *Radical Social Work Today*. London: Unwin Hyman.

Lasch, C. 1978: *The Culture of Narcissism*. New York: Norton.

Lash, S. and Bagguley, P. 1988: Labour Relations in Disorganized Capital-ism. *Environment and Planning D: Society and Space*, 6 (3) 321–38.

Lash, S. and Urry, J. 1987: *The End of Organized Capitalism*. Cambridge: Polity.

Le Grand, J. and Estrin, S. (eds) 1989: *Market Socialism*. Oxford: Clarendon Press.

Leman, C. 1977: Patterns of Policy Development: Social Security in the US and Canada. *Public Policy*, 25 (2) 261–91.

Levine, D. 1983: Social Democrats, Socialism and Social Insurance in Ger-many and Denmark, 1918–1933. In R. F. Tomasson (ed.), *Comparative Social Research: The Welfare State*, 6, pp. 67–86. London: Jai Press.

Lewis, J. and Piachaud, D. 1987: 'Women and Poverty in the Twentieth Century'. In C. Glendinning and J. Millar (eds), *Women and Poverty in Britain*, pp. 28–52. Brighton: Wheatsheaf.

Lipset, S. M. 1969: *Political Man*. London: Heinemann.

Luhmann, N. 1990: *Political Theory in the Welfare State*. Berlin: De Gruyter

McEvedy, C. and Jones, R. 1978: *Atlas of World Population History*. Har-mondsworth: Penguin.

McIntosh, C. A. 1983: *Population Policy in Western Europe*. Armonk, NY: Sharpe.

McIntosh, M. 1978: The State and the Oppression of Women. In A. Kuhn and A. Wolpe (eds), *Feminism and Materialism: Women and Modes of Produc-tion*. London: Routledge and Kegan Paul.

Mackie, T. T. and Rose, R. 1982: *The International Almanac of Electoral History*, 2nd edn. London: Macmillan.

Maddison, A. 1984: Origins and Impact of the Welfare State. *Banca Nazionale del Lavoro Quarterly Review*, 148, 55–87.

Madison, B. Q. 1980: *The Meaning of Social Policy*. London: Croom Helm.

Maguire, M. 1986: Ireland. In P. Flora (ed.), *Growth to Limits*, vol. 2, pp. 241–384. Berlin: De Gruyter.

Maillat, D. 1987: Long-Term Aspects of International Migration Flows: The Experience of European Receiving Countries. In OECD, *The Future of Migration*, pp. 38–63. Paris: OECD.

Malthus, T. R. 1890: *An Essay on the Principle of Population*. London: Ward, Lock and Co.

Mann, M. 1970: The Social Cohesion of Liberal Democracy. *American Sociological Review*, 35 (3) 423–39.

Mann, M. 1987: Ruling Class Strategies and Citizenship. *Sociology*, 21, 339–54.

Marcuse, H. 1972: *One Dimensional Man*. London: Sphere.

Marshall, T. H. 1963: *Sociology at the Crossroads*. London: Heinemann.

Marshall, T. H. 1975: *Social Policy in the Twentieth Century*. London: Hutchinson Education.

Marwick, A. 1967: The Labour Party and the Welfare State in Britain 1900–1948. *American Historical Review*, 73 (2) 380–403.

Marx, K. 1973a: *Capital*. Harmondsworth: Penguin.

Marx, K. 1973b: *Surveys from Exile*. Harmondsworth: Penguin.

Meidner, R. 1978: *Employee Investment Funds*. London: Allen and Unwin.

Middlemas, K. 1979: *Politics in Industrial Society: The Experience of the British System since 1911*. London: André Deutsch.

Miliband, R. 1969: *The State in Capitalist Society*. London: Weidenfeld and Nicholson.

Millar, J. 1987: Lone Mothers. In C. Glendinning and J. Millar, (eds), *Women and Poverty in Britain*, pp. 159–77. Brighton: Wheatsheaf.

Millar, J. 1989: *Poverty and the Lone-Parent: The Challenge to Social Policy*. Aldershot: Avebury.

Miller, D. 1989: *Market, State, and Community: Theoretical Foundations of Market Socialism*. Oxford: Clarendon.

Minami, R. 1986: *The Economic Development of Japan: A Quantitative Study*. London: Macmillan.

Minford, P. 1987: The Role of the Social Services: A View from the New Right. In M. Loney (ed.), *The State or the Market: Politics and Welfare in Contemporary Britain*, pp. 70–82. London: Sage.

Mishra, R. 1984: *The Welfare State in Crisis*. Brighton: Wheatsheaf.

Mitchell, B. R. 1975: *European Historical Statistics 1750–1970*. New York: Columbia University Press.

Mommsen, W. J. (ed.) 1981: *The Emergence of the Welfare State in Britain and Germany*. London: Croom Helm.

Moran, M. 1988: Crises of the Welfare State. *British Journal of Political Science*, 18, 397–414.

Morris, R. (ed.) 1988: *Testing the Limits of Social Welfare*. London: Brandeis University Press.

Moynihan, D. P. 1965: *The Negro Family: The Case for National Action*. Washington, DC: Office of Planning and Research, US Department of Labor.

Murray, C. 1984: *Losing Ground: American Social Policy 1950–1980*. New York: Basic Books.

*New Statesman and Society* 1988: Charter 88. *New Statesman and Society*, 1, 26.

*New Zealand Official Year-Book* 1882– : Wellington: Census and Statistics Office.

Niskanen, W. A. 1971: *Bureaucracy and Representative Government*. New York: Aldine-Atherton.

Niskanen, W. A. 1973: *Bureaucracy: Servant or Master?*. London: Institute of Economic Affairs.

Nordlinger, E. A. 1981: *On the Autonomy of the Democratic State*. Cambridge, Mass.: Harvard University Press.

Nozick, R. 1974: *Anarchy, State and Utopia*. New York: Basic Books.

O'Connor, J. 1973: *The Fiscal Crisis of the State*. New York: St Martin's Press.

O'Connor, J. 1987: *The Meaning of Crisis*. Oxford: Blackwell.

O'Connor, J. S. 1988: Convergence or Divergence? Change in Welfare Effort in OECD Countries, 1960–1980: *European Journal of Political Research*, 16, 277–99.

O'Connor, J. S. and Brym, R. J. 1988: Public Welfare Expenditure in OECD Countries: Towards a Reconciliation of Inconsistent Findings. *British Journal of Sociology*, 39 (1) 47–68.

Oakley, A. 1974: *Housewife*. Harmondsworth: Allen Lane.

OECD (Organization for Economic Cooperation and Development) 1966: *Economic Growth, 1960–1970*. Paris: OECD.

OECD 1977: *Towards Full Employment and Price Stability*. Paris: OECD.

OECD 1981: *The Welfare State in Crisis*. Paris: OECD.

OECD 1984: *OECD Observer*, 126.

OECD 1985a: *Social Expenditure 1960–1990: Problems of Growth and Control*. Paris: OECD.

OECD 1985b: *The Integration of Women into the Economy*. Paris: OECD.

OECD 1986a: *OECD Observer*, 138.

OECD 1986b: *Employment Outlook*. Paris: OECD.

OECD 1987: *The Future of Migration*. Paris: OECD.

OECD 1988: *The Future of Social Protection*. Paris: OECD.

OECD 1989: *Economies in Transition*. Paris: OECD.

Offe, C. 1984: *Contradictions of the Welfare State*. London: Hutchinson Education.

Offe, C. 1985: *Disorganized Capitalism*. Cambridge: Polity.

Offe, C. 1985/6: New Social Movements: Challenging the Boundaries of Institutional Politics. *Social Research*, Winter. (A version is reprinted as 'Challenging the Boundaries of Institutional Politics: Social Movements since the 1960s' in C. S. Maier (ed.) 1987: *Changing Boundaries of the Political: Essays on the Evolving Balance between the State and Society, Public and Private in Europe*, pp. 63–105. Cambridge: Cambridge University Press.

Offe, C. 1987: Democracy Against the Welfare State? *Political Theory*, 15 (4) 501–37.

Offe, C. and Wiesenthal, H. 1985: Two Logics of Collective Action. In C. Offe (ed.), *Disorganized Capitalism*, pp. 170–220. Cambridge: Polity.

*Official Year Book of the Commonwealth of Australia* 1923: Melbourne.

*Official Year Book of the Commonwealth of Australia* 1932: Canberra.

Ohlin, B. 1938: Economic Progress in Sweden. *The Annals of the American Academy of Political and Social Science*, 197, 1–6.

Olson, M. 1965: *The Logic of Collective Action: Public Goods and the Theory of Groups*. Oxford: Oxford University Press.

Olson, M. 1982: *The Rise and Decline of Nations: Economic Growth, Stagflation, and Social Rigidities*. New Haven, Conn.: Yale University Press.

Olsson, S. 1986: Sweden. In P. Flora, *Growth to Limits* vol. 1, pp. 1–116. Berlin: De Gruyter.

Orban, O. 1908: *Le Droit Constitutionnel de la Belgique: II: Les Pouvoirs de l'Etat*. Liège: Dessain.

Orloff, A. S. 1988: The Origins of America's Belated Welfare State. In M. Weir, A. S. Orloff and T. Skocpol (eds), *The Politics of Social Policy in the United States*. Princeton, NJ: Princeton University Press.

Orloff, A. S. and Skocpol, T. 1984: Why not Equal Protection? Explaining the Politics of Public Social Spending in Britain, 1900–1911, and the United States, 1880s–1920. *American Sociological Review*, 49 (6) 726–50.

Oshima, H. T. 1965: Meiji Fiscal Policy and Agricultural Progress. In W. W. Lockwood (ed.), *The State and Economic Enterprise in Japan*, pp. 353–89. Princeton, NJ: Princeton University Press.

Owen, R. 1927: *A New View of Society and Other Writings*. London: Dent.

Paine, S. 1974: *Exporting Workers: The Turkish Case*. Cambridge: Cambridge University Press.

Paine, T. 1958: *The Rights of Man*. London: Dent.

Pampel, F. C. and Williamson, J. B. 1988: Welfare Spending in Advanced Industrial Democracies, 1950–1980. *American Journal of Sociology*, 93 (6) 1424–56.

Pampel, F. C. and Williamson, J. B. 1989: *Age, Class, Politics and the Welfare State*. Cambridge: Cambridge University Press.

Pampel, F. and Stryker, R. 1990: Age Structure, the State, and Social Welfare Spending: a Reanalysis. *British Journal of Sociology*, 41 (1) 16–24.

Panitch, L. 1986: *Working Class Politics in Crisis*. London: Verso.

Parry, R. 1986: United Kingdom. In P. Flora (ed.), *Growth to Limits*, vol. 2, pp. 155–240. Berlin: De Gruyter.

Pascall, G. 1986: *Social Policy – A Feminist Analysis*. London: Tavistock.

Pateman, C. 1988: The Patriarchal Welfare State. In A. Gutmann (ed.), *Democracy and the Welfare State*, pp. 231–60. Princeton, NJ: Princeton University Press.

Peacock, A. and Wiseman, J. 1961: *The Growth of Public Expenditure in the UK*. Oxford: Oxford University Press.

Pearce, D., Markandya, A. and Barbier, E. B. 1989: *Blueprint for a Green Economy: A Report*. London: Earthscan.

Pelling, H. 1968: The Working Class and the Origins of the Welfare State. In H. Pelling (ed.), *Popular Politics and Society in Late Victorian Britain*. London: Macmillan.

Pemberton, A. 1983: Marxism and Social Policy: a Critique of the 'Contradictions of welfare'. *Journal of Social Policy*, 12 (3) 289–308.

Pen, J. 1987: Expanding Budgets in a Stagnating Economy: The experience of the 1970s. In C. S. Maier (ed.), *Changing Boundaries of the Political*. Cambridge: Cambridge University Press.

Piachaud, D. 1984: *Round About Fifty Hours a Week*. London: Child Poverty Action Group.

Piccone, P. 1976: Gramsci's Marxism: Beyond Lenin and Togliatti. *Theory and Society*, 3, 485–512.

Pierson, C. 1986: *Marxist Theory and Democratic Politics*. Cambridge: Polity.

Pierson, C. 1990: The 'Exceptional' United States: First New Nation or Last Welfare State? *Social Policy and Administration*, 24 (3) 186–98.

Pierson, C. 1991: Welfare States and Social Democracies: Sweden's 'Austro-Marxism' and the 'Social Democratic Road to Power'. *Research in Political Sociology*, 5.

Pigou, A. C. 1912: *Wealth and Welfare*. London: Macmillan.

Pigou, A. C. 1929: *The Economics of Welfare*. London: Macmillan.

Pimlott, B. 1988: The Myth of Consensus. In L. M. Smith (ed.), *The Making of Britain: Echoes of Greatness*, pp. 129–41. London: Macmillan.

Piore, S. 1979: *Birds of Passage: Migrant Labour and Industrial Societies*. Cambridge: Cambridge University Press.

Piven, F. F. and Cloward, R. 1971: *Regulating the Poor: The Functions of Public Welfare*. New York: Pantheon Books.

Piven, F. F. and Cloward, R. 1977: *Poor People's Movements: Why They Succeed, How They Fail*. New York: Pantheon Books.

Piven, F. F. and Cloward, R. 1985: *The New Class War: Reagan's Attack on the Welfare State and Its Consequences*. New York: Pantheon.

Piven, F. F. and Cloward, R. A. 1986: The New Class War in the US. In E. Oyen (ed.), *Comparing Welfare States and their Futures*, pp. 47–63. London: Gower.

Poguntke, T. 1987: New Politics and Party Systems: The Emergence of a New Type of Party? *West European Politics*, 10 (1) 76–88.

Polanyi, K. 1944: *The Great Transformation*. New York: Rinehart.

Poulantzas, N. 1973: *Political Power and Social Classes*. London: Verso.

Poulantzas, N. 1978: *State, Power, Socialism*. London: Verso.

Przeworski, A. 1985: *Capitalism and Social Democracy*. Cambridge: Cambridge University Press.

Przeworski, A. and Sprague, J. 1986: *Paper Stones: A History of Electoral Socialism*. London: University of Chicago Press.

Pulzer, P. 1987: The Paralysis of the Centre-Left: A Comparative Perspective. *Political Quarterly*, 58 (3) 378–88.

Quadagno, J. 1984: Welfare Capitalism and the Social Security Act of 1935. *American Sociological Review*, 49, 632–47.

Quadagno, J. 1987: Women's Welfare Benefits and American Exceptionalism. *Comparative Historical Sociology Newsletter*, 4 (2) 1–2.

Quadagno, J. 1988a: *The Transformation of Old Age Security, Class and Politics in the American Welfare State*. Chicago: University of Chicago Press.

Quadagno, J. 1988b: From Old-Age Assistance to Supplemental Security Income: the Political Economy of Relief in the South, 1935–1972. In M. Weir, A. S. Orloff and T. Skocpol (eds), *The Politics of Social Policy in the United States*, pp. 235–63. Princeton, NJ: Princeton University Press.

Quadagno, J. 1990: Race, Class, and Gender in the U.S. Welfare State: Nixon's Failed Family Assistance Plan. *American Sociological Review*, 55 (1) 11–28.

Rader, M. 1979: *Marx's Interpretation of History*. New York: Oxford University Press.

Raison, T. 1990: *Tories and the Welfare State*. London: Macmillan.

Rawlings, H. F. 1988: *Law and the Electoral Process*. London: Sweet and Maxwell.

Rawls, J. 1973: *A Theory of Justice*. Oxford: Oxford University Press.

Reede, A. H. 1947: *Adequacy of Workmen's Compensation*. Cambridge, Mass.: Harvard University Press.

Rein, M. 1985: Women, Employment and Social Welfare. In R. Klein and M. O'Higgins (eds), *The Future of Welfare*, pp. 37–58. Oxford: Blackwell.

Rein, M., Esping-Andersen, G. and Rainwater, M. 1987: *Stagnation and*

*Renewal in Social Policy: The Rise and Fall of Policy Regimes.* New York: Sharpe.

Richter, M. 1964: *The Politics of Conscience: T. H. Green and his Age.* London: Weidenfeld and Nicolson.

Rimlinger, G. V. 1974: *Welfare Policy and Industrialization in Europe, America and Russia.* New York: John Wiley.

Ritter, G. A. 1985: *Social Welfare in Germany and Britain.* Leamington Spa: Berg.

Roberts, D. 1960: *Victorian Origins of the Welfare State.* New York: Yale University Press.

Roche, M. 1987: Citizenship, Social Theory and Social Change. *Theory and Society,* 16, 363–99.

Rosanvallon, P. 1988: The Decline of Social Visibility. In Keane, J. (ed.), *Civil Society and the State.* London: Verso.

Rose, H. 1981: Rereading Titmuss: The Sexual Division of Welfare. *Journal of Social Policy,* 10, 477–501.

Rose, R. and Peters, G. 1978: *Can Governments Go Bankrupt?* New York: Basic Books.

Rosenblum, G. 1973: *Immigrant Workers: Their Impact on American Labor Radicalism.* New York: Basic Books.

Samuelsson, K. 1968: *From Great Power to Welfare State: Three Hundred Years of Swedish Social Development.* London: Allen and Unwin.

Saville, J. 1975: The Welfare State: An Historical Approach. In E. Butterworth and R. Holman (eds), *Social Welfare in Modern Britain,* pp. 57–69. London: Fontana. This is an edited version of the original which appeared in *The New Reasoner,* 1, 1957/8.

Scase, R. 1977a: *Social Democracy in Capitalist Society: Working Class Politics in Britain and Sweden.* London: Croom Helm.

Scase, R. 1977b: *Readings in the Swedish Class Structure.* London: Pergamon.

Schmidt, M. G. 1983: The Welfare State and the Economy in Periods of Economic Crisis: A Comparative Study of 23 OECD Nations. *European Journal of Political Research,* 11, 1–26.

Schmidt, M. G. 1989: Social Policy in Rich and Poor Countries: Socioeconomic Trend and Political-institutional Determinants. *European Journal of Political Research,* 17 (6) 641–59.

Schneider, S. K. 1982: The Sequential Development of Social Programs in Eighteen Welfare States. *Comparative Social Research,* 5, 195–219.

Schottland, C. 1969: *The Welfare State.* New York: Harper and Row.

Schumpeter, J. 1954: The Crisis of the Tax State. *International Economic Papers,* 4, 5–38.

Schumpeter, J. 1976: *Capitalism, Socialism, Democracy.* London: Allen and Unwin.

Selbourne, D. 1985: *Against Socialist Illusion.* London: Macmillan.

Senior, N. A. 1865: *Historical and Political Essays.* London: publisher unknown.

Shalev, M. 1983: The Social Democratic Model and Beyond: Two 'Generations' of Comparative Research on the Welfare State. In R. F. Tomasson (ed.), *Comparative Social Research,* 6, 315–51. London: Jai Press.

Shaver, S. 1988: 'Design for an Australian Welfare State'. Paper presented to the BSA Annual Conference, Edinburgh, 28–31 March, 1988.

Shaver, S. 1989: Gender, Class and the Welfare State: The Case of Income Security in Australia. *Feminist Review*, 32, 91–108.

Sked, A. and Cook, C. 1984: *Post-War Britain*. Harmondsworth: Penguin.

Skidelsky, R. 1979: The Decline of Keynesian Politics. In C. Crouch (ed.), *State and Economy in Contemporary Capitalism*, pp. 55–87. London: Croom Helm.

Skocpol, T. 1980: Political Response to Capitalist Crisis: Neo-Marxist theories of the State and the case of the New Deal. *Politics and Society*, 10, 155–201.

Skocpol, T. 1985: Bringing the State Back In: Strategies of Analysis in Current Research. In P. B. Evans, D. Rueschemeyer and T. Skocpol (eds), *Bringing the State Back In*, pp. 3–37. Cambridge: Cambridge University Press.

Skocpol, T. 1987: America's Incomplete Welfare State. In M. Rein, G. Esping-Andersen and M. Rainwater (eds), *Stagnation and Renewal*. New York: Sharpe.

Skocpol, T. and Amenta, E. 1986: States and Social Policies. *Annual Review of Sociology*, 12, 131–57.

Skocpol, T. and Ikenberry, J. 1983: The Political Formation of the American Welfare State. An Historical and Comparative Perspective. In R. F. Tomasson, (ed.), *Comparative Social Research*, 6, pp. 87–148. London: Jai Press.

Smith, A. 1976a: *The Wealth of Nations*. Oxford: Clarendon Press.

Smith, A. 1976b: *Theory of Moral Sentiments*. Oxford: Clarendon Press.

Smith, H. L. 1986: *War and Social Change: British Society in the Second World War*. Manchester: Manchester University Press.

Smith, T. W. 1987: The Polls – A Report: The Welfare State in Cross-national Perspective. *Public Opinion Quarterly*, 51, 404–21.

Smith, T. W. 1989: Inequality and Welfare. In R. Jowell, S. Witherspoon and L. Brook (eds), *British Social Attitudes: Special International Report*, 6th edn, pp. 59–86. Aldershot: Gower.

*Social Europe* 1990: *Social Europe*, 1.

Sombart, W. 1976: *Why is There no Socialism in the United States?* New York: Sharpe.

Stallard, K., Ehrenreich, B. and Sklar, H. 1983: *Poverty in the American Dream: Women and Children First*. Boston: South End Press.

Steering Group on Equal Opportunities for Women in the NHS 1988: *Equal Opportunities for Women in the NHS*. London: Jason Press, NALGO.

Stephens, J. 1979: *The Transition from Capitalism to Socialism*. London: Macmillan.

Stockman, D. A. 1986: *The Triumph of Politics*. London: The Bodley Head.

Swann, M. 1985: *Education for All: The Report of the Committee of Inquiry into the Education of Children from Ethnic Minority Groups*. London: HMSO.

Tampke, J. 1981: Bismarck's Social Legislation: A Genuine Breakthrough? In W. Mommsen (ed.), *The Emergence of the Welfare State in Britain and Germany 1850–1950*, pp. 71–83. London: Croom Helm.

Taylor, A. J. P. 1965: *English History 1914–1945*. Oxford: Clarendon Press.

Taylor, C. L. and Hudson, M. C. 1983: *World Handbook of Political and Social Indicators*. New York: Yale University Press.

Taylor-Gooby, P. 1985: *Public Opinion, Ideology and State Welfare*. London: Routledge and Kegan Paul.

Taylor-Gooby, P. 1986: Privatization, Power and the Welfare State. *Sociology*, 20 (2) 228–46.

Taylor-Gooby, P. 1988: The Future of the British Welfare State: Public Attitudes, Citizenship and Social Policy under the Conservative Governments of the 1980s. *European Sociological Review*, 4 (1) 1–19.

Taylor-Gooby, P. 1989: The Role of the State. In R. Jowell, S. Witherspoon and L. Brook (eds), *British Social Attitudes: Special International Report*, (6th edn), pp. 35–58. Aldershot: Gower.

Taylor-Gooby, P. and Dale, J. 1981: *Social Theory and Social Welfare*. London: Arnold.

Taylor-Gooby, P. and Papadakis, E. 1987: Consumer Attitudes and Participation in State Welfare. *Political Studies*, 35 (3) 467–81.

Temple, W. 1941: The State. In *Citizen and Churchman*. London: Eyre and Spottiswoode. Reproduced in C. Schottland (ed.), *The Welfare State* (1967). London: Harper and Row.

Temple, W. 1942: *Christianity and the Social Order*. London: Penguin.

Thane, P. 1982: *Foundations of the Welfare State*. London: Longman.

Thane, P. 1984: The Working Class and State 'Welfare' in Britain, 1880–1914. *The Historical Journal*, 27 (4) 877–900.

Thane, P. 1987: The Coming Burden of an Ageing Population? *Journal of Social Policy*, 7 (4) 373–87.

Thatcher, M. 1989: Introduction to Department of Health (UK), *Working For Patients*. London: HMSO.

Therborn, G. 1986: Karl Marx Returning. *International Political Science Review*, 7 (2) 131–64.

Therborn, G. 1987: Welfare State and Capitalist Markets. *Acta Sociologica*, 30 (3/4) 237–54.

Therborn, G. 1989: States, Populations and Productivity: Towards a Political Theory of Welfare States. In P. Lassman (ed.), *Politics and Social Theory*. London: Routledge.

Tingsten, H. 1973: *The Swedish Social Democrats: Their Ideological Development*. Totowa, NJ: Bedminster.

Titmuss, R. M. 1963: *Essays on the Welfare State*. London: Allen and Unwin.

Titmuss, R. M. 1970: *The Gift Relationship*. London: Allen and Unwin.

Titmuss, R. M. 1974: *Social Policy*. London: Allen and Unwin.

Tomasson, R. F. 1969: The Extraordinary Success of the Swedish Social Democrats. *Journal of Politics*, 31 (3) 772–98.

Tomasson, R. F. 1970: *Sweden: Prototype of a Modern Society*. New York: Random House.

Tomasson, R. F. (ed.) 1983: *The Welfare State, 1883–1983: Comparative Social Research*, 6. London: Jai Press.

Trattner, W. 1988: The Federal Government and Needy Citizens in Nineteenth-Century America. *Political Science Quarterly*, 103 (2) 347–56.

Tullock, G. 1976:  *The Vote Motive: An Essay in the Economics of Politics, with Applications to the British Economy*. Princeton: Princeton University Press.

Turner, B. S. 1986:  *Citizenship and Capitalism: The Debate over Reformism*. London: Allen and Unwin.

Turner, B. S. 1990:  Outline of a Theory of Citizenship. *Sociology*, 24 (2) 189–217.

Ullman, H. P. 1981:  German Industry and Bismarck's Social Security System. In Mommsen, W. J., (ed.): *The Emergence of the Welfare State in Britain and Germany*, pp. 133–149. London: Croom Helm.

United Nations 1948:  *Universal Declaration of Human Rights*. New York: United Nations.

United Nations 1949:  *National and International Measures for Full Employment*. New York: United Nations.

Urquhart, M. C. 1965:  *Historical Statistics of Canada*. Cambridge: Cambridge University Press.

Urry, J. 1981:  *The Anatomy of Capitalist Societies*. London: Macmillan.

US Bureau of the Census 1987:  *Statistical Abstract of the US* (107th edn). Washington, DC: US Bureau of the Census.

US Bureau of Statistics 1975:  *Historical Statistics of the United States: From Colonial Times to 1970*. Washington, DC: US Government Printing Office.

US Department of Commerce 1975:  *Historical Statistics of the US*. Washington, DC: Department of Commerce.

Uusitalo, H. 1984:  Comparative Research on the Determinants of the Welfare State: The State of the Art. *European Journal of Political Research*, 12, 403–22.

Vincent, A. and Plant, R. 1984:  *Philosophy, Politics and Citizenship: The Life and Thought of the British Idealists*. Oxford: Blackwell.

Waldron, J. 1986:  John Rawls and the Social Minimum. *Journal of Applied Philosophy*, 3 (1) 21–33.

Walker, A. 1987:  The Poor Relation: Poverty among Old Women. In C. Glendinning and J. Millar (eds): *Women and Poverty in Britain*, pp. 178–98. Brighton: Wheatsheaf.

Walzer, M. 1983:  *Spheres of Justice*. Oxford: Martin Robertson.

Weale, A. 1983:  *Political Theory and Social Policy*. London: Macmillan.

Wane, A. (ed.) 1989:  *Charities and Government*. Manchester: Manchester University Press.

Webb, S. and Webb, B. 1910:  *English Local Government: English Poor Law History*, vols. 7–10 London: Longmans, Green.

Webb, S. and Webb, B. 1927:  *English Local Government: English Poor Law History: Part 1: The Old Poor Law*. London: Longmans, Green.

Weber, M. 1968:  *Economy and Society*, 3 vols. New York: Bedminster.

Weir, A. 1974:  The Family, Social Work and the Welfare State. In S. Allen, L. Sanders and J. Wallis, *Conditions of Illusion*, pp. 217–28. Leeds: Feminist Books.

Weir, M. and Skocpol, T. 1985:  State Structures and the Possibilities for 'Keynesian' Responses to the Great Depression in Sweden, Britain and the United States. In P. B. Evans, D. Rueschemeyer and T. Skocpol (eds),

*Bringing the State Back In*, pp. 107–63. Cambridge: Cambridge University Press.

Weir, M., Orloff, A. S. and Skocpol, T. 1988a: *The Politics of Social Policy in the United States*. Princeton, NJ: Princeton University Press.

Weir, M., Orloff, A. S. and Skocpol, T. 1988b: Understanding American Social Politics. In M. Weir, A. S. Orloff and T. Skocpol (eds), *The Politics of Social Policy in the United States*. Princeton, NJ: Princeton University Press.

Wilensky, H. 1975: *The Welfare State and Equality: Structural and Ideological Roots of Public Expenditure*. Berkeley, Calif.: University of California Press.

Wilensky, H. 1976: *The 'New Corporatism', Centralization and the Welfare State*. London: Sage.

Wilensky, H. 1980: Introduction to R. Coughlin, *Ideology, Public Opinion, and Welfare Policy*. Berkeley, Calif.: University of California Press.

Wilensky, H. L. 1981: Leftism, Catholicism, and Democratic Corporatism: The Role of Political Parties in Recent Welfare State Development. In P. Flora and A. J. Heidenheimer (eds), *The Development of Welfare States in Europe and America*, pp. 345–82. London: Transaction.

Williams, F. 1989: *Social Policy: A Critical Introduction: Issues of Race, Gender and Class*. Cambridge: Polity.

Wilson, E. 1977: *Women and the Welfare State*. London: Tavistock.

Wilson, W. J. 1987: *The Truly Disadvantaged: The Inner City, the Underclass, and Public Policy*. London: University of Chicago Press.

Winter, J. M. 1982: The Decline of Mortality in Britain 1870–1950. In T. Barker and M. Drake (eds), *Population and Society in Britain 1850–1950*, pp. 100–20. London: Batsford.

Wolfe, A. 1979: *The Limits of Legitimacy*. London: Macmillan.

Zimmern, A. 1934: *Quo Vadimus*. Oxford: Oxford University Press.

# Index